ROBIN HOOD

ROBIN HOOD

GREEN LORD
OF THE
WILDWOOD

JOHN MATTHEWS

FOREWORD BY MARK RYAN
PREFACE BY RICHARD CARPENTER

AMBERLEY

To the late, lamented Richard 'Kip' Carpenter
To Mark Ryan, our very own Nazir
and to Chesca Potter –
explorers of the Greenwood

First published 2016

Amberley Publishing
The Hill, Stroud
Gloucestershire, GL5 4EP

www.amberley-books.com

Copyright © John Matthews, 2016

The right of John Matthews to be identified as
the Author of this work has been asserted in
accordance with the Copyrights, Designs and
Patents Act 1988.

ISBN 978 1 4456 5601 4 (hardback)
ISBN 978 1 4456 5602 1 (ebook)

British Library Cataloguing in Publication Data.
A catalogue record for this book is available
from the British Library.

Typesetting and Origination by Amberley
Publishing.
Printed in the UK.

CONTENTS

GREAT SEAL of HENRY II, AND RICHARD COEUR de LEON

A MAP TO SHOW THE SITUATION of ROYAL HUNTING
FORESTS WHERE ROBIN HOOD LIVED. A·D 1160~1247

STRATHCLYDE

PLOMPTO
FOREST

BARNESDALE
FOREST

YORK

IRELAND

DUBLIN

IRISH SEA

NORTH
SEA

MANCHESTER

CHESTER

SHERWOOD
FOREST

NOTTINGHAM

LINCOLN

DERBY

WALES

R. SEVERN

SHERWOOD
FOREST

WARWICK

R·AVON

WATLING STREET

LONDON

R·THAMES

CANTERBURY
DOVER

CALAIS

FLANDERS

EXETER

ENGLISH CHANNEL

NORMANDY

R·SEINE

BRITTANY

FOREWORD BY MARK RYAN

Part myth, part man. Living and surviving deep within the forbidding and primal heart of a massive woodland sanctuary, some twenty miles long and ten miles wide, a labyrinthine Wildwood fortress known as Sherwood Forest, owned and administered by a rich and ruthless Norman royal hierarchy. A place where to be caught taking a deer, or even a rabbit, for food, or simply cutting down a tree for shelter or fuel, means blood-chilling mutilation, cruel physical disfigurement or even a swift, ignominious death by hanging at the hands of merciless foresters commanded by powerful Norman overlords, Sherwood Forest remains a compelling psychological battleground of the heart and the spirit.

The ghost of Robin Hood lurks stoically and constantly in our enduring tribal memory, not just in the English psyche but also within the collective subconscious of human beings around the globe, irrespective of cultural and social backgrounds or even national history. This phenomenon I have experienced for myself whenever the subject of *Robin of Sherwood* and the lethal struggles with the fascist-like authority of the Normans comes up in conversation.

Robin is a cheerful fellow, a gifted archer and experienced woodsman living off the land, followed by a small and disparate band of likeminded individuals who share a common sense of justice and loyalty and for whom 'the robbing from the rich and providing for the poor' and downtrodden is key. This sacred bond holds this unlikely and desperate cadre of 'wolf's head' outlaws together.

Though they face formidable odds, always outnumbered by a well-armed and provisioned Norman foe, led by a cunning, astute and psychotically cruel nemesis in the form of the Sheriff of Nottingham, the band survive by guile, skill and daring. They hold fast to their loyalty to each other, their cause and to their charismatic leader, Robin Hood.

The reality of the historic landscape in which I grew up is the backdrop of this iconic mixture of esoteric mythos, rebellious defiance and individual courage that has been woven together over eight hundred years and maybe even more to form the rich, thorny and tangled tapestry that is the legend of Robin Hood and his Merry Men.

More recently the band acquired the semi-permanent fixture of a quiet and deadly foreigner who says little but whose actions speak volumes. The addition of a 'stranger from a strange land' who also hears the ancient voice of the Wildwood and is willing to serve the greater cause of justice for all and the resistance of oppression was a masterstroke by Richard 'Kip' Carpenter in the now iconic *Robin of Sherwood* TV show of the 80s, an icon which evokes the international cultural and social appeal of this enduring legend, as well as such mystically resonating concepts as: 'Nothing's forgotten. Nothing is ever forgotten.' My small contribution to the cast was ably imagined and administered by Kip and has passed the test of time.

Old Watling Street morphs into the Great North Road as it meanders its ancient way along the southern edge of the forest from London, then tracks north to Ermine Street and onward to Barnsdale, near Doncaster, eventually arriving at the original Pilgrim's point of departure at the medieval exchequer in York. Here the Pilgrims began the arduous and oft-times fatal sojourn into the parched and tortured killing fields of the Holy Land.

So too the tale of the men and women of Sherwood snakes sinuously through the history and the memory of the landscape and breathes life into such arcane concepts as loyalty, justice and a moral calling greater than the individual, sometimes demanding a final and selfless sacrifice.

Who better to guide, challenge and cajole the reader throughout this rich, splendid adventure than my wise and good friend John Matthews, a sage fellow indeed, in touch with the ethos of the Wildwood and the denizens that keep it alive and relevant in our modern age. I can think of none better than John to guide and accompany the wanderer in the deep woods.

So! Once more into the Wildwood with Robin and his merry band!

Nothing's forgotten ...

Mark Ryan, 2016

PREFACE BY RICHARD CARPENTER

The investigation of any myth leads us back to fundamental and deep-rooted questions about our place in this environment and the reason for our existence: who are we and why are we here? What, in fact, is our purpose, both individually and collectively?

The twentieth century has seen an explosion of technological achievement, and with it has come a very materialistic view of the world. Yet, at the same time, almost as if to counteract this, magic has been reborn. As a result of this mysterious happening, there has been a considerable and growing interest in the paranormal and occult.

Mythology is as intertwined with magic as the mistletoe is with the oak. It is vitally important to all of us. It chronicles our quest for identity: the great myths and the magic elements in world religions forming the basis of all storytelling. They are the mystery behind history. The archetypes of every aspect of human character and behaviour are to be found in myth, affecting each one of us to the very core of our being. Because they are truer than fact.

John Matthews has gone deep into the leafy shadows of the Greenwood in search of the elusive folk hero we call Robin Hood. His own Wild Hunt has led him through the magic of the changing seasons to reveal the Green Man as the ancient archetype lurking behind the legend of the Outlaw of Sherwood Forest.

In an age of computers, electronics and widespread pollution – both physical and mental – perhaps it is synchronistically right and proper that

England's most famous rebel should now appear in this fascinating book as the very spirit behind today's Green movement; the embodiment not only of freedom but of the power of Nature, and a potent symbol of our disillusion with a dulling, wasteful and poisonous technocracy.

> Bring me my bow of burning gold
> Bring me my arrows of desire

So wrote Blake. Perhaps he was thinking of Robin Hood.

Richard Carpenter, 1993

ACKNOWLEDGEMENTS

A number of people have helped in researching this book and offered general support over a many years. First and foremost my friend Mark Ryan, known to all followers of the TV show *Robin of Sherwood* as 'Nazir', for his cheerful insights into the myth and his skill with the longbow. His generous preface adds a considerable weight to this new edition, and I still laugh when I recall the stories of the adventures that took place off camera. My thanks must also go to the late, great Richard 'Kip' Carpenter, creator of the show, who kindly wrote the original foreword. His work was an early inspiration in the writing of this book, and all who love the Greenwood owe him a debt. Marian Green, whose work is an embodiment of so many of the principles underlying the Robin Hood mythos, gave helpful advice and information relating to the Morris plays. R. J. Stewart telephoned me out of the blue one evening and set me off on a whole new line of reasoning. Gareth Knight shared some of his own insights into the mystery of Robin Hood, and made me see the potentiality of the material. Seldy Bate expounded her not inconsiderable knowledge of folklore and the Morris dance and pointed out a few of my howlers. Thanks also to Barbara Green of the Yorkshire Robin Hood Society for allowing me to reproduce the photograph of Kirklees Priory that appears on p. oo. I must, as ever, thank my fabulous wife Caitlín for her tireless support, and our son Emrys for sharing *Maid Marian and Her Merry Men* with me, and insisting that she was far more interesting than Robin.

Nor would these acknowledgements be complete without a mention of my brothers in the Beneficent Order of the Greenman (www.bogbrothers. org) – especially Shane Odom, whose enthusiasm for the subject is total. Nor would this list be in any way complete without a mention of the redoubtable Billy Scudder (the Green Man himself) and the astonishing Mark Lewis, whose demise in 2014 left a huge gap for all who love these stories.

Finally I must pay tribute to the scholars and antiquaries, past and present, whose work inspired mine and helped me to find my way through occasionally unfamiliar territory. In particular the indefatigable Joseph Ritson, whose collection of ballads is still the best compiled, and Lewis Spence, who, as so often before, was years ahead of contemporary researchers. Among modern authorities no one should fail to be aware of Maurice Keen and J. C. Holt, with whom I can travel only so far but in whose company I spent many a pleasant hour. Needless to say, any mistakes in this book are my own responsibility and not theirs.

John Matthews
Oxford, 2016

'A SONG OF SHERWOOD' BY ALFRED NOYES

Sherwood in the twilight, is Robin Hood awake?
Grey and ghostly shadows are gliding through the brake,
Shadows of the dappled deer, dreaming of the morn,
Dreaming of a shadowy man that winds a shadowy horn.

Robin Hood is here again: all his merry thieves
Hear a ghostly bugle-note shivering through the leaves,
Calling as he used to call, faint and far away,
In Sherwood, in Sherwood, about the break of day.

All the gnarled old thorn-trees are blossom white for June.
All the elves that Marian knew were here beneath the moon –
Younger than the wild thyme, older than the trees,
Lob and Mab and Bramblescratch, on their unbridled bees.

Oaken-hearted England is waking as of old,
With eyes of blither hazel and hair of brighter gold:
For Robin Hood is here again beneath the bursting spray
In Sherwood, in Sherwood, about the break of day.

Love is in the Greenwood building him a house
Of wild rose and hawthorn and honeysuckle boughs:
Love is in the Greenwood, dawn is in the skies,
And Marian is waiting with her laughter-loving eyes.

Robin Hood

Hark! The dazzled laverock climbs the golden steep!
Marian is waiting: is Robin Hood asleep?
Where the last dark arrow fell, the white scuts flash away,
In Sherwood, in Sherwood, about the break of day.

Oberon, Oberon, the hazel copses ring,
Time to hush the night-jar and let the throstle sing,
Time to let the blackbird lift a bonny head,
And wake Will Scarlet from his leafy forest bed.

Friar Tuck and Little John are riding down together
With quarter-staff and drinking-can and grey goose feather.
The dead are coming back again, the years are rolled away
In Sherwood, in Sherwood, about the break of day.

Softly over Sherwood the south wind blows.
All the heart of England hid in every rose
Hears across the Greenwood the sunny whisper leap,
Sherwood in the red dawn, is Robin Hood asleep?

Hark the voice of England wakes him as of old
And, shattering the silence with a cry of brighter gold,
Bugles in the Greenwood echo from the steep,
Sherwood in the red dawn, is Robin Hood asleep?

Where the deer are gliding, down the shadowy glen,
All across the glades of fern he calls his merry men –
Doublets of the Lincoln green glancing through the may
In Sherwood, in Sherwood, about the break of day –

Calls them and they answer: from aisles of oak and ash
Rings the Follow! Follow! And the boughs begin to crash,
The ferns begin to flutter and the flowers begin to fly,
And through the crimson dawning the robber band
goes by.

Robin! Robin! Robin! All his merry thieves
Answer as the bugle-note shivers through the leaves,
Calling as he used to call, faint and far away,
In Sherwood, in Sherwood, about the break of day.

Alfred Noyes

INTRODUCTION

THE GREEN GROVE

The merry pranks he play'd, would ask an age to tell,
And the adventures strange that Robin Hood befell ...
How often he hath come to Nottingham disguis'd,
And cunningly escap'd, being set to be surpriz'd.
In this our spacious isle, I think there is not one
But he hath herd some talk of him and Little John;
And to the end of time, the tales shall ne'er be done,
Of Scarlock, George a Green, and Much the miller's son,
Of Tuck the merry friar, which many a sermon made
In praise of Robin Hood, his outlaws, and their trade.
                    Michael Drayton, *The Polyolbion*, song xxvi

The question as to the identity of Robin Hood has been asked many times
since the Outlaw of Sherwood first sprang to fame in the twelfth century.
No two authorities seem able to agree as to his origins and antecedents,
or even whether or not he was a historical personage or a mythical figure.

  Historians, both amateur and professional, have for years been bringing
out new books in which they claim to have found 'the real Robin Hood'.
Among the more recent are those of J. C. Holt (1982), John Bellamy (1985),
R. de Vries (1988) and Yoshiki Ueno (1985). All have sought to push the
boundaries of the story further out into recorded time – seeking Robin
Hood among the records of government and law enforcement, in the ballads
lore of the twelfth to fourteenth centuries, and in the folk-memory of the
people of Britain. For them, Robin is either a product of the ballad maker's

muse, or a literary fabrication based on the lives and deeds of several outlaws, or on the garbled memory of an actual person whose real life bore little or no resemblance to the romanticised songs of the ballad makers.

The so-called 'mythological school' has, at the same time, poured scorn on these attempts, maintaining that Robin never existed as a real person at all, and that to seek him among the fragmentary records of the Middle Ages is a waste of time. Such luminaries as Lord Raglan, Thomas Wright, Lewis Spence and Margaret Murray have made a case for Robin Hood (or Hode or Robehod) as a figure of myth and folklore. However, in every case their conclusions were summary in nature, briefly stated, and lacking the detailed study of tradition and myth required. They have thus, in their turn, been dismissed.

Neither side has, to the best of my knowledge, seriously considered that they might both be right, that a historical personage or personages might have inherited the qualities and archetypal demeanours of an older figure or figures. The present book sets out to show that this is indeed what occurred – that one or more people bearing the name Robin Hood (or one of the several variants of that name) really did exist, and that because of their location, the time in which they lived, as well as various other factors, they assumed the mantle of an older character, one known originally from ancient myth and later from literary history and folkloric belief. This ancient character was the Green Man, a personification of the power of the natural world, who has continued to haunt the minds and imaginations of people in many different parts of the world ever since, becoming something of a mascot for the ecological movement.

In this book I have therefore begun with the premise that Robin was known, first and foremost, as a mythic figure, and that he came only later to be associated with more than one historical personage. I have set out to show how he was perceived in the medieval period, when the stories still circulating today were given birth.

Another little-understood strand in the puzzle that surrounds the identity of Robin Hood is his association with the Faery race, and in particular with his namesake Robin Goodfellow. It is my belief that the story of this sprightly elf and his merry pranks added significantly to the picture of Robin as he was perceived by the minds of the medieval ballad makers, and that the ages-old traditions of the Faery people in Britain are still an integral part of the story.

To this must be added the association of Robin and of his consort Maid Marian with the great tradition of mumming plays, and to songs and dances of the Morris teams, who still perform their ancient rituals to this day. Behind them lies one of the oldest themes in myth: the struggle of the Winter and Summer Kings for the possession of the Spring Maiden. Others of Robin's outlaw band – Little John, Will Scarlet, Friar Tuck, Much the Miller's Son and the rest – offer surprises of their own, proving, in some cases, to be far older than expected.

Thus from many varied strands the figures of Robin, Marian, John, Tuck and the rest of the Merry Men emerge from the shadows to which historical speculation and mythic dreaming alike have consigned them. Through an exploration of the archetypes behind them we learn not only their true identities, but also something of the way ancient traditions are preserved – in fragmentary form maybe, but still retaining the clear outlines of their original shapes.

The very fact that the presence of Robin – and through him of the Green Man – has come down to us at all is due to a number of complex reasons, one of the foremost being the continuing popularity of the Robin Hood mythos in modern dress through film, TV and novelisation. As I write a whole string of new films and TV shows are in the making, and an audio adventure of what is still one of the best of its kind, *Robin of Sherwood*, is soon to be recorded. Both Robin and the Green Man have fed each other; and it is at the centre of this interaction that the most powerful elements of the living Greenwood myth are born.

It is this mythic tradition that informs the ballads and plays, the songs and dances of Robin Hood. It enlivened the dark days of Winter for our medieval ancestors, and it helped them welcome back the Spring. It is still with us, still present in our hearts and minds even as we wander far from the fields and rivers, woods and valleys of this old land. Robin and Marian represent a freedom we have lost, the freedom to escape to the woods and live at peace there. They remind us of the times when, in our childhood, we made bows and arrows out of pieces of stick and played at Robin Hood and the Sheriff of Nottingham. As the banished Valentine, in Shakespeare's *Two Gentlemen of Verona*, muses:

How use doth breed a habit in a man!
This shadowy desert, unfrequented woods,
I better brook that flourishing peopled towns.
Here can I sit alone, unseen of any,
And, to the nightingale's complaining notes,
Tune my distress, and record my woes.

Act V, sc. iv

Even in the midst of the harsh reality of medieval life, where outlawry was anything but a romantic idyll, there was a kind of rough camaraderie and a sense of freedom that we can scarcely grasp in this day and age.

The mystery that lies at the heart of the Greenwood is a green mystery. When the greenness is brought inside – as in the Green Man carvings in churches, for example – it is pent, it dies. Robin sets it free, and with it all who seek to experience the joyous celebrations of May Day, when Robin and Marian come together and are crowned with the blossom that signifies the birth of the new season. In this book I shall therefore explore the nature of the historical Robin Hood only in order to set the context for the more detailed exploration of the mythic figure, which takes the Outlaw of Sherwood both further back and further forward in time – to the very beginning of history, and on to the future where generations yet unborn will, it is my belief, come to view the myths of the Green Man and of the Wildwood as ever more important.

At the end of the book will be found a generous selection of the ballads featuring Robin Hood. They are there because they reflect the spirit and drama of the Wildwood, where Robin and Marian and the Merry Men found shelter and where most of their adventures took place. It is to their memory, and in the hope that their adventures will never be forgotten, that this book is ultimately dedicated.

I

WHO WAS ROBIN HOOD?

Courtesy, good temper, liberality, and manliness are his chief
marks; for courtesy and good temper he is a popular Gawain.
Yeoman as he is, he has a kind of royal dignity, a princely
grace, and a gentleman-like refinement of humour. This is ...
Robin Hood.
F. J. Child, *The English & Scottish Popular Ballads*

The Ballad Muse

Aside from a few scattered references in medieval chronicles, the
main textual sources for the legend of Robin Hood are a series of
popular ballads; some thirty date from the thirteenth and fourteenth
centuries and are judged to be genuine products of the Middle Ages,
and a great many more date from the sixteenth and seventeenth
centuries and even later. Even here, as in the character of Robin
himself, there is disagreement as to which of the ballads is the oldest
(and how old that is), which are genuine and which pastiche, and
which contain clues to the historical contenders. A selection of these
will be found in Appendix 3, enabling readers to make their own
judgement.

Despite the various attempts to date the ballads or their sources,
there is no denying that they were well known by 1380, when the great
religious poem *Piers the Plowman* was written by William Langland. In
this we find the following, much quoted, lines:

> I know not perfectly my paternoster,
> As the priest would sing:
> But I know rhymes of Robin Hood,
> And Randolf Earl of Chester ...
>
> (author's trans.)

This makes it clear enough that the ballads had already reached a degree of familiarity where even a Christian cleric – who might not normally be supposed to know of such things – was more conversant with them than his prayers!

Francis Child, in his scrupulously researched collection *The English and Scottish Popular Ballads* (17), lists four which he regards as being particularly authentic and which date, in all probability, from the fourteenth century. These are 'Robin Hood, the Knight and the Monk', 'Robin Hood, Little John and the Sheriff', 'Robin Hood and the King' and 'Robin Hood's Death'. These ballads together form the basis for the much longer *Little Gest of Robin Hood* (*Gest*), the earliest surviving version of which was printed in 1508, though earlier fragments exist which date from 1492. Child believes the original version of the ballad (really more of a mini-epic, running to 456 stanzas) may have been composed as early as 1400 or even before that. What is certain is that by the time the work was committed to print a large number of ballads featuring the famous outlaw were circulating widely. As John Major (or Mair) in his *History of Greater Britain* (1521) remarks:

> The Feats of this Robin are told in song all over Britain. He would allow no woman to suffer injustice nor would he rob the poor, but rather enriched them from the plunder taken from abbots. The robberies of this man I condemn, but of all thieves he was the prince and the most gentle thief. (41)

This also gives us some idea of the respect in which Robin was held – even by those who could not outwardly condone his deeds. He was indeed seen as essentially a 'good' man, despite the fact that many of the ballads contain scenes of violence and cruelty.

Child sums it up for us in the words that head this chapter. Robin is courteous, liberal, good-tempered and possessed of an almost royal dignity.

He lives by stealing the King's deer, but has the utmost respect and love for the King – though just *which* king is, again, uncertain. Child adds that if this is what Robin Hood is, 'it is equally important to say what he is not. He has no sort of political character ... and this takes the ground from under the feet of those who seek to assign him a place in history.'

This might well stand as an epitaph to the many Robin Hoods identified 'beyond reasonable doubt' by historians right from the very beginning of the Outlaw of Sherwood's career. Early chroniclers like Wyntoun, Fordun and Bower all assign him to specific places and times. (23) Wyntoun says Robin was alive in 1283 in the reign of Edward I; Bower attaches him to the era of Simon de Montfort (1208–65); Major to Richard I (1157–89). Later, in the nineteenth century, Joseph Hunter says that evidence from the *Gest* places Robin in the time of Edward II, making him an adherent of the Earl of Lancaster's doomed insurrection of 1332; though in the text itself the reference is simply to a 'King Edward', and we are not told which king to bear that name is intended.

The *Gest* itself is a remarkable document, combining the best of the Robin Hood stories with a firm grasp of narrative and a considerable variance in style and content. As it opens – interestingly enough in Barnsdale Forest, South Yorkshire rather than Sherwood, which lies in Nottinghamshire – Robin and the outlaws are already established in the forest, and the Merry Men listen as their leader describes the proper way for them to behave in a scene reminiscent of that in which the Round Table knights learn of their chivalric duties from King Arthur:

> Look you do no husband harm,
> That tilleth with his plough;
> No more you shall on good yeoman,
> That walked in Greenwood shawe;
> Nor no knight nor squire
> That would be a good fellow ...

However:

> These bishops and archbishops
> You shall them beat and bind;
> The high sheriff of Nottingham
> Him hold you in your mind ...

Having said which, Robin then declares that he will not have supper until a guest has been brought to his table, again echoing Arthur's prescription of never beginning a feast until he has seen some wonder.

Little John and two others at once set off to nearby Watling Street (the old Roman road which was still the chief artery for travel through the North of England at this time) and soon espy a somewhat sad and poor-looking knight named Sir Richard-at-Lee, who readily accepts the invitation of the outlaws to dine with them, having heard 'much good' of Robin.

After supper Robin asks politely for payment, as he is given to doing after he has feasted with a noble-born person on the King's deer, and hears a sad tale from the knight, who claims to have no more than ten shillings to his name – a fact quickly verified by Little John after searching his baggage. In some surprise Robin asks how this is possible, and Sir Richard tells how his son had killed another knight in a tournament, because of which Sir Richard was forced to purchase a pardon by mortgaging his land for the sum of £400 to the Abbot of St Mary's Abbey in York. He was now on his way to ask for an extension of time in which to pay off the debt.

Robin generously offers to lend Sir Richard the money, and to send Little John with him as a squire, since he cannot afford one of his own. He even gives him a gift of a pair of gilt spurs – presumably stolen from a less worthy 'guest' on a previous occasion. Sir Richard swears by the Virgin to repay the loan in twelve months.

Arriving in York, Sir Richard pleads with the greedy abbot for longer to pay his debt. He is, of course, refused – then produces the bag of gold given him by Robin and throws it down in front of the abbot with a grand gesture, before returning home to tell his wife that they have been saved from ruin by the generosity of Robin Hood.

A year passes, during which time Little John apparently continues in the service of Sir Richard. At the given time the knight – dressed now in fine clothes and with a hundred retainers at this back – sets out again for Barnsdale to repay his debt. On the way he passes through a village where a fight is about to break out because a yeoman from another part of the country has just defeated the local wrestling champion. Sir Richard intervenes and awards a prize of a white bull to the winner 'for love of Robin Hood', an interesting episode which seems to hark back to an earlier time when the presentation of such a valuable, and probably sacred, beast would have represented an offering to the gods (see also the account of the Tutbury Bull-Running in Chapter 5).

The author's attention now switches abruptly to the adventures of Little John, who – under the assumed name of Reynold Greenleaf – enters an archery contest organised by the Sheriff of Nottingham. He is so successful at this that the Sheriff asks him if he would like to join his own soldiery, and to this Little John agrees as he had always meant to do so.

There follows a curious scene in which, while the Sheriff is away hunting, John asks the cook for a meal. When the latter refuses him, John draws his sword and the two fall to fighting. However, the cook is such a mighty fighter that neither can gain the advantage, and John suggests they be friends and that the cook should join Robin's band. When the man agrees the two of them break into the Sheriff's treasury and steal £300 and all the silver plate they can carry.

Still not done with his 'master', Little John now follows the hunting party and, going by ways known only to those who live in the forest, overtakes the Sheriff. When his surprised master asks where he has been, John answers:

> I have been in this forest:
> A fair sight I can see:
> It was one of the fairest sights
> That ever yet saw I me.
>
> Yonder I saw a right fair hart,
> His colour is of green:
> Seven score of deer in herd,
> Be with him at bedene ... [wearing]

This has been interpreted as simply Little John's cryptic way of referring to Robin and the Outlaws, and while this is true on one level, on another it is describing Robin as a green stag with a herd of deer – terms applicable not only to a forest setting, but also to an older time when he who 'wore the horns' represented an ancient forest god.

In this instance the Sheriff proves ignorant of the hidden reference and is thus led right to the outlaws' camp, where he is at once imprisoned, along with his men. He is then stripped of his outer garments and wrapped in a green cloak and subsequently made to put on the green garb of the outlaws. He is then invited to a feast at which poached venison is served on his own silver plate! Next day Robin releases him on the promise that he will never harm any of the outlaws again – once again demonstrating that the outlaw is more chivalrous than his opponent, who of course has no intention of honouring his promise.

It is now time for Sir Richard-at-Lee to repay the £400, and Robin refuses to eat until he has received the money. Since there is no sign of the knight, Little John, Will Scarlet and Much the Miller's son speed off to Watling Street to find a suitable victim to ambush. They soon spy two black-cowled monks with an escort of fifty men, who flee at the first sight of the outlaws, leaving their charges to be taken to join the outlaw's feast.

One of the monks turns out to be the cellarer of St Mary's Abbey – the very same to which Sir Richard had made good his debt a year before. Not satisfied by this, the greedy abbot has sent the two monks to London to establish a lawsuit against the knight. Asked how much gold they carry, the monks assure Robin they have only £80. However, at that moment, Little John triumphantly shows the £800 he has discovered in their baggage. Declaring that the Virgin, in whose name Sir Richard had sworn, has returned his investment twofold, Robin sends the disgruntled monks on their way, minus their gold.

Shortly after this Sir Richard appears, explaining his delay and offering to repay the debt. Robin responds that he would certainly not hear of taking the money twice and instead gives Sir Richard half what he had taken from the monks. Thus all is well and Sir Richard returns home better off than when he had started, while the monks are repaid in kind for their greed.

A change of mood and tone now enters the ballad, as the author evidently begins a new story from a different source. So far all has been fairly innocent, knockabout stuff. Now a darker stand enters, as the Sheriff, furious at his humiliation in the forest, prepares to set a trap. In a famous episode, often retold, he announces an archery contest in which the winner will be presented with the prize of a golden arrow. Of course, as the Sheriff knows, Robin cannot resist such a prize, and sure enough the outlaw comes to Nottingham in disguise, accompanied by a large number of his men, who mingle with the crowd.

At the end of the day Robin is clearly the winner, and is presented with the golden arrow. At that moment horns blow and pandemonium breaks loose as the Sheriff's men attempt to capture Robin. The hidden outlaws at once spring to his defence and they all escape – though Little

John is slightly wounded. As they flee, pursued by the Sheriff's men, they find themselves close to the castle of Sir Richard-at-Lee and seek sanctuary there. Sir Richard is glad of the opportunity to repay his debt, and when the Sheriff appears he refuses to give up the outlaws, adding that only 'King Edward' could decide the matter.

The Sheriff at once sets off to London to petition the King, who in turn promises to come to Nottingham in two weeks to take the castle and capture both Robin and Sir Richard. Still unsure that he will win the case, the Sheriff then abducts Sir Richard while the latter is out hunting and prepares to execute him on trumped-up charges. Sir Richard's wife sends a message to Robin and the outlaws set out to rescue their ally.

In a dramatic episode the outlaws make their way to Nottingham and mingle with the crowds assembling for the execution. When he sees the Sheriff, Robin lets fly an arrow that transfixes his enemy. In the ensuing melee Sir Richard is released and Robin beheads the Sheriff, sticking the severed head on his bow and mutilating it savagely – an uncharacteristic action which was, in fact, quite in keeping with the actions of real outlaws at this time.

Having thus freed Sir Richard, Robin advises him to remain with the outlaws until such time as the King arrives and matters can be set straight. However, when the King arrives in Nottingham and learns of the Sheriff's death he declares Sir Richard an outlaw also, and offers a large reward for his – and Robin's – capture.

Six months pass, however, and there is no sign of the outlaws. A forester finally advises the King that the only way to reach Robin Hood is for the monarch to disguise himself as a monk and travel through the forest with a small escort. The King does this, and is inevitably captured by Robin. Over a meal of royal venison, Robin declares that he and his fellows are poor yeomen forced to live in this way, and asks for 'alms'. The King declares that he has only £40 and Robin generously takes only half, returning the rest to the 'monk'. The King then produces a document sealed with the royal seal, demanding the presence of Robin at Nottingham to 'dine' with him. Robin at once kneels to the disguised monarch and declares that he will answer the summons, for he loves his king above all men.

An archery contest is then proposed in the Greenwood. Two garlands of roses are set up on poles, and the winner must knock his down with each of three arrows or lose his equipment and receive a buffet from the winner. In fact Robin himself misses one of the three shots and requests the monk to administer the blow. Somewhat reluctantly the disguised monarch obliges, and hits Robin so powerfully that the outlaw is amazed. Realising only a warrior could have administered such a blow he looks more closely at the face of his guest and recognises the King. At once all the outlaws, as well as Sir Richard, fall to their knees and beg pardon of the King. Edward is so impressed by the generosity of Robin that he agrees, on two conditions: that the outlaws leave the forest and that Robin becomes his man and joins him at the court.

Robin agrees and the Merry Men disband, returning to their homes. Only Little John and Will Scarlet go with him, while Sir Richard goes home.

A year passes and Robin is already bored with life at court. He asks leave to go on pilgrimage to a chapel in Barnsdale and is given a week. Once in the Greenwood again he cannot leave, and summons his old followers to join him. For the next twenty-two years he continues to live out his life in the forest as an outlaw.

After this the *Gest* peters out with a brief reference to Robin's death at the hands of the Abbess of Kirklees. We have to turn to one of the several versions of another ballad, 'The Death of Robin Hood', for the end of the story. Even here the versions that have survived are curiously conflicting and fragmentary, and there has been much debate as to their real meaning. However, it is possible, with only a little effort, to understand what is being said.

Growing old and ill, Robin decides to visit his 'kinswoman', who is the Abbess of Kirklees Priory near Peterborough and a famed healer. Apparently knowing that she was also the mistress of Roger of Doncaster, an old enemy of Robin's, and sensing trouble, Little John tries to persuade his master to take fifty men with him, but Robin refuses and in the end is accompanied only by John.

On the way they encounter a strange old woman beside a stream who appears to curse Robin. John is filled with foreboding but cannot persuade his master to turn back. At the abbey John is locked out of the room where Robin is to be treated, and the abbess begins to bleed her kinsman – a common enough treatment for most ailments in that time. However, as the ballad says:

> And first it bled, the thick, thick blood,
> And afterwards the thin,
> And well then wits good Robin Hood
> treason there was within ...

With failing strength he blows his horn and Little John breaks in – too late to save his master. As John rages and begs to be allowed to burn Kirklees and all within it to the ground, Robin rallies enough to say that he had never made war on women and will not begin now. He then begs to be helped to the window, and from there looses his last arrow, declaring that where it falls there should he be buried. John carries out this duty and erects a stone above the grave bearing only the words (in this version):

HERE LIES BOLD ROBIN HOOD.

Thus ends the story. There are any number of other ballads, of varying date and quality, but these add little to the essential version of the *Gest* beyond adding adventures that are often little more than variations on the essential theme.

The fragmentary nature of the ballads relating to Robin's death – the fullest dates from the eighteenth century and though it may well contain echoes of earlier stories, cannot be relied upon without hesitation – have made the serious writer's task fraught with problems. It is easy to see – as other commentators such as Margaret Murray have already done – a version of the death of the Divine King in this account, his end foretold by the old woman who seems very like the Celtic *bean sidhe* or Washer-at-the-Ford. However, we should be cautious at leaping to such conclusions on the evidence of a few broken lines. Only the strength of traditions relating not only to Robin himself but to the figure of the Green Man, which will be examined in succeeding chapters, bring us to the conclusion that the above is a correct reading of the text. Robin is indeed an aspect of the Divine King, and even though there is little evidence in the rest of the ballads, this is the only realistic way to understand the story.

The Birth and Life of an Outlaw

For evidence of the birth and life of Robin Hood we must look to both literature and historical speculation. A ballad collected in the nineteenth century by Robert Jamieson tells a different story of Robin's birth, which may preserve an older truth than any of the medieval ballads. Here we read of one 'Willie', a servant to 'Earl Richard', who loves his master's daughter and gets her with child. The couple flee to 'the good green wood' and there the girl gives birth to a 'bonny young son, among the

leaves so green'. When the earl misses his daughter he sends men out to
find her, and eventually they do so and bring her home. The earl looks
at the child, and

> He took the bonny boy in his arms
> And kissed him tenderly;
> Says, though I should your father hang,
> your mother's dear to me.

> He kissed him o'er and o'er again:
> My grandson I thee claim;
> And Robin Hood in good green wood,
> And that shall be your name.

> And many one sings of grass, of grass,
> And many one sings of corn,
> And many one sings of Robin Hood,
> Kens little where he was born. (53)

Whether or not one accepts this as a viable version of the story, there is
no escaping the idea that it was founded on a still living tradition in which
Robin is born illegitimate and, like many heroes before him, in the forest –
perhaps in one of the 'Beltane Weddings' (so-called) which lasted only for
a night and a day. That his putative grandfather recognises the spirit of
his conception and birth is clear enough, and that he chooses to call him
Robin Hood suggests an older derivation for the Outlaw of Sherwood.

The notion that Robin Hood was really the Earl of Huntingdon – or
sometimes his son and heir – seems to stem entirely from the writings of a
ballad maker of the seventeenth century named Martin Parker, in whose
'True Tale of Robin Hood' (23) we find that he died in 1198, and that his
epitaph, which could be 'read within these hundred years, though in old
broken English' read, somewhat more elaborately than in the older ballads:

> Robert Earl of Huntington
> Lies under this little stone.
> No archer like him was so good:
> His wildness named him Robin Hood.

Full thirteen years, and something more,
These northern parts he vexed sore.
Such outlaws as he and his men
May England never know more.

All this really says is that Robert of Huntington was an outlaw whose deeds earned him the title of Robin Hood – a fact that we shall see recurring again and again as successors appear jostling for the title of the famous outlaw.

There are, indeed, a number of instances where the name 'Robin Hood' appears in historical documents dating from the Middle Ages. Professor Child mentions a Thomas Robinhood, who is one of six witnesses to a grant of land in 1380 or 81. (17) Sir Edmund Chambers lists five further references from the Sussex area between 1296 and 1332, in Wakefield between 1316 and 1335, and at the royal court in 1324. (16) In the *Great Roll of the Pipe* for 1230 there is a reference to one 'Robertus Hood, *fugitivus*', which has led at least one commentator to suggest that this was 'the' Robin. But, as Professor Hodgart remarks in his study of *The Ballads* (39),

It ... looks as if Robin Hood were a fairly common name, perhaps one used generically for outlaws in the thirteenth and fourteenth centuries.

This idea, that 'a Robinhood' was a title applied generically to outlaws from the thirteenth century onwards, is an interesting one, borne out by later evidence of a number of men said to bear this name, but for whom there is little evidence to connect them with the more substantial figure of the ballads. Later, in the same work quoted above, Hodgart includes a fragment dating from about 1400, scribbled in a MS found in Lincoln Cathedral:

Robyn hod in scherwod stod
hodud and hathud hosut and schod
ffour and thuyrti arowus he bar
in his hondus.

This seems to hint at an older figure, 'hooded and clothed, with hose and shoes', but the truth is that no one really knew who Robin Hood was, when he lived, or even, with any certainty, where. Scholars have placed him, variously, in Sherwood, Barnsdale or Wakefield, and can point out his grave, along with that of Little John, in at least two separate places. Yet, try as they might, they cannot pin him down. He remains as elusive now as in the ballads, slipping into and out of the forest of history as he does in the stories and songs that tell of his adventures.

I have already stated that I do not believe there was ever a single person called Robin Hood (or any variants of the name), but that he is rather a principle of the natural world, a Green Man of the forest rather than a Saxon yeoman 'courteous and free'. However, in order to get a correct frame of reference for the way in which this character has continued to haunt the consciousness of people all over the world (his popularity is not confined to England alone), it is necessary to look briefly at some of the contenders who have emerged from the diligent enquiries of various commentators through the ages.

In the first instance we find references to Robin in several chronicles dating from the Middle Ages more or less at the time he is supposed to have lived – if we accept the testimony of the ballads. From these we pick up a few details of chronology – though none are to be strictly believed.

The Sloane Manuscript *Life of Robin Hood* (*c.* 1600), included as Appendix 2 of the present book, records the date of Robin's birth as 1160 at Thoresby in Ducatus Leodensis (better known as Leeds), and that of his death at Kirklees Priory as 1274, when he would have been eighty-seven years old. Richard Grafton refers to the much-debated epitaph, which goes through so many versions after its first appearance in the ballads, in more detail in 1596. He says that the Prioress of Kirklees

caused him [Robin] to be buried by the highway side, where he used to rob and spoil those that passed that way. And upon his grave the said prioress did lay a very fair stone, wherein the names of Robert Hood, William of Goldsborough, and others were graven. (4)

This is curious, as it suggests that rather than a grave what we actually have here is a memorial stone listing several outlaws, including the well-known William of Goldsborough.

Apparently the stone remained in place for several hundred years, though by the seventeenth century the inscription was almost illegible and by the eighteenth it was unreadable – despite an attempt by the antiquary Samuel Gale (or possibly his brother Roger) to pass off a version they claimed to have copied down from the original stone.

Close to one of the many supposed sites of Robin Hood's grave, this one near Bradford in West Yorkshire is another supposedly belonging to one Elizabeth Stainton, who may perhaps be the infamous prioress. The gravestone believed to be Robin's was once lifted, but no bones were found there. Indeed, the earth seemed as though it had never been disturbed, making it even more likely that the stone was either a fake or had been placed there simply as a memorial to the outlaw and others of his ilk.

Other documents add little or no information. The Parliamentary Rolls for 1437 mention one Piers Venebles, who was arrested on the grounds that he had taken to robbery and then hidden in the woods 'like it had been Robyn Hood and his meynie', while statutes set down during the reign of Edward III refer to the term 'Roberdsmen' as a general term for 'outlaw'. John Fordun, in his *Scottichronicon* of *c.* 1446, mentions both Robin Hood and Little John in the entry for 1341, in terms that suggested that they were already well known in England.

The nineteenth-century historian John Gutch, who gives Robin's birth as 1225, says that the title 'Earl of Huntington' was once used to refer to any skilled huntsman – from which we may suppose that many bore it as a title. Another source says that the title was held during Robin Hood's own (supposed) time by King David of Scotland, brother to William the Lion.

Curiously, as pointed out to me by David Elkington, in the pedigree of the Scottish kings there is a Robert of Huntington, born sometime before 1207. He appears to be the eldest child of seven of David Earl Lennox, 2nd Earl Huntingdon. The area over which this nobleman ruled would appear to be Huntingdon in what is now Cambridgeshire but was then Huntingdonshire. Robert's mother was Mathilda (Maund/ Maud) of Chester, Countess de Keveliock (Ceuelioc, Wales) whose father, Hugh, was the Earl of Chester. Among the oldest of the Robin Hood ballads is one entitled 'Robyn Hood and Randolf Erl of Chestr.' This Robert should have inherited the title 'Earl Huntingdon' but because he predeceased his father he did not acquire the title. According to John Fordun, Robert Ceann mhor died in infancy. Robert's younger brother Jean le Scot appears to have inherited the title 'Earl of Huntingdon' as well as the earldom of Chester. Interestingly, the sixth child of David and Mathilda was Isabella Ceann mhor [FitzDavid] of Huntingdon, who married Robert Bruce, 4th Lord of Annandale, which led to the line of the Bruces, including the great Robert le Bruis I, King of Scotland.

Thus the title Earl of Huntingdon was once part of the Scottish line. Jean/John le Scot/Cean mhor, Earl of Chester and Huntingdon was probably the last in the line to hold the title. This may well account for the popularity of Robin Hood plays and ballads throughout Scotland as late as the seventeenth century.

Another oft-repeated assertion is that Robin was in reality Robert Fitzooth, born at Loxley, Nottinghamshire in 1274. No less a person than the great eighteenth-century antiquarian William Stukeley published a pedigree to support this theory in his 1746 work *Paelographica Britanicca*. It is reproduced overleaf as a curiosity, though there is almost certainly no shred of truth in it. Stukeley based his conclusion on a late ballad (1621), 'The Birth, Breeding, Valour and Marriage of Robin Hood'. He showed that 'Robert' became Earl of Huntington through his descent from Judith, a niece of William the Conqueror, who married Wathlof, the last Saxon Earl of Northumberland and Huntington. Joseph Ritson revived this unlikely belief in his valuable collection of the ballads, but subsequent historians have generally discredited it. Despite this, Stukeley's list gave rise to yet another theory, proposed by Jim Lees of Nottingham, that Robin was a man named Robert de Kyme (see below).

The Yorkshire Robin Hoods

One of the most interesting suggestions for the identity of the Outlaw of Sherwood was put forward by Joseph Hunter in 1852 in a tract called *The Great Hero of the English Minstrelsy of England, Robin Hood, his period, real character...* Hunter believed Robin to have been a Yorkshireman, born at Wakefield between 1285 and 1295, who took

The Pedigree of Robin Hood, Earl of Huntingdon.

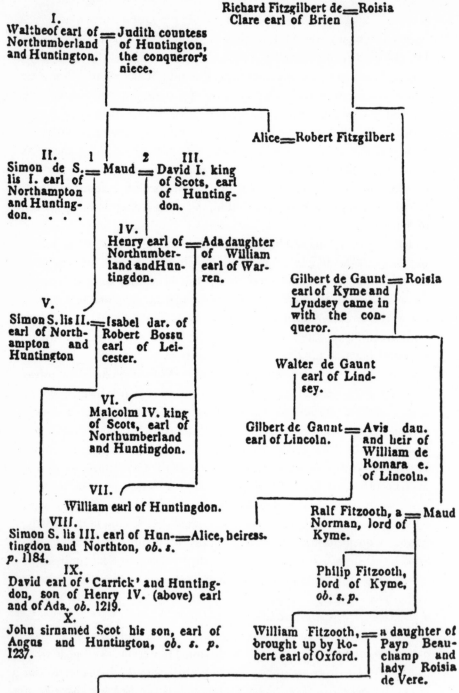

Robert Fitzooth, commonly called Robin Hood, pretended ſearl of Huntington, *ob.* 1274 [1247].

The fanciful Pedigree of Robin Hood, Earl of Huntingdon from the Paleographica Brittanica *of William Stukeley, 1788.*

part in an ill-fated rebellion on the part of the Earl of Lancaster against Edward II in 1322. This does seem, on the surface, to tie in with the *Gest*, in which 'a' King Edward does indeed travel to Barnsdale in search of Robin. Also, Edward II did go on a tour of his realm, taking him through Lancashire in 1323. He also stayed for some weeks in Nottingham. In the Court Rolls relating to the following year, 1324, a man named Robin or Robert Hood was apparently Groom of the Chamber, but did not remain so for long. This Robin is said to have pined so much for the forest that he fled back there within a year of taking service with the king.

Further details may be added. Adam Hood, a forester in the service of John de Warenne, Lord of the Manor of Wakefield, had a son named Robert who was educated in the school run by John of Wakefield, a clerk in service to the earl. In time he married a local girl named Matilda, of whom nothing more is known. It is possible that this is the same man as Hunter's contention.

Sometime before this, in 1316, when Edward II began gathering an army to subdue rebellious Scots along the Borders, we find mention of one Robert Hood being fined for failing to answer the summons of his liege lord, John, Earl of Warenne. Soon after, this same nobleman became involved in the abduction of the Earl of Lancaster's wife, with whom he was apparently in love, and subsequently the manor of Wakefield changed hands when John de Warenne granted it to Lancaster in reparation for the wrongs done to him. Thus Robert Hood became the liegeman of a new lord, the Earl of Lancaster, who in 1322 became involved in a rebellion against Edward II. Lancaster was defeated and beheaded at the battle of Boroughbridge, and Robert, who seems to have answered the call to arms on this occasion, lost his lands and either chose or was forced to become an outlaw. Matilda, it is said, went with him, and from this point the legends of Robin's female counterpart began.

Hunter is one of the earliest of those who set out to identify the 'real' Robin Hood. His claim that Robert Hood was later pardoned by King Edward and became for a time a royal bodyguard may or may not be true, but there is still sufficient evidence here to give us pause. Even supposing that this is the 'real' Robin, however, it still proves nothing. It seems likely that there would have been some more significant accounts of this identification of the most famous outlaw in England, and even if such accounts were to be produced, it would still not disprove the belief that there were probably several men called 'Robin Hood' who were all outlaws and who either identified themselves, or were so identified by the people, with an older and more primal figure.

The fact that the name of the reigning monarch changes from story to story – as do details like the use of the longbow at a time when the shorter Saxon bow was in use – suggests nothing more than the effect of the retelling of the stories by new generations of balladeers – who, just as they did with King Arthur, fitted Robin into the clothing of the time and gave his enemies appropriate titles. The setting of the Robin Hood stories and ballads has entered into mythic time – a period before the present time of the singer, composer or listener. The 'feel' of the stories retains a sense of belonging to an earlier historical period than that of Edward II, to a time when the Norman and Saxon had still not fused into the English. The adversaries of the great outlaw are nearly always 'Norman' rather than simply 'the rich'.

Internal evidence provided by the ballads themselves offers little by way of precise information, though they do reflect the society of the early Middle Ages. The treatment meted out to yeoman farmers, or worse to the ordinary tenants, by the powerful Norman landowners was certainly unfair and cruel. The sheriffs, appointed by the King to oversee rents, taxes and general law enforcement, were often greedy and self-seeking. There is no evidence that the Sheriff of Nottingham was any worse than the rest, but he obviously became a caricature of all sheriffs everywhere.

Even worse than the sheriffs or the landowning nobles were the churchmen, whose grip on their lands was at times even tighter than that of the barons. Small wonder that abbots and monks became frequent targets for Robin and the merry men.

More Bold Outlaws

One of the oldest surviving references to anyone with the name Robert or Robin Hood dates from between 1213 and 1216, when a servant of the Abbot of Cirencester is said to have murdered a man named Ralph in the abbot's garden; however, not only is this too early to have influenced the stories of Robin, there is no mention of this man being an outlaw living with a band of others in a forest setting.

We can easily dismiss the Robert Hod recorded as being in a Rockingham jail for poaching the king's deer in 1354 as being far too isolated an account, though it must be said that the reference discovered in the Court Rolls for 1354–56 possesses a certain ring of authenticity:

May 16 1354, Westminster

To Thomas de Brewer, keeper of the forest this side of the Trent or to him who supplies his place in the forest of Rokyngham. Order to bail Robert Hod, imprisoned at Rokyngham for trespass of vert and venison in the forest of Rokyngham, if he shall find twelve mainpernors of that bailiwick who will undertake to have him before the justices next in eyre for pleas of the forest in the county of Northampton, to stand to right for the said trespass, if he is replievable according to the assize of the forest.

The fact that this Robert Hod is accused of poaching in the king's forest does not, unfortunately, offer sufficient evidence to make him the original Robin, nor do the claims of Nottingham researcher Jim Lees, suggesting that a man named Robert de Kyme was the real Robin, since these are based on a much-challenged genealogy compiled by William Stukeley in the eighteenth century, and a supposed manuscript which has unfortunately remained 'missing' to this day.

One can see why one Roger (or Robin) Godberd (d. *c.* 1276) has been considered as a possible origin for Robin Hood, since his career does in many ways parallel that of the great outlaw. He served for a time under Simon de Montfort, 6th Earl of Leicester, and took part in the Barons' War of 1264–67 against Henry III. Having fought on the losing side at the Battle of Evesham in 1265, Roger was outlawed and fled for his life, ending up in Sherwood Forest in 1267, where he continued to hold out for four years. He certainly seems to have lived a life similar to that of Robin Hood, attacking monasteries and demanding reparation for lands 'stolen' by the Church. It was reported that he had as many as a hundred men at his command, but this did not prevent him from being captured in 1272, by no less a person than the then Sheriff of Nottingham, Reginald de Grey. Godberd ended up in Nottingham Castle, having been captured in the grounds of the Cistercian abbey of Rufford. However, again following a similar path to that of his famous namesake, Robin escaped – helped, it seems, by a local knight named

Richard Foliot, who it has been suggested is the origin of Sir Richard of the Lee.

Foliot certainly offered Robin Godberd shelter and protection for several months in his castle at Fenwick, until a sheriff (it is disputed whether this was of Yorkshire or Nottingham) arrived with a small force and laid siege to it. Fortunately for Godberd and his friends they got word of the impending attack and made good their escape, but Foliot was accused of harboring the outlaws and was himself arraigned and forced to give up his holdings, including the castle, for a time – though he seems to have regained his title later on.

As to Godberd, he is said to have been held in three different prisons while awaiting trial for his misdeeds. Finally he ended up in the Tower of London, but his subsequent fate is uncertain. One source says he was pardoned by Edward I on the king's return from the Ninth Crusade in 1274, perhaps as part of a general order of clemency or in celebration of his coronation in that year. In this version Godberd is said to have returned to his farm to live out the rest of his life in peace, but the *Oxford Dictionary of National Biography* has him dying in Newgate prison in 1276.

In the end, as with most historical contenders, all one can say is that the life of this man may well have inspired the ballad makers to adopt scenes from the life of Roger Godberd to that of the Outlaw of Sherwood.

The Naming of Robin Hood

In the end it is to the name that we may look to see why so many people have been extracted from medieval documents to be identified with the Outlaw of Sherwood. Much has been made of the derivation of the name 'Hood' (or Hode, etc.) and it is noted that it was a common name, as was Robin, and that they often appear in tandem in records of the thirteenth and fourteenth centuries. However, no one seems to care that it is the way in which the name was applied to the hero that is important. 'Robin-i-the-Hood' is as much a part of the matter of outlawry as is 'Robin Wood'. This latter was also a common name, which had older associations. Thomas Wright, much maligned for his careless scholarship, pointed out that the name 'Witikind', a famous outlaw opponent of the Emperor Charlemagne, derives from 'Witu-Chint' in Old High Dutch, and means 'the Son of the Wood'. The Old Norse words *skoggangar* and *skogarmadr*, frequently applied to outlaws, literally mean 'one who goes into the woods'. This equates well with the detail noted by several other writers that 'wode' also means 'twig' or 'bush', and that in the context Robin is quite rightly called 'Robin of the Woods' or 'Robin of the Bushes'.

Other, less tenuous memorials are the number of place names that derive from Robin or his men. In Sherwood, as one would expect, these proliferate. Robin Hood's Pot is a stone near Oxton; his Larder is at Birklands; the River Leren rises near Robin Hood's Hills; Friar Tuck's Cell stood at Copmanhurst. There is a Robin Hoods Well in Sherwood itself, near Beaubale Hall, and another on the bank of the River Skell, while in Cheshire there is Robin Hood's Barrow near Tilston Fearnell and in Yorkshire Robin Hood's Bay, where he is supposed to have hidden. In Cheshire and East Yorkshire the bitterly cold wind that ushers in the thaw after a long frost is still called Robin Hood's Wind, and is said to be the only discomfort he could not stand. In 1700 at Robin Hood's Well (also known as St Anne's Well) the hero's cap, chair, slipper and horn were kept on show. The custom was that travellers sat in the chair and were crowned with the hat – a distant memory, perhaps of the crowning of the May King. As with Arthur, once a hero has attained this stature it is fairly certain that we are no longer dealing with a simple human being. (41)

The point of all this, as we shall see, is not simply that the name Robin Hood was applied to a succession of outlaws from the twelfth to the fifteenth centuries (though this may well be true), but that the name Robin Hood derived from a far older figure, that of the Green Man, and that in time the exploits of the legendary outlaw began to be confused with memories of this ancient ritual character and the long-remembered events which celebrated him – especially those revolving around the May Day Games, which came in time to be known simply as 'Robin Hood's Games'.

The Myth of Robin

Having looked at the story as it is told in the *Gest* and elsewhere, we can see that the life of Robin Hood conforms very well to that of an archetypal hero. Lewis Spence, one of the most outright champions of the mythological theory, summarises the argument thus:

He was, indeed, King of the May, and his Maid Marian the May Queen ... His May Day ceremonies seem to have given rise to tales capable of arrangement into three classes: stories of single combat, stories of feats with a bow, and tricky stories ... These are all suggestive of a system by which the king reigned from one May Day to the next, when he had to fight for his title, if not for his life, and possibly also for the possession of his consort. Here, then, we are ... face to face with the ... theory of the king whose waning vigour made it necessary to remove him or put him to death and replace him by another. The second class of story is due to the popularity of the longbow in England in the fifteenth century ... Lastly, the tricky stories may be due to a confusion between Robin Hood and Robin Goodfellow, the familiar fairy. (85)

Lord Raglan, another influential authority, in his excellent, if at times aberrant book *The Hero* (73) suggests a number of signs by which we may recognise the typical life story of a classic hero-figure. He lists these as follows:

1. The hero's mother is a royal virgin.
2. His father is a king, and
3. Often a near relative of his mother, but
4. The circumstances of his conception are unusual, and
5. He is also reputed to be the son of a god.
6. At birth an attempt is made, usually by his father or his maternal grandfather, to kill him, but
7. He is spirited away, and
8. Reared by foster parents in a far country.
9. We are told nothing of his childhood, but
10. On reaching manhood he returns or goes to his future kingdom.
11. After a victory over the king and/or a giant, dragon, or wild beast,
12. He marries a princess, often the daughter of his predecessor, and
13. Becomes king.
14. For a time he reigns uneventfully, and
15. Prescribes laws, but
16. Later he loses favour with the gods and/or his subjects, and

17. Is driven from the throne or city, after which
18. He meets with a mysterious death,
19. Often at the top of a hill.
20. His children, if any, do not succeed him.
21. His body is not buried, but nevertheless
22. He has one or more holy sepulchres.

Raglan then applies this to Robin Hood, revealing how he fits into the pattern:

> His father is a Saxon yeoman, but he is also (5) reputed to be the son of a great noble. We (9) hear nothing of his youth, but on reaching manhood he leads a life of debauchery [*sic*] until compelled to fly (10) to Sherwood, where he (11) gains victory over the Sheriff of Nottingham, (12) marries Maid Marian, the Queen of May, and (13) becomes King of May and ruler of the forest. For a long time he reigns, and (15) prescribes the laws of archery, but eventual illness overtakes him, and he (17) has to leave the forest, and meets (18) a mysterious death in (19) an upper room. He (20) has no children. The place of his death and burial are (21) variously given, but (22) miracles were performed at his tomb at Kirklees, in Yorkshire.

Some of these points are undoubtedly stretching the story somewhat to make it fit, but enough are true to the ballad mythos to suggest that Raglan was correct, and that Robin really does fit the pattern sufficiently to assure him a place in the heroes roll of honour.

It is this basic premise that we shall follow throughout the remainder of this book.

2

THE GREEN DANCERS

The fairy-tale universe is often a fragmentary memory if not of
actual events, then of psychological processes of social change.
Sometimes, as in many nursery rhymes, it evades censorship
by disguising home truths not in rubbish but in nonsense. It
survives, like Robin, because it is evoked by unending longings
and prejudices, maintaining Harlequin restlessness and Punch
lawlessness and violence ... keeping alive quicksilver movement
and never-never, the dance of the emotions.

Peter Vansittart, *Green Knights, Black Angels*

Dancers in the Green
The people of Faery – the Fair Folk, the Good People, the Mothers;
by whatever name we call them, the Faeries are probably the earliest
level in the multi-layered strata that has gone into the making of
Robin Hood.

It may well be a truism that the Faery folk tended to dress in green
and wore hoods, and that Robin and his men did likewise – but it is from
this point that we should begin our investigation into the connections
between Robin and the Faery race.

No one knows the origins of the Faeries. Perhaps they were the first
people in this land, the Little Dark People, or the Picts, the Old Ones.
Perhaps they were gods once; perhaps we only dream them – but no
two people can ever agree as to their appearance. Some say they are

small, others of normal human size, while still others see them as tall and stately; and though it is generally accepted that it was the Victorians who opted for small and cute, and who added the tinsel wings still associated in many people's minds with the idea of faeries, there seems little reason to doubt that just as they were sometimes perceived as tall, beautiful and powerful, they were equally often seen as small in stature. As J. A. MacCulloch notes in his entry on Faeries in the *Encyclopaedia of Religion and Ethics:*

> Frequently fairies are regarded as diminutive folk, but there is much contradiction on this subject, and many fairies (the fees of Southern Europe, the Slavic vilas, and the sid folk of Ireland) are hardly to be distinguished in size from mortals. In the same region some groups of fairies may be tall, others pygmies, but the varying size is sometimes due to their power of changing their form. Once fairies were regarded as small, their smallness would tend to be exaggerated.

One of the few things that most accounts agree upon is that the favourite colour of the Faery folk was green. It is for this reason that some people still think of green as unlucky, since the people of Faery alone could wear it and to copy them was to court their anger.

'Virtually all the elfin folk of Britain and Ireland dress in green, a colour, indeed, that is pretty generally characteristic of fairies,' says Professor Wimberley in his book *Folk Lore and the Ballad*, going on to cite a number of Faery ballads such as *Tam Lin* and *Thomas Rhymer* (Child Ballads Nos 37 and 39), where we read of Thomas being provided with green shoes:

> He has gotten a coat of the even cloth,
> And a pair of shoes of velvet green,
> And till seven years were past and gone
> True Thomas on earth was never seen.

While in the description of the second Faery court in Tam Lin we read how:

> The next court that comes along
> Is clad in robes of green,

And it's the head court of them all,
For in it rides the queen.

As to the reason, if any is needed, why the Faery folk should choose this colour, one may decide whether one sees it as a natural reflection of their closeness and participation in the natural world, or whether the folklore association of the colour green with death and witches derives from the Faery tradition, or whether it influenced that tradition in turn.

The tradition that Robin and the Merry Men wore 'Lincoln Green' is probably a late one, though if we are right in supposing that Robin is a relative of the Green Man, then it would be natural enough for him to wear this colour. The name actually refers both to the woollen cloth woven by the weavers of Lincoln, and to the colour, produced by dying the cloth blue using woad (*Isatis tinctoria*), then overdyeing it yellow with weld (*Reseda luteola*) or dyers' broom (*Genista tinctoria*). In the ballads there are numerous references to the outlaw's costume, including the following from part eight of the *Gest*:

Haste thou any green cloth? said our King
That thou will sell now to me.
Ye, before God, said Robin,
Thirty yards and three ...

The king cast off his cote then,
A green garment he did on.
And every knight had so, I wys,
They clothed them full soon.

When they were clothed in Lincoln Green,
They cast way their grey.
Now we shall to Nottingham,
All thus our king 'gan say ...

All the people of Nottingham
They stood and beheld,
They saw nothing but mantles of green,
That covered all the field;

Then every man to the other 'gan say,
I dread our king be slain;
Come Robin Hood to the town, I wys,
On life he leveth not one ...

In another ballad, *Robin Hood's Birth, Breeding, Valour, and Marriage at the Tutbury Bull-Running*, he encounters Clorinda, Queen of the Shepherdesses, who is dressed 'in a gown of velvet as green as the grass', showing that not only the male members of Robin's band wore green. (See also Chapter 5.) Ritson points out that green was also a colour generally adopted by archers, to whom Robin was something of an unofficial patron. As we read in Spenser's *Fairy Queen*:

All in a woodman's jacket he was clad
Of Lincoln greene, belaye'd with silver lace;
And ion his head an hood with aglets sprad,
And by his side his hunter's horne he hanging had.

Canto VI. ii. 5

The importance given to the episode in the *Gest* where the Sheriff, having been captured, is made to put on the dress of an outlaw is evidence that the colour was still regarded as important even then. Certainly all the references to the clothing bought for those taking the role of Robin Hood in the May-Day Games, or in the Robin Hood plays of the sixteenth to eighteenth century, refer to this colour. Until recent times 'to wear the green' was another way of saying that one followed the old religion of this land.

Another aspect of all this is the association between Robin Hood and fairs and between Faery folk and fairs. According to the Elizabethan writer Henry Fuller, wherever Robin went 'he carried a fair along with him, chapmen crowding to buy his stolen goods', and there are certainly frequent references to fairs in the ballads. In Ireland, of course, there was the Puck Fair, held at Killorglin in County Kerry every August, where there was a general disposition towards wild behaviour and unbridled licence.

Puck, in this instance, comes from the Gaelic *poc*, meaning a he-goat. (Though, as we shall see, there is reason to connect Puck with Robin Hood.) Every year a goat is chosen, decorated, and paraded through the town to the accompaniment of music and song. It is regarded as the King of Fair, and is ceremonially crowned and placed on a platform, where it remains throughout the duration of the fair. Despite the derivation of the name, there are echoes of Puckish goings on at the fair, with possible factional combats, and there are a number of stories about people unlawfully trying to steal the goat and finding that their hands were mysteriously stuck to its shaggy coat.

Several fairs of this kind – popularly known as 'Faery Fairs' – were held in Ireland up until at least the end of the nineteenth century. Another such, at Ballycotton, revolved around a figure known as 'Muck Olla', who seems to have been represented by a horse's skull on a pole, also called the *Lir Bhan* or the 'White Mare', which was paraded between Ballycotton and Trabolgan on the eve of Samhain (31 October). The followers of this famous spirit went from house to house demanding money in return for a good crop and were seldom refused. An almost identical ceremony, enacted in Kent, was called 'Hoodening', the horse here known as 'The Hoden Horse', while in Wales the Mari Llwyd, another decorated horse skull, is paraded from house to house with elaborate riddling exchanges by those within and those without. The connection between these fairs, the Puck, Muck Olla and the 'Hooded' Horse, may be circumstantial, but cannot be entirely dismissed, as we shall see.

There is also the matter of the 'Robin Hood's Bowers', constructed as part of the May Day celebrations. In tandem with the Maypole these had a deeper significance than is at first apparent. They were certainly the scenes of amorous trysts between the participants of the fairs, and are also described as Faery bowers, supposedly in imitation of such magical shelters believed to be constructed by the Fair Folk themselves.

Even Robin's skill in archery is a Faery trait, since the discharging of 'elf-shot', flint-tipped arrows, at both human and beast, is among the most prominent features in the Faery tradition. (Significantly so, if the theory that relates the Faery race to the earliest inhabitants of these islands is true, since the people of that time would have carried bows and used flint arrowheads.)

Aside from these factors, we must look elsewhere, to the Faery tradition itself, in order to understand why we should perceive Robin as one of the personnel of Faery, as at least one particular member of the Faery race – the outlaw of Sherwood's namesake, Robin Goodfellow – helps to make clear.

Merry Robin

Almost everything we know about Robin Goodfellow comes from a curious seventeenth-century pamphlet which rejoices in the title *Robin Goodfellow, alias Puck, alias Hob: his mad pranks, and merry jests, full of honest mirth, and is a fit medicine for melancholy. (74)* It was printed in 1628 but almost certainly drew on a whole range of earlier Faery lore as well as, we may infer, lore concerning Robin Hood and the Green Man. The story contained in the pamphlet may be summarised as follows.

This Robin's nascence is described in a manner very reminiscent of the birth of Merlin. Oberon, the Faery King, visits a maiden at night, but in the day vanishes 'wither she knew not, he went so suddenly'. As with Merlin's mother, the outcome of these nightly visits is a child, who shows no unusual traits until age six, when he begins to be so troublesome and to play such knavish tricks upon the neighbours that his mother is in despair. Finally she promises him a whipping, and since this did not please him he runs away. A day from his home he settles to sleep in a field, and there dreams of bright-eyed folk who dance around him all night to music he deems as fair as Orpheus might have made. In the morning he wakes to find a scroll beside him on which is written, in words of gold:

> Robin, my only son and heir,
> How to live take thou no care:
> By nature thou hast cunning shifts,
> Which I'll increase with other gifts.
> Wish what thou wilt, thou shall it have;
> And for to fetch both fool and knave,
> Thou hast the power to change thy shape,
> To horse, to hog, to dog, to ape.
> Transformed thus, by any means,
> See none thou harm'st but knaves and queans:
> But love thou those that honest be,
> And help them in necessity.
> Do thus and all the world shall know
> The pranks of Robin Goodfellow,
> For by that name thou called shall be
> To age's last posterity;
> And if thou keep my just command,
> One day thou shall see Fairy Land.

Robin at once tested the promise of wish-granting by asking for food; a dish of fine veal was set before him. He wished for plum pudding; it appeared. Then, being weary, he wished himself to be a horse. At once he became a fine-spirited beast, and thereafter changed himself into a black dog, a green tree, and so on until he was sure he could change himself into anything he wished. Then he wished to try out his newfound skills by playing more of the tricks for which he had been recently chastised, and forthwith set out into the world, where he played so many merry jests that soon his name was known throughout the land. He played tricks on clowns, on burghers, on old and young; he turned himself into a chimney sweep (for which reason he was a patron of sweeps until the Victorian era and appeared in procession with them in the May Day Games). Finally, so great was the noise about the world complaining of Robin Goodfellow's trickery that his father Oberon summoned him to Faery with these words:

> Robin, my son, come quickly rise:
> First stretch, then yawn, and rub your eyes:
> For thou must go with me to-night,
> And taste of Fairy-Land's delight.

Robin rose from his bed at once and went where he was called. Here he met with Oberon and many other fairies, all clad in green. Throughout the night they danced to Faery music, and as they danced Oberon said:

> Whene'er thou hear the piper blow,
> Round and round the fairies go!
> And nightly you must with us dance,
> In meadows where the moonbeams glance,
> And make the circle, hand in hand –
> That is the law of Fairy-Land!
> There thou shalt see what no man knows;
> While sleep the eyes of men doth close!

After this Robin is said to have remained in Faery for 'many a long year'.

Thus ends the curious little story, which on the face of it bears little resemblance to anything to do with Robin beyond the name of its hero. However, if we dig a little deeper into the origin of the work we begin to glimpse some common points, which suggest its origin in a more distant past.

Kathleen Briggs, the great historian of Faery, catalogues this Robin, together with Puck, as a type of Brownie, a hobgoblin or sprite whose characteristics were chiefly to cause trouble for mortals and to clean up houses where they were made welcome. (11) This is generally in line with the instructions given to Robin in the scroll by his father – that he harm none who do not deserve it. Generally, the victims of his pranks are indeed unworthy people, and despite the anger he causes by his at times outrageous deeds, there is little or no real spite or cruelty in them. Indeed, like Robin Hood he more often helps the poor at the expense of the rich.

Like other heroes of myth, such as Taliesin, he is able to change shape at will – not only into animal, bird and fish, but also into such things as trees, bushes, rocks and clouds. In this, and by the nature of his birth, he proclaims himself more than a simple Faery. Like Robin he is a hero of the common people, with powers far greater than his pranks would suggest. Indeed, it seems that he really never grows up, but remains forever the little six-year-old boy, even after he has attained his rightful place beside his father in Faery. Like the young Merlin and the youthful Taliesin he loves playing tricks, which more often resolve mysteries or display his abilities to make things happen. His characteristic 'ho, ho, ho' is reminiscent of Merlin's laughter, while his shape-shifting abilities are like those of the famous Welsh bard. Alfred Nutt, in his essay on *The Fairy Mythology of Shakespeare* (71), even compared him to the Irish God Manannan mac Lir, who was also the son of a mortal and a human mother, and who eventually attained the Celtic otherworld after being watched over for many years by his father.

There are many other descriptions of Robin Goodfellow, showing that he was seen in a remarkably unified way – as witness the following extract from Thomas Rowlands' *More Knaves Yet*:

> Amongst the rest, was a good fellow devil,
> So called in kindness, cause he did no evil,
> Known by the name of Robin (as we hear)
> And that his eyes as bigge as sawcers were,
> Who came a nights, and would make kitchens cleane
> And in the bed bepinch a lazie queane ...(11)

Lewis Spence, in his study of seasonal games (84), argues that 'many of the Mad Pranks and Merry Gests recounted of Robin Goodfellow in the old pamphlet of that name make it clear that the goblin in question had more than a nominal connection with Robin Hood in his 'tricky' stories.' He goes on to discuss the belief in the 'great dead' or tribal ancestors, who were believed to preside over the growth of vegetation – hence, perhaps, the attribution of the colour green to the world of the dead – and with whom the faeries have a close association.

> Of such a type, I believe, was Robin Hood, or Rob, or Hob of the Wood or Forest, who presided over that particular demesne, whence both timber and venison were forthcoming … The facts that his traditional tomb was situated among a grove of trees [see Chapter 1] and that it consisted of a standing stone which was capable of self-propulsion and miraculous motion … bring him into line with those other spirits who haunt such standing stones, and who were formally worshipped at them. In a word his gravestone behaves like the traditional fairy monolith … Robin Hood I believe, then, is a reminiscence of an early departmental deity or godling associated with afforested places, and as such his festival would be celebrated at the seasons of vernal growth. That Robin Goodfellow, the Mad Hob, or wild goblin, is a later and more elfin phase of him appears more than probable. (84)

Whether we see this Robin as an elf, a Faery, a hobgoblin or an ancestral guardian of the land, we can be sure that he was at one time recognised as a far more powerful being than we can imagine today. Folklorist Sydney Hartland reached the same conclusion when he wrote in his book *The Science of Fairy Tales*:

> Do you imagine that Robin Goodfellow – a mere name to you – conveys anything like the meaning to your mind that it did to those whom the name represented a still living belief, and who had the stories about him at their fingers' ends? Or let me ask you, why did the fairies dance on moonlit nights? Or have you ever thought why it is that in English literature, and in English literature alone, the fairy realm finds a place in the highest works of the imagination?

This makes it clear that we would not be far wrong in seeing Robin Goodfellow (and therefore, perhaps, Robin Hood) as a native British trickster figure akin to the Native American Coyote, or the West Indian Anansi. The other leading contender for this title is the subject of the next part of our investigation into the Faery traditions associated with Robin Hood.

The Puck

Puck is, of course, most familiar to us from his appearance in Shakespeare's *A Midsummer Night's Dream* and Kipling's wonderful *Puck of Puck's Hill* (114). Shakespeare makes it clear how much he knows about the character, describing him as:

> ... that shrewd and knavish sprite
> Call'd Robin Goodfellow. Are not you he
> That frights the maidens of the villagery,
> Skim milk and sometimes labour in their quern,
> And bootless makes the breathless housewife churn
> And sometimes make the drink to bear no balm,
> Mislead night-wanderers, laughing at their harm?
> Those that Hobgoblin call you, and sweet Puck,
> You do their work, and they shall have good luck
>
> Act 2. sc. 1

Puck, as nearly always, is here seen as virtually interchangeable with Robin Goodfellow, as the title of the old pamphlet discussed above also makes clear. Yet he does have an existence of his own, and is still remembered all over Britain in place names like Pickwell, Pickhill, Pickmere, Peckham, Puckholm, etc.

His name, in fact, is probably derived from the Middle English *pook*, or *pouke*, meaning an elf or sprite, and there is in fact a remarkable commonality between this word and the name attributed to similar characters over a wide area. Thus we have

Puki	Icelandic	Imp
Puckle	Old English	Spirit
Buckie	Scots	Sprite
Pech	Scots	Faery
Spuck	German	Hobgoblin
Spook	Dutch	Ghost
Bwca	Welsh	Faery
Pooka	Cornish	Faery

To this list we may perhaps add 'Bogey', 'Bogle' and 'Boggart', all of which may possible derive from the Slavic word *bog* ('God'), suggesting again that in many cases the Faery folk are a diminished form of the early gods of the land.

An old rhyme says:

> Turn your cloaks,
> For Fairy Folks
> Are in old oaks. (82)

This may well refer to the spirit listed by Reginald Scott as 'the Man in the Oak', a good name indeed for either Robin, Goodfellow or Hood, or for Puck himself.

Another argument for Robin as a Faery being is his name. Hood or Wood are both appropriate – the latter because of the strong association of the Faery folk with woodland, and the former for their traditional use of the hood as a garment to cover their heads.

It is tempting to speculate whether the 'cucullati' or 'hooded folk', a species of local Romano-Celtic deity or spirit usually represented by small figurines (usually in groups of three) dressed in a hooded cloak called the cucullus, might not be related to Puck and Pook, and that this might have given rise to the idea that elves and fairies themselves wore hoods. If this were the case then we might well be close to the reason for the name Robin Hood or Robin-o-the-Wood as applied to the Outlaw of Sherwood. (In at least one relief, found at Aquae Sulis (Bath) in Somerset, three hooded figures are shown standing beneath a representation of the Roman god Mercury – widely known to be the god of thieves.) Professor Toynbee calls the cucullati 'deities of death and after-life, or life through death, of healing and of fertility' (95) which would be in keeping with the idea of Robin as the focus of a fertility cult and a type of the sacrificed god (see Chapters 3 and 4).

Margaret Murray (70) lists a number of instances of Faery folk wearing hoods and of being extremely protective of them, to the extent that to lose one's hood or cap was considered disastrous to one of the Faery kind. She also mentions the goblin named Hudekin or Hodekin, which may itself derive from 'Hod' or 'Hob' or 'Hood'. It has been suggested that this may also connect Robin to the Saxon Woden, through the intermediary name

'Hoda'. As a primarily Saxon hero, this is at least a possibility, and given the association of Robin with Herne the Hunter (see below), we should not dismiss this out of hand.

Robin and the Devil

While on the subject of the anthropologist Margaret Murray, this would seem to be a good point at which to examine her theories regarding Robin Hood, which have received a good deal of attention since she first propounded them in her book *The God of the Witches* (70) in 1931.

She begins by listing Robin as one of the names of the God in the Old Religion of these islands, quoting an account of the 'confession' of one Dame Alice Kytler to the effect that when summoning the Devil they called upon 'Some Robin the Devil, or I wot not spirit of the Ayre'. Somerset witches referred to the grand master of their coven as Robin, while others called upon Robin Filius Artis or Robin Artisson during their ceremonies.

'It [Robin] is so common a term for the "Devil" as to be almost a generic name for him,' Mead remarks, adding, 'The cult of Robin Hood was widespread both geographically and in time, which suggests that he was more than a local hero in the places where his legend appears ... He was always accompanied by a band of twelve companions, very suggestive of a Grand Master and his coven ... If there were more than one Robin Hood at the same time in different parts of the country his ubiquity is explained; the name would mean Robin with a Hood, and would be the generic appellation of the god.'

The trouble with all of this is that it does not stand up to close scrutiny at all. Most of the information we have on medieval witchcraft derives from the confessions, extracted under torture or duress, of a few ignorant old women who could – and did – say anything to ease their pain. They may well have been calling upon confused memories of folklore concerning Puck and Robin Goodfellow or other elemental spirits, but it is unlikely that they were referring to Robin Hood. 'Robinus Filius Artis' is probably no more than a reference to a common Irish name, Robert Mac Art. Nor is it anywhere explicitly stated that Robin always had twelve companions – the numbers of the Outlaw band fluctuated wildly, as one would expect, so that there are sometimes two or three, at other five or six, rising to 150 in some of the ballads. While there is no denying that Robin does indeed possess many of the attributes of a god, it is unlikely that his name was ever considered as a proper title for the grandmaster of any coven.

Herne and the Wild Hunt

Though not strictly part of the Faery tradition, Herne the Hunter deserves mention here since he shares many of the attributes of the Faery folk, and since the creation of a more recent mythology in the TV series *Robin of Sherwood* is forever associated with the great Outlaw. Like Robin he has assumed the mantle of earlier archetypes, being a descendant of the Norse god Woden and a leader of the Wild Hunt, just as Arthur, Charlemagne and Francis Drake among others are said to lead this Faery pack across the hills of Britain.

The first recorded mention of Herne is in 1623, in Shakespeare's *The Merry Wives of Windsor*. In act IV scene 4 Mistress Page recites the legend:

> There is an old tale goes, that Herne the hunter,
> Sometime a keeper here in Windsor forest,
> Doth all the Winter-time, at still midnight,
> Walk round about an oak, with great ragg'd horns –
> And there he blasts the tree, and takes the cattle,
> And makes the milch-kine yield blood, and shakes a chain
> In a most hideous and dreadful manner ...
> You have heard of such a spirit, and well you know
> The superstitious idle-headed eld
> Received, and did deliver to our age,
> This tale of Herne the Hunter for a truth.

Despite the doubt expressed in these last lines, there is also a clear indication that the story is an old one. Though the seventeenth century may seem comparatively recent, just because there are no written records does not mean that the figure of Herne was unknown before this time. We know that Shakespeare's knowledge of folklore was considerable, and he seldom invents when he can refer to a genuine story. A variant version of the above scene, altered by an anonymous author who probably lived in the Windsor area, adds the following:

> Oft have you heard since Horne the hunter [*sic*] dyed
> That women to affright their little children,

Ses that he walkes in shape of a great stagge.
Now for that Falstaffe hath been so deceived,
As that he dare not venture to the house,
Weele send him word to meet vs in the field,
Disguised like Horne, with huge horns on his head,
The houre shal be just betweene twelue and one,
And at that time we will meet him both:
Then would I have you present there at hand,
With little boyes disguided and dressed like Fayries,
For to affright fat Falstaffe in the woods. (72)

Here Herne is clearly associated with the Faeries and is shown to wear horns, a fact which helps us to identify him as something more than a simple 'keeper here in Windsor forest'. Whatever story Shakespeare knew, it seems more likely that whoever the author of these additional lines was (it is still possible that they were written by Shakespeare himself and form part of an earlier draft of the play) knew better. He seems to have drawn upon an older story associated with Windsor Great Park, which until the seventeenth century proudly displayed 'Herne's Oak', a vast and ancient tree supposed to commemorate regular sightings of a mysterious and terrifying huntsman and his ghostly hounds.

In fact, as stated above, Herne is easily identifiable as one of the numerous leaders of the Wild Hunt, references to which are found in many cultures and at many different times through the ages. A dramatic account from Sweden, recorded in the nineteenth century, gives an idea of the effect their presence had.

Sometimes, if you sleep with an open window during the Summer, when the weather is fine and the nights are light, you might suddenly be woken up by a frightful hurly-burly out in the forest, right behind the house. There is shrieking and shouting, and the barking of a whole pack of dogs, the thud of horse hoofs, the cracking of broken branches and so on. It's dreadful, and it's no time to be out in the forest, for the hind hunt's on. You shake and quiver and your heart pounds at the sound of it. Sleeping's out of the question. If you're brave enough to take a peep out of the window in spite of it – O good gracious, seeing the hind hunt is even worse than hearing it! (72)

Other accounts verify the fear experienced by all who hear, let alone see, the Hunt. Its coming is often announced by a terrible din, flashes of lightning, wind in the treetops, the rattling of chains and the ringing of bells. The rider himself is variously described as carrying a whip, as wearing antlers on his head, as having a skull for a face or no face at all. In Germany an old man named Honest Eckart goes in front of the Hunt, warning people to get out of the way. He is often described, like Woden or Odin, as having a long grey beard and a broad-brimmed hat, and as riding a white horse. In one version of the story he calls out:

> Fly then, quickly, make no stay
> For Herne the Hunter rides this way. (72)

In the Welsh collection known as the *Mabinogion* (32), Pwyll Prince of Dyfed encounters the Underworld king Arawn with his ghostly pack:

> And of all the hounds he had seen in the world, he had seen no dogs the colour of these. The colour that was on them was a brilliant shining white, and their ears red; and as the whiteness of their bodies shone, so did the redness of their ears glisten ... and ... he saw a horseman coming towards him upon a large light-grey steed, with a hunting horn round his neck, and clad in garments of grey ...

This is the Celtic image of the huntsman, and it is borne out further by accounts of Gwynn ap Nudd, who dwells beneath Glastonbury Tor and leads his pack of hounds to hunt across the Somerset Levels on certain feast days throughout the year.

The huntsman then is horned, rides a wild horse and leads a pack of hounds – or sometimes, wildmen – over the hills. In most of the accounts of him he chases the souls of the dead, capturing them and carrying them off to the Otherworld. The Wild Hunt is also said to exact retribution from individuals who have neglected their debts – a feature of Robin and his band. These are all factors that help us to identify the Huntsman. But Herne is not a Celtic god, any more than Robin Hood is a Celtic hero – they both spring from Saxon tradition, and it is to that tradition that we must look to find Herne's origins – and maybe a further clue to the mythological identity of Robin.

Woden and the Hoodeners

It is perhaps inevitable that Robin Hood and Herne should become associated. Both are huntsmen, lords of the Forest and its inhabitants. Both dress in green and lead a band of wild followers. But there is a deeper connection than this.

Woden (or Odin) is the premier god of the Norse people. He is a father god, like Zeus or Jupiter or the Dagda, and he also brings life and fertility to his people, as well as the wisdom of the runes, which he discovers by sacrificing 'himself to himself, for nine nights on the windy tree' as the *Norse Sagas* have it. He is also a god of the hunt, and trees are sacred to his name.

Etymologically the names Woden and Herne are connected, as are the names 'Hood', or 'Hod'. When Woden leads his select band of warriors, the *herjar*, he is given the name Herian, which mutates into Harilo, Hevela, Herlake, Herla – and, later on, Herne. The Herlingas referred to by the Anglo-Saxon poet Widsith are the followers of Woden's *herjar*. Norse Tradition tells us further that Woden rides an eight-legged horse named Sleipnir, which seems to have given some of its attributes to the 'Hobby-Horse' in the English mumming plays; Herne rides a wild mount which sometimes has two legs and sometimes six or eight. Herne also seems to have been associated with the cult of the dead, as was the stag, whose antlers he wears, from very early times. The combination of the terrible horse with its spectral rider wearing stag's horns, suggests a long history of interconnected tradition, dealing with a phantom rider who chases the souls of the dead, leads a pack of white hounds, and rides through the heavens.

Even star lore bears this out. The various names for the constellation of the Great Bear include Charles' Wain (after Charlemagne who was also a leader of the Wild Hunt), Arthur's Wain (for similar reasons) and Carleswain (Saxon) which probably refers to Woden as lord (Carl) of the heavens.

Although the Wild Hunt appears most often in association with Winter, it also makes an appearance at certain other feast days – 24 June (St John's Day), 29 June (St Peter's Day), and also 1 May, which aside from being St Walpurga's Day is also traditionally the time of the Robin Hood games. If we are correct in thinking that the name Hood derives from the disguise or masks worn by the participants in the games (mummers are also referred to as 'guisers') then we can at once perceive a further link between Herne and Robin.

The Hodening or Hoodening revels, which took place at Christmas, particularly in Kent, are somewhat like the May Games in that they consist of the same manifestation of otherworldliness erupting into the everyday world. Groups of young men went from house to house in villages, carrying with them a horse's skull mounted on a pole, and with strings that enabled its jaws to clash. It was a deliberately terrifying object, which actually caused one woman in 1839 to die of fright, after which the custom died out for a time. However it is undoubtedly of great antiquity, and seems to reflect the image of the Huntsman and his ghostly pack. The Hodening horse is related as well to the mummers 'Obby 'Oss, which we shall discuss in Chapter 6, as well as to the Lir Bhan of the Muck Olla fairs and the Marie Llwyd of Welsh tradition.

Herne has been connected both with the semi-mythical Scottish Saint Kentigern, and with the Gaulish god Cernunnos, who is depicted as a horned figure and a protector of animals. Kentigern, though never depicted as a leader of the Wild Hunt, certainly has a reputation as a guardian of animals, especially cattle, which were sacred to the Celts. Cernunnos, despite a somewhat tenuous history, is only one aspect of a central horned figure in Celtic myth – again a guardian of animals. He is portrayed on the great ceremonial bowl known as the Gunderstrup Cauldron, which in turn relates to the myth of Bran the Blessed and Arawn, the lord of the Underworld, both of whom possess wondrous cauldrons.

Margaret Murray believed Cernunnos to be a precursor of Herne, while Lewis Spence suggested another figure, Gurgintius or Guriunt, mentioned in Geoffrey of Monmouth's *History of the Kings of Britain* (28), as an intermediary. Gurgintius was, like various other rulers listed by Geoffrey, descended from the semi-legendary King Coel. His direct father was Beli or Belinus, a Celtic deity remembered in the nursery rhyme as 'Robin the Bobbin, the big bellied Ben, who ate more meat than four score men'. (36)

Nor should we forget the phallic Cerne Abbas Giant, sketched into the chalk downland near Sherborne in Dorset. No one can say with any certainty who is represented by this figure, though he is widely recognised as a fertility figure and has been, at various times, identified with the

Greek hero Hercules, the German god Donar, and the Celtic Nodens. It is also possible that he is related to the Dorset Ooser, a kind of wild bull-man who used to caper through the streets in Dorsetshire villages as recently as the beginning of this century. This character bears a resemblance both to Herne and to the Green Man and King of the May. If we allow the attribution to Nodens then we are brought back to both Gwynn ap Nudd and Cernunnos, both of whom are believed to be aspects of Nodens – who, as a god of healing, is appropriately associated with the green strength of the earth.

The whole subject of 'wearing the horns' is of considerable interest here. 'Old Horny' is an ancient name for the Devil, who was believed, literally, to be constantly 'horny', and the association of horns with potency and fertility is widespread in folklore traditions throughout most of Europe. An illustration accompanying some of the earlier editions of *The Merry Pranks of Robin Goodfellow* depicts Robin as leading a rout of dancers. He is horned, wears a hunting horn slung round his neck and carries a distinctly phallic staff.

Traditions still extant, and which reflect this symbolism, include the famous Abbot's Bromley Horn Dance, performed by a team of Morris dancers every year in September in the village that bears its name in Staffordshire. The dance involves six dancers who carry sets of antlers which are certainly very ancient – though just how old is hard to say. Carbon analysis dates them to the eleventh century, but they may well be replacements for an even older set. A man dressed as Maid Marian, a Fool with a bladder and a boy with a bow and arrows who is generally recognised as Robin Hood accompany the dancers. The whole occasion may well be the last remnant of a far older ceremony, possibly even as old as prehistoric times, of a shamanic ritual that either celebrated or enacted the hunting of the deer.

An additional old ceremony that still takes place, at Highgate in London, is called 'the Swearing on the Horns'. Its purpose is to bestow the freedom of the village of Highgate on those who take an oath while holding on to the horns. Traditionally this takes place twice a year, in May and September, so that we can see this as another aspect of the May Day revels. A further account, from the *Chronicle of Lanercost Priory* for 1282, mentions the terrible religious lapse of John, the parish priest of Inverkeithing. During Easter week he gathered a party of girls from local villages and lead them in a circling dance, while carrying a pole on which were displayed 'the human organs of reproduction'! A similar event seems to have taken place regularly during the Middle Ages at Cerne Abbas, where a Maypole was erected in a field above the giant's head and became the setting for 'wild rites' and dancing.

Shakespeare, familiar with many of the ancient traditions of this country, preserves another old notion in *As You Like It*, where Jacques sings:

> What shall he have that kill'd the deer?
> His leather skin and horns to wear.
> Then sing him home:
> Take no scorn to wear the horn;
> It was a crest ere thou wast born.
> Thy father's father wore it;
> And thy father bore it.
> The horn, the horn, the lusty horn,
> Is not a thing to laugh to scorn.

This same song is included in the Helston 'Furry Dance', a possibly ancient ceremony revived in Victorian times and still celebrated to this day, which connects Robin and Marian to the celebration of the life force in nature (see Chapter 6). Shakespeare's song has all kinds of echoes with the idea of wearing the horns, both as a symbol of 'lustiness' and as a reward to he who has 'killed the deer'. What more appropriate symbol for Robin Hood and Herne the Hunter than to put on the skin and horns of the animal – tokens of hunting skills and virile power?

We have, then, several connecting links between Woden, Herne, Nodens, Cernunnos and Gurgintius, whose father, Beli, is remembered as Robin. Woden himself, as Wod or Herla, relates to the name Hood or Hod. Herne is associated with Robin as a guardian of the forest, whose rites involved 'Hodening'. The wearing of the horns is associated with fertility and the hunt. Such links may seem tenuous, but in the light of the interrelationship of Celtic and Saxon (Norse) cultures in England, we should not be surprised to find such overlaps and blurring of the lines between such archetypical figures as Herne and Robin Hood.

3

THE FACE IN THE LEAVES

Like antlers, like veins of the brain the birches
Mark patterns of mind on the red Winter sky;
'I am thought of all plants,' says the Green Man,
'I am thought of all plants,' says he.

William Anderson, *The Green Man*

The King of the Wood

In 1936 Sir James George Fraser, who is generally seen as one of the founding fathers of modern anthropology, published the thirteenth and final volume of his book *The Golden Bough* (27). It had taken him forty-six years to complete and was to revolutionise the study of myth and religion. The central theme of this monumental work is the worldwide myth of the sacrificed god-king whom Fraser called 'the King of the Wood'. This figure, who could be regarded either as king, god or priest, was usually selected to reign for a year, at the end of which time he was killed and his slayer took over his role for a further year. In this way the eternal round of the seasons are preserved, without hindrance, and the human and animal realms remained in balance and harmony with the rest of Creation.

Fraser's description of the selection rite, which he pictured as taking place in the temple of Diana at Nemi in the Alban hills near Rome, is dramatic and powerful:

In the sacred grove there grew a certain tree round which at any time of day, and probably far into the night, a grim figure might be seen to prowl. In his hand he carried a drawn sword, and he kept peering wildly about him as if at every instance he expected to be set upon by an enemy. He was a priest and a murderer; and the man for whom he looked was sooner or later to murder him and hold the priesthood in his stead. Such was the rule of the sanctuary. A candidate for the priesthood could only succeed to office by slaying the priest, and having slain him, he retained his office until he was himself slain by a stronger and craftier ... and if he slew him he reigned in his stead with the title of King of the Wood (*Rex Nemorensis*). (27)

Such is the essence of Fraser's account, and from it he elaborated a theory that took up many hundreds of pages, drawing on traditions from around the world. Much of his argument has been questioned in more recent times, and its precise application to classical, specifically Roman, tradition may be flawed. However, even his most stringent critics have admitted that, while the evidence may at times fail to stand up to a detailed scrutiny, the ideas – and especially the themes – within the book are still worthy of attention. It is in this light that we may see them here – not as far-fetched or nonsensical, but as a genuine effort to gather together the fragmentary memories of a past age and to find the beliefs that underpinned the ancient world.

When he looks at the beliefs of the Celtic people of Britain, Ireland and Gaul in particular, Fraser draws our attention to the large number of celebrations centring on two periods of the year: the Spring and Autumn equinoxes. These two gateways (coupled with the Summer and Winter solstices) are key turning points in the progression of the seasons, and it is during this time that the most significant examples of sacrificial rituals are to be observed.

Among the examples Fraser selects for discussion is the burning of huge, man-shaped wickerwork cages containing human and animal sacrifices. These sacred rites, according to Caesar's account of the Celts, took place at the time of the Beltane or Beal-tain fires, around the period of May Day and Midsummer. Later on, as the Celts became, at least nominally, Christianised, such rituals were replaced by token ceremonies in which a man and woman representing the King and Queen of the

Wood took part in a mock-sacrifice in which no blood was actually spilled and no one was burned (see Chapter 5). Fraser notes also that the wicker-clad dancers in the May Day revels may possibly be a last survival of earlier, more literal ceremonies.

One should perhaps add that Caesar's account is almost certainly biased and exaggerated, and that modern evidence of the ritual sacrifices practised by the Celts seems to have involved the killing either of criminals or of voluntary and therefore willing victims, rather than the wholesale slaughter suggested by the Roman accounts.

However one feels about the question of human or animal sacrifice, or the validity or otherwise of its practice, it is a fact which remains to be considered as part of our examination of the Robin Hood mythos. We will find, as we look at the material available, that Robin fits very well into the role of King of the Wood, and that as such his life and death may well be seen as paralleling that of the King's. He thus crosses from the socially integrated world of the forest, entering instead into a liminal place and state as an outlaw, a person without house or citizenship. Conforming to this new location he evolves the likeness of the Spirit of the Wood, becoming in effect his priest, dispensing freedom and liberality.

To understand how this came to be, we need to look at two specific strands of tradition – that pertaining to the figure known as the Green Man, and the traditions surrounding an ancient ritual combat between the kings of Winter and Summer.

The Green Man

A large number of the medieval Christian churches in Britain contain carvings representing the figure known as the Green Man. These generally take the form of foliate heads, faces from the eyes and lips and ears of which sprout leaves, so that the faces sometimes seems to be peering from amid the leafage, and at others to be actually made of leaves.

Writing in the journal *Folk-Lore*, Vol. 50 in 1939, the distinguished anthropologist Lady Julia Raglan described how she first became interested in these carvings. Eight years previously she had been shown a carving in the roof of the church at Llangwm in Monmouthshire by its then vicar the Revd J. Griffith. It was of 'a man's face, with oak leaves growing from the mouth and ears, and completely encircling the head. Mr Griffith suggested that it was intended to symbolise the spirit of inspiration, but it seemed to me certain that it was a man and not a spirit, and moreover that it was a "Green Man".'

Lady Julia's resulting researches showed that she was wrong in believing that the Green Man was 'not a spirit'. She also very quickly learned that foliate heads were to be found in churches across Britain and elsewhere throughout Europe. She next noticed that the predominant foliage sprouting from the ears and lips of these foliate heads was oak, a tree long known to be sacred in northern climes. Where this varied, the tendency was towards ivy, also a sacred plant.

Raglan was initially convinced that the faces she observed were portraits, and sought for a figure from real life from which the grinning, leafy faces could derive. She would soon be forced to acknowledge that the basis for the leafy faces was not of a real man but a figure of great antiquity. As she wrote, 'There is only one [character] of sufficient importance, the figure variously known as the Green Man, Jack-in-the-Green, Robin Hood, the King of May, and the Garland, who is the central figure in the May-Day celebrations throughout Northern and Central Europe. In England and Scotland the most popular name for this figure ... was Robin Hood.'

In these guises we shall meet the Green Man again and again throughout this book, and though we shall postpone talking of each one until the appropriate place, it is worthwhile noticing at this point the extraordinary amount of evidence indicating that each of the figures listed by Lady Raglan derive from the same source – the Green Man himself, who was, of course, far more than a man, more even than a spirit, perhaps even a God.

The idea of the Green Man as a representative of the natural world probably dates back to the first agrarian peoples of the ancient world, who felt the power of nature and gave it a face and form. We have only to look at the way in which the green thrusts through, rampantly overcomes, and glories in its strength to understand why a masculine image was chosen. Certainly among the tribal people who lived in the vast woodlands that once covered much of the European continent, the Green Man ruled supreme as a spirit of these woods, a representation, in semi-human guise, of the abiding life force of the trees.

Both as an actual presence and as symbolic entities in their own right, the vast woodlands made a deep and lasting impression on the imagination of those who dwelt close to their shaded depths. Individual sacred trees featured in many cultures and often possessed the qualities of the deities to which they were dedicated. Though no truly ancient image of this kind has survived, we may imagine that certain trees could have been seen as representatives of the Green Man, and may well have been carved into his likeness. Even if this were not the case, the connection between trees and the sustaining of the world provided links with the energy of nature that the Green Man represented.

For the Norse people the entire world was founded on the roots and branches of the world tree Yggdrasil, while in ancient Ireland, the great yew, Eo Mugna, was considered a source of Druidic and territorial power. In the Mediterranean world the cult of the dying and rising god Attis, himself a type of Green Man, was represented by a pine tree, which was borne in procession.

In a severely deforested world, it is hard to imagine just how dense our woodlands once were. Forests were places of awe and mystery, into whose depths few would venture during the day, although the resources of the wood shore were useful to those who lived nearby. In North West Europe, these dense forests often contained groves of sacrifice or spiritual mystery. From trees in the groves dedicated to the Norse cult of Odin both human and animal offerings were hung, indicators of the powerful force of the ancient forest gods.

The oak groves of the Celtic world were the haunt of strange forest beings and fantastic tree-spirits, their mysteries known only to the Druids, whose knowledge and understanding of the natural world was second to none.

According to Kathleen Basford, the leading modern expert in the study of foliate heads, these first emerged in Roman art in the second half of the first century AD. (5) It seems, however, that they can be traced back still further to Mesopotamian and Sumerian leaf mask carvings dating from as early as 700 BC. These lead us to the Sumerian epic of *Gilgamesh* where we encounter a figure that represents the power of the natural world: Enkidu, a wild and primitive being whose great strength and passionate soul embodies the energy of Nature itself. Enkidu can be seen as a distant progenitor of the wildmen who, as we shall see, were themselves influential on the ballad makers' lore of Robin Hood. In the *Gilgamesh* poems the gods themselves are jealous of Enkidu's power, and condemn Enkidu to die, prompting his friend, the hero Gilgamesh, to undertake a journey to the otherworld in search of a cure for death itself, a plant called 'The Old Man has Become a Young Man Again'. Although Gilgamesh finds the plant, he loses it again to a serpent, which at once sloughs its skin in a symbolic image of rebirth.

In the poems that make up the Gilgamesh epic Enkidu represents an overflowing life force, wild and untamed. He stands out as one of the oldest representations of the potent energy of the Green Man that was to reappear during the Middle Ages as the Wildman, who represented the idea of living closer to the natural world.

In ancient Egypt, where water was scarce and the annual rising of the Nile waters was essential to all life, green gods and goddesses played an important part in the spirituality of the two lands. The colour green was honoured above all, and to 'do green things' came to mean doing good; while 'to do red things' meant to do evil. Osiris, perhaps the most important deity in Egyptian life, was both a god of vegetation and resurrection. In the Pyramid Texts, he is known as 'the Great Green' and is depicted as green-skinned in acknowledgement of his life-giving energy.

The story of Osiris told of his murder and dismemberment at the hands of the jealous god Set. Afterwards his wife Isis recovered the scattered parts of his body and restored him to life. Thereafter this cycle of dismemberment, death and resurrection was honoured as a symbolic reference to the flooding of the Nile delta, by which the fields were greened with new growth when the waters rose. In token of this, miniature mummy cases representing Osiris were sown with grain and left out in the rain until they sprouted – an emblematic statement of life rising from death and a perfect expression of the energy that flowed in the veins of the Green Man.

The Green Thread

The thread of the natural force continues like a green serpent throughout the classical world. The orderly deities of Mount Olympus were not the only ones to hold sway. There were older, wilder forces also; every tree, stream, hill and grove had its own dryad, nymph and tutelary spirit.

The god Pan, whose name means 'universal', was a major deity of nature. As the protector of the wild, he could appear anywhere in the natural world. Those who came across him at lonely, unfrequented places were said to be consumed with panic at the sight of him. This experience of solitude, of a numinous sense of wild, god-filled nature, is one seldom experienced in a world that has tamed so much of the earth. But Pan could not be tamed or controlled, any more than Dionysus (Roman Bacchus), another representative of unfettered nature, could be made to obey the desires of his followers.

Before his later association with vines and drunkenness, Dionysus is credited with the fostering of agriculture among the Greeks, and his power manifests often in images of growth and wildness. At one point he is said to have undertaken a journey to India, spreading the word about the intoxicating power of the vine. During the journey some sailors captured him and tried to ransom him for a vast sum, but Dionysus caused a huge vine to grow out of the deck of their ship, and ivy and vines to twine throughout the rigging. The oars became serpents and the whole ship was filled with animals, with the god, in lion form, as their leader.

The wild green power of Dionysus, like that of Pan, overcomes the ordered world of humanity in much the same way that plants penetrate concrete. His growth overwhelms man-made structures, and his ferment enters into the human body so that we can experience for ourselves the ecstatic life of plants. Both gods represent an energy that is an essential aspect of the Green Man.

In Britain the leafy faces of the Green Man can be recognised in the blurred outlines of faces carved onto Romano-British tombs dating from the period of the Roman occupation of Britain. At this point it is clear that they became associated with earlier, Celtic representations of the human head, which were regarded as sacred. Thus when we look, for example, at the pediment of the temple to Sulis Minerva in Bath, we see not what has misguidedly been referred to as a 'Male Medusa' (*sic*) but a representation of a sacred oracular head from Celtic tradition. Such a thing can be best exemplified by the god Bran the Blessed, who, according to the story of 'Bran and Branwen' in the *Mabinogion*, commanded his followers to cut off his head and carry it with them to an island off the Welsh coast, where it continued to speak and to entertain them for twenty-two years, until one of the group broke a taboo which forced them to carry the head to London and inter it in the mound beneath the present Tower of London.

Lady Raglan's brief article (no more than ten pages) gave fuel and substance to ideas that had been in the air for much longer. She herself referred to *The Golden Bough* and to Fraser's theories concerning the sacrificed god, chosen to reign for a year and then killed (usually by decapitation) and hanged from a tree, acknowledging that it was still to be explored as part of the story of the foliate heads.

Some twenty-two years later the historian of religion E. O. James, in his book *Seasonal Feasts and Festivals* (46), called Robin Hood 'a further development ... [in] ... themes associated with the Green Man, or Jack-in-the-Green, as the annual victim in the vegetation drama, the prototype of the Fool garlanded in greenery', and went on to associate the cult of the Green Man with the 'Al-Khider' or 'green thing' of the Indus Valley culture, to the Hebrew Elijah myth, to Mesopotamia and the myth of Tammuz, and finally to St George of Cappadocia, who became the patron Saint of England – still to be seen in the figure of 'King George' in the mumming plays alongside Robin, Marian and Tuck (see Chapter 6).

James adds that

his equation with the Green Man and the May Day revels and Maid Marian brought him into the fertility drama and its seasonal death and resurrection ritual. As its central figure he had to die by the chance flight of an arrow and like Adonis bleed to death, and then be restored to life, while Maid Marian assumed the role of the Man-Woman. In the capacity of Robin-of-the-Wood, he was essentially a vegetation sacral hero rather than the leader of a robber band in the forest, of the highly skilled archer of the ballad and romance, or even the shepherd of the French pastourelles.

The most important aspect of the Green Man remains his association with vegetation myths and kingly sacrifice. William Anderson in a recent book (2) takes Lady Raglan's essay as his starting point, asserting that the foliate heads in medieval churches are not necessarily the same as the Green Men of folklore, but that both derive, ultimately, from the youth who dies and is reborn, 'the son lover and guardian of the Great Goddess'. This has opened the whole story of the Green Man far more widely than before, although Anderson has chosen to dismiss the earlier, pre-Christian evidence as too insubstantial or irrelevant to his argument. Despite this he brings forward a great body of material that supports our current thesis. In particular Anderson puts forward the theory of colour symbolism, in which the green of the forest god gives way to the gold of transformation and rebirth. He traces this through alchemy, Mayan poetry, the myth of Osiris and the medieval poem *Sir Gawain and the Green Knight* (see below). The second pattern presented by Anderson is that of the relationship between the Green Man and the Goddess. I have myself written at length about this in my book *Gawain, Knight of the Goddess* (63), the findings of which will be outlined in the section dealing with the Green Knight.

Anderson points to the presence of the Green Man in medieval stained glass, where he is frequently associated with the Virgin Mary. This leads him to a third supposition, that the Green Man in Christian architecture is the outcome of a fusion between Christianity and Paganism. Certainly the presence of both Christian and Pagan motifs in the May Day revels and in the Robin Hood myths is considerable, nor is it unreasonable to suppose that the master masons of the medieval era, who themselves were the guardians of many mysteries, saw in the Pagan imagery of the Green Man a chance to express the Christian story of death and resurrection in terms familiar to the ordinary people for whom doctrine and theology were far from accessible. That they chose to do so secretively, hiding the Green Men in the highest rafters of the buildings, where they remained largely invisible until the advent of electric light, is part of a pattern of Pagan beliefs lying just beneath the skin of Christianity.

For the medieval churchmen, the symbolism was something other. In the man-made forests of the gothic cathedrals the Green Man is pent, the old pagan wildness tamed in frozen stone. Perhaps it amused the medieval Church Fathers to imagine an image they regarded as 'devilish' caught and pinned on the roof-bosses of their own stone forests. That the masons and worshippers perhaps had the last laugh is a matter of conjecture – certainly the protruding tongues and grimacing faces of the foliate heads may be interpreted in more ways than one – as strangled or beheaded gods on the one hand, or as grinning, nose-thumbing caricatures on the other.

Nor should we forget the relationship of the foliate heads and Green Man to the idea of the Wildman, a widely acknowledged figure who represented untamed nature throughout the medieval world (see below).

The Green Knight

In the fourteenth century there appeared a poem of such strength and beauty that it has remained essential reading for all who love the Arthurian mythos, or who love poetry for its own sake. In the manuscript in which it was written, somewhere in the area of Cumbria, it is called *Sir Gawain and the Green Gome*; we know it better as *Gawain and the Green Knight* (54), though perhaps its original title would be more appropriate as 'gome' can mean a wild, goblin-like character with a far more ancient pedigree than that of a knight. It tells the story of an adventure which begins at Christmastide in Camelot. Just as Arthur and his knights and their ladies are sitting down to dinner, there is a loud crash of thunder and into the hall rides a terrifying figure.

> From his neck to his loins so square set was he, and so long and stalwart of limb, that I trow he was half a giant. And yet he was a man, and the merriest that might ride. His body in back and breast was strong, his belly and waist were very small, and all his features
>
> > full clean.
> > Great wonder of the knight
> > Folk had in hall, I ween,
> > Full fierce he was to sight,
> > And all over bright green. (54)

This powerful and threatening figure offers to play 'a Christmas game' in which he will exchange blows with any man there, on condition that whoever gives the blow will accept a blow in return. Gawain alone has the courage to face the giant, and with the Green Knight's own axe cuts off his head. To the horror of all the company, however, the monstrous visitor does not fall – instead he rises and takes up his head, holding it aloft. The lips move and the voice speaks, telling Gawain that he must journey to the Green Chapel one year hence to receive back the blow he has given. The Green Knight then mounts his horse and rides from the court, leaving everyone stunned and horrified and Gawain wondering what he has promised.

Before continuing with the second part of the story, let us pause for a moment to examine this first episode.

The Green Knight comes with an offer – to play a game with his opponent in which he will allow himself to be sacrificed, his head severed from his neck – if only the challenger will submit himself to the same test in a year's time. This kind of exchange is an age-old concept. The otherworldly intruder, whom we would not be mistaken in calling a god, offers his life-blood for the sake of the people in return for their courage and self-sacrifice. This exchange, which in another turning of the story becomes a central theme within the Grail myth, is at the heart of the Green Man's story. As the guardian of the natural world he challenges all people to acknowledge his yearly sacrifice by offering their own love, trust and service to the natural world.

The challenge offered at the Christmas feast at Camelot is told in other stories, in particular the early Irish tale of *Bricriu's Feast*, where the semi-divine trickster Curoi mac Daire offers a similar test that is accepted by the hero Cuchulainn. Nor should we be surprised to learn that Cuchulainn and Gawain are closely related. Both are recognisably solar heroes: Gawain because his strength waxes and wanes towards midday, following the course of the sun, and because he dresses in red; Cuchulainn because of the battle madness which overtakes him and turns him into a radiantly fiery being with a single eye. The Green Knight is very evidently a representative of Winter and of the natural world. His green colouring and appearance announced by thunder at the Christmas court alone would suggest this. The challenge is thus seen to be between the champions of Summer and Winter which, as we shall see, is significant to the story of Robin Hood for a number of reasons.

The second part of the poem relates the turning of the seasons and Gawain's approach to his terrible challenge. He sets out in search of the Green Chapel and is at first unsuccessful, until he arrives as the castle of Sir Bercilak, a fiercely hearty lord who tells Gawain that the place he is seeking lies close at hand and offers him hospitality and a guide when the day of the trial dawns. Gawain willingly accepts the offer and settles down to enjoy the elaborate hospitality of his host. Every day Bercilak rides forth to the hunt, returning with various beasts he has captured and killed to the table. Before leaving he proposes an exchange: since Gawain prefers to stay at home, he will give whatever he catches in the hunt in exchange for whatever prize Gawain wins at home. Reluctantly Gawain agrees, expecting to win nothing. But his host's wife, the beautiful Lady Bercilak, has her own ideas about this. Every morning, as soon as her husband has departed, she enters Gawain's bedroom and blatantly offers herself to him. Gawain, who is described as the soul of chivalry and courtesy, refuses all but a chaste kiss, which he awards to the lord of the castle when he returns.

This curious exchange is repeated three times, and each time Gawain, fearing the inevitability of his death at the hands of the Green Knight, finds it harder to refuse the lady. At last he is persuaded to accept a gift – a green baldric that, she tells him, will protect him from the death he fears. The day dawns when he must make his way to the Green Chapel, and as promised Bercilak provides a guide. Soon Gawain finds himself in a strange place. The poem describes it thus:

> At length a little way off he caught sight of a round hillock by the side of a brook, and there was a ford across the brook, and the water therein bubbled as though it had been boiling. The knight ... walked round about it, debating within himself what place it might be. It had a hole at the end and on either side, and it was overgrown with tufts of grass and was all round and hollow within ... (54)

Gawain now hears the unmistakable sound of an axe being sharpened, and the Green Knight appears. Gawain kneels to receive the blow, and twice his adversary feints, mocking Gawain's courage. Finally he nicks Gawain's neck and declares himself satisfied, then to Gawain's astonishment and wonder reveals that he is really Sir Bercilak, and that he and his wife were placed under enchantment by 'the Goddess Morgane', whom Gawain had seen disguised as an ugly old woman in the castle. The whole business had been set up to test the courage of Arthur's court, and Gawain in particular. The only reason for the slight wound to Gawain's neck was because he had failed at the last and accepted the green baldric.

This story contains so many levels of interpretation that it is undoubtedly one of the most important medieval texts in which are preserved the seeds of older material. Though ostensibly a Christian poem, it extols virtues far more ancient than those of Christianity. As John Spiers says in his study *Medieval English Poetry: The Non-Chaucerian Tradition*:

> It is Christian rather as some of the medieval Christmas carols are, as Christmas itself is: Christian in harmony with pre-Christian nature belief and ritual, a Christian re-interpretation of these ...

The underlying theme of the poem, which harks back to the rituals of the Year King and to the battle of the challenge between Winter and Summer for the possession of the Maiden of Spring, or of the May, here represented by Lady Bercilak, overshadowed by Morgane the Goddess. This character, better known as Morgan le Fay, Arthur's half-sister and bitterest opponent throughout the Arthurian saga, has her own pedigree. In this text, as in one other, the thirteenth-century Middle High German poem *Diu Crone* (*The Crown*) (92) she is recognised as a goddess. In Irish mythology she is the Morrighan, a wild battle-goddess closely related to Cuchulainn.

Thus the circle is completed. Morgane is to Gawain as the Morrighan is to Cuchulainn; Bercilak (the Green Knight) is to Gawain as Curoi is to Cuchulainn. In each case the pattern is the same. A fearsome creature of otherworldly origin comes to challenge a hero to play the Beheading Game; the period of the challenge is for one year, and the objective, embedded just beneath the surface in the Gawain poem, is the winning of the Maiden of Spring, who in time, as we shall see, becomes known as Maid Marian.

Gawain, as I have shown elsewhere (63), is the son/lover of the Goddess, who must undergo repeated tests and trials to win her; Robin Hood, as King of the Wood, must undergo similar trials in order to win the hand of Marian. He is the latest in a long line of sacrificial kings, whose term was for a year, after which his place was taken by another, and so on throughout the ages. It is thus that the latest account of the story of the dying and rising god of field and forest, which we find echoed in the ballad of the 'Death of Robin Hood', is remembered (see Chapter 4).

Nor must we forget the actions of the mummers in the traditional sword dance that accompanies the ancient folk-plays still performed around Christmas time throughout much of Europe. As we shall see in Chapter 5, the forming of a five-pointed star and the miming of the beheading of one of their number echoes both the symbol emblazoned on Gawain's shield (known as the Knot of Wisdom, or Solomon's Seal) and the story of the Beheading Game and the ritual death of the King of the Wood.

Such is the pattern underlying the story both of Robin and of the Green Man. We shall examine the nature of the May Day Games and the mumming plays as they relates to these themes in the following chapters. For the moment a single quotation will serve to illustrate the theme. It comes from an anonymous seventeenth-century pamphlet entitled *The Way to Things by Words, and Words by Things*. Under the heading of May, its author recounts the following:

> May was considered the boundary day that divided the confines of Winter and Summer, allusively to which there was instituted a sportful war between two parties; the one in defence of the continuance of Winter, the other for bringing in the Summer ... The mock battle was always fought for booty; the Spring was sure to obtain the victory, which they celebrated by carrying triumphantly green branches with May flowers, proclaiming and singing the song of joy ... (10)

That Robin, alias the King of Summer, alias the King of the Wood, fights the King of Winter, alias the Green Man, for the hand of the Queen of the May, alias Maid Marian, is a pattern that becomes increasingly clear as we journey deeper into the folklore of the year. Gradually, as time passes, the roles become increasingly blurred. Robin becomes a permanent resident of the Greenwood, a full-time Champion of the Goddess of Spring, indeed her son/lover, just as Gawain and Cuchulainn are the champions of Morgane and the Morrighan respectively. In time, Robin becomes the Green Man again, and rules over the time between Summer and Winter, the time of the May Day revels which we shall consider in the next chapter. Later still he becomes the Outlaw of Sherwood.

Green Jack

Another aspect of the Green Man that remains to be considered is the Green Jack or Jack-in-the Green, who has been an essential part of the Midsummer Games from early times, and is still part of them to this day.

Despite the antiquity of the character's origins, the earliest written reference appears to be in a book called *Sports and Pastimes of the People of England* by J. Strutt, published in 1801. Here the description is of the May Day festival and refers in particular to chimney sweepers, who 'have also singled out the first of May for their festival'. Strutt goes on:

> Some of the larger companies have a fiddler with them, and a Jack-in-the-Green, as well as a Lord and Lady of the May, who follow the minstrels in great stateliness, and dance as occasion requires. The Jack-in-the-Green is a piece of pageantry consisting of a hollow frame of wood or wicker-work, made in the form of a sugarloaf, but open at the bottom, and sufficiently large to receive a man. The frame is covered with green leaves and bunches of flowers interwoven with each other, so that the man within may be completely concealed, who dances with his companions, and the populace are mightily pleased with the oddity of the moving pyramid. (47)

This is very evidently not a description of something that was new to the writer, or to the people; the casual mention of the Jack's presence in the Sweep's entourage makes it clear that this was a well-founded tradition. We shall see in Chapter 4 that in at least one instance a leaf-clad figure was symbolically sacrificed and hung upon the tower of the church at Castletown in Derbyshire.

The variety of ways in which the Jack is perceived makes it difficult to arrive at a definite picture. Robert Judge, the author of the most detailed study on the Jack, dismisses the opinions of Fraser, Douglas Kennedy, E. O. James and Violet Alford as 'unwarranted assumptions', while Maureen Duffy in her book *The Erotic World of Faery* (25) is unequivocal in her support of the idea:

> The Green Giant is the Robin Hood of the May revels and the Jack-in-the-Green, covered all in leaves, who came to town with London chimney sweeps. His face, breaking into tendrils and

foliage, looks down from cloister bosses. He is John Barleycorn who 'became a man', and, like the Green Knight, was beheaded but sprang up again and 'so amazed them all'.

This relates both Jack and, by extension, Robin Hood to the Corn King, also known as John Barleycorn, of whom the traditional English folk song says:

> There were three men came out of the west
> Their fortunes for to try,
> And these three men made a solemn vow,
> John Barleycorn should die.
>
> They ploughed him in the earth so deep,
> With clods upon his head.
> Then these three men they did conclude
> John Barleycorn was dead.
>
> There he lay sleeping in the ground
> Till rain from the sky did fall;
> Then Barleycorn sprang a green blade
> And proved liars of them all ...

Here Barleycorn is the spirit of the grain that is cut down and made into bread and beer, as used in the ancient sacrament of the Eleusinian mysteries of which the orator Cicero writes:

> Nothing is higher than these mysteries. They have sweetened our characters and softened our customs; they have made us pass from the condition of savages to true humanity. They have not only shown us the way to true humanity, but they have taught us to die with a better hope...
>
> *On the Eleusinian Mysteries: Laws II*, xiv, 36

The fact that the Jack-in-the-Green ceremony was most often performed by chimney sweeps is significant. In Celtic literature 'sooty' characters like the smith Eccet were considered powerful, related perhaps to smith gods like Gofannon and Goibniu, while Robin Goodfellow often takes the shape of a sweep to play his tricks on mortals. Perhaps the symbolism here is of those who enter the underworld and are able to return again, but who retain for a time the coloration of that place. Similarly, the sweeps themselves were associated with ashes, a fertilising element that possibly linked them to more ancient fertility rites.

Wildmen and Others

Yet another aspect of the spirit of the Wood is the Wildman, prevalent in both medieval literature and art. He is usually described as

> a hairy man curiously compounded of human and animal traits, without, however, sinking to the level of an ape. It exhibits upon its naked human anatomy a growth of fur, leaving bare only its face, feet, and hands, at times its knees and elbows, or the breasts of the female of the species. Frequently the creature is shown wielding a heavy club or mace, or the trunk of a tree; and since its body is usually naked except for a shaggy covering, it may hide its nudity under a strand of twisted foliage worn around the loins. (7)

This may well be the same figure that accompanied the May Day pageant, as mentioned in the diary of one Henry Machlyn from 1647: 'and then came two great wodyn (wodwose, wildmen) with two great clubs all in green, and with squibs burning'. Similarly, there is the Burryman's Parade at Queensferry, East Lothian in Scotland, where traditionally a tall man is wrapped in flannel and then covered from head to foot in burrs. He thus become a walking bush, and is led from house to house through the village and the money thus collected spent at the fair that takes place at the same time. Looking back to the myths of Mesopotamia we see at once how the wild and hairy figure of Enkidu prefigures these living representatives of the natural world.

Nor should we forget the figure of the Fool in all of this. He, who as Lord of Misrule presided over the games of Summer and Winter alike, was never far from the minds of the ordinary people. He was their safety valve, their way of answering back with impunity the lords who suppressed them so cruelly the rest of the year round. Small wonder if the daring Outlaw of Sherwood was seen to possess more than a little of this character's qualities. He alone dared to cock a snook at the greedy sheriffs and their brutal men. Who else could be seen to do this if not the figure in green with the power of Faery and of the earth itself at his back, who stood for the ordinary folk and for the oppressed and, at another remove, represented the ancient gods of the land itself?

The presence of these figures was an essential part of the folklore of the year – as indeed it still is in many places throughout Europe to this day – and without which the year could not be seen to turn though the seasons. The Green Man and his retinue of champions and followers were also present in the Morris dances and mumming plays which, from the Middle Ages onward, became a principle expression of human longing for the greenness of life. The great medieval mystic Hildegard of Bingen called this the *veriditas*, the greening of the soul, showing that even within the mysteries of Christianity, the spirit wildness was present. Medieval people saw 'dryness' of soul as aridity and celebrated the 'moisture' of the soul as the juice or sap of life. Nowhere is this more evident than in medieval dance traditions which maintained the verdant glory of the spirit attuned to the body. Clerics saw dancing as inherently lascivious, but were not slow to utilise it as part of sacred drama and dance.

One sure way of gauging the degree of importance attributed to any figure of Pagan origin is the way in which the medieval church dealt with it. Thus the ancient horned god of the Celts was transformed, iconographically, into a demon, and finally into the Devil. In the case of the foliate heads, numerous examples exist where these have been transformed into the grinning malevolent faces of horned daemons with protruding tongues – though, as we saw, these can also be seen as the carvers' joke at the expense of the clergy ranged far below them. The vital, elemental energy of the Green Man easily transcends this crude attempt to distort the original meaning of the image, but the very fact that it inspired enough fear to necessitate such treatment shows how deeply the medieval churchmen were moved by the presence of an ancient 'enemy' within the very buildings erected to their God.

The Morris dances and mumming plays, which we shall examine in greater detail in Chapter 6, are particularly important as vehicles for the preservation of pre-Christian traditions. As Douglas Kennedy writes in his history of folk-dance:

> The particular Green Man who has a proprietary interest in the Morris Dance is that semi-mythical character, Robin Hood, the hero of so many stories and ballads and the patron of our ancient English cult of the long bow. Robin-of-the-Wood is another name for Jack in the Green, and long before the reigns of King Richard and King John he was a local medicine man – a character in the ritual drama concerned with the restoration of life after the Winter death. The Robin Hood games, which included such characters known as Maid Marian, Friar Tuck, Hobby Horse and Little John, were romanticised versions of the ritual Folk Play. Robin Hood, the central figure, had to die and come to life again like the ritual actor, and his Maid Marian was the common symbol of fertility, the man-woman. If the fertility aspect of Robin Hood and Maid Marian kept the game popular with the English peasantry, it was his symbolic death with maintained him in the myth preserved by tradition and literature. He was killed by the chance flight of an arrow and bled to death. Comparative folk-lore has shown that other local gods, who were constrained to give their lives for their people, have suffered death from a shaft. The association of this ancient myth of Robin-of-the-Wood with the leader of a band of rob-the-rich-help-the-poor outlaws in Sherwood Forest, and with the national need for a high level of skill with the long bow, has provided us with enough dramatic substance to serve popular taste for romance, mixed with magic, for the last seven hundred years. (51)

In this we begin to see the true outlines of the being that stands behind Robin Hood, the Outlaw of Sherwood. Here he is compared with the dying and rising gods of the age-old vegetation myth, with Adonis and Tammutz, with the very spirit of fertility itself. In the next chapter we shall begin to explore how the folk-belief of the ordinary people preserved far more ancient ideas and saw the figure of the Outlaw of Sherwood as a representation of those distant but still vital themes.

All of which leads us back to a basic premise: that the Green Man (and indeed the Green Woman, though she is a much rarer presence within the churches of old Europe) derive from a central theme – that of the vegetation myth described by Fraser, Hone, Bryant, Alford, Speirs and many others. This is denied by some modern folklorists precisely on account of the variety of evidence and the disparate nature of the various figures such as the Green Jack, the Wild Man, the Green Knight and Robin himself. However, when we look at the underlying meaning embodied by *all* of these figures, we see a pattern that is impossible to ignore, a pattern where each character represents, in some way, the fertility and greenness of life. Essentially Robin Hood is one of the great fertility and vegetation figures of this land. As the Wild Man he is a representative of the old shamanic traditions of this country, dating from the most distant times and refocused by the Celts and the Saxons. Such figures as Suibhne Gelt in Ireland, Lailoken in Scotland, Merlin in Britain and Taliesin in Wales all in their own way represent the vital, life-giving greenness, just as Green Jack, the Burryman, the May King and the Summer Lord, Robin-o-the-Wood and Maid Marian all express the strength and importance of greenness, of growing things, of the ripening corn.

The symbolic death and resurrection of these figures, from the Green Knight to Robin himself, is part of a vast, ongoing cycle that will continue until the end of time (or until we become so mechanised that we forget our origins entirely). All the green and wonderful figures outlined in this study exist to remind us that we are a part of the natural world, and that we are still able to celebrate the ancient holy traditions of the earth and the Greenwood, however far we may have come from the days of Robin and the May Day and Midsummer Games.

4

THE GAMES OF ROBIN HOOD

The hedges of quick are thick with may blossom
As the dancers advance on the leaf-covered King;
'It's off with my head,' says the Green Man,
'It's off with my head,' says he.
William Anderson, *The Green Man*

The Games of Summer

During the Middle Ages and beyond, once the May blossom flowered, a kind of divine madness took possession of the people of England. Everyone, from kings to commoners, took part in a variety of celebrations of the dawning Spring, when the shackles of Winter were thrown off and a new light was everywhere apparent. The May Day Games, or 'Revels', in fact took place at almost any time throughout the Summer, as well as on 1 May, and from at least the 1500s until the end of the seventeenth century were almost continually ruled over by Robin Hood, to the extent that the celebrations became known as 'Robin Hood's Games'. Maid Marian was present as well, though not specifically named until later, taking upon herself the role of the May Queen just as Robin assumed the guise of the May King – thus bringing back to his role characteristics which had originally belonged to him but which had been absent for generations.

The story of how this came about is a complex one and involves our taking a journey that follows the winding path through the historical and folkloric traditions surrounding the May Games.

The earliest reference to a festival of the kind that must once have been celebrated throughout Britain is to be found in the *Brut or Chronicle of Britain* by a Saxon priest named Layamon. (55) He is better known for a powerful account of the days of King Arthur, which he derived in turn from the earlier *Roman du Brut* of Wace, a Norman French writer who hailed from Jersey in the Channel Isles. (93) Both of their accounts were written between 1155 and 1200, and derived in turn from the earlier *Historia Regum Britanniae* of Geoffrey of Monmouth, a Latin pseudo-history dating from *c.* 1130. (28) Geoffrey himself drew on still earlier documents, now lost, and on oral traditions dating back generations. The traditions thus preserved in all three works are therefore far older than their actual dates of composition.

Geoffrey's account is of a religious festival celebrating the Celtic King Cassivellaunus' defeat of Julius Caesar in *c.* 53 BC. All the barons of Britain and their wives were summoned to London to make offerings to their gods.

> They accordingly all came without tarrying and made sacrifice of divers kinds, and profuse slaying of cattle. Forty-thousand kine did they offer, a hundred thousand sheep, and all manner fowl at a number not lightly to be reckoned, besides thirty thousand in all of every sort of forest deer. And when they had paid all due honour unto the gods, they feasted them on the remainder ... and the day and the night they spent in playing games of divers kinds. (28)

Layamon elaborates this somewhat, beginning with an account of the sacred rites.

> The King began the rite after the heathen laws of the time. There were ten thousand men in the temple, the best of all Britons, standing before the mighty idol of Apollin. Each man held a torch, and each was clothed in gold, while the king wore a crown on his head. In front of the altar was a great fire set, and into this the King

and all his greatest men cast gifts ... Thereafter they feasted on twelve thousand oxen, three thousand harts, three thousand hinds and countless fowl ... then all the company repaired to the fields nearby, where they began to ride, and to run, and to play, while others fought with spear and shield, cast great stones, or played games on the table-board. (Author's trans.)

Both these accounts were written by Christian scribes long after the event, but in each case there is a sense of actuality which implies the use of existing earlier documentation and oral memory. Modern archaeological investigations at sacred sites such as Windmill Hill in Dorset have discovered ample evidence of such feasts. There is little doubt that the games described here were a celebration of the sun god Belinus, whom the Romans identified with Apollo. Indeed, in the writings of the Greek historian Diodorus Siculus, we find a description of a ceremony held at a great circle of stones in the island of the Hyperboreans. There Apollo makes an appearance every nineteen years, and there is to be found 'a city sacred to the same god, most of the inhabitants of which are harpers who continually play upon their harps in the temple and sing hymns to the God extolling his actions'. (29)

Another classical writer, the Roman poet Pindar, added in his 'tenth Pythian Ode':

In the banquets and praises of that people Apollo chiefly rejoiceth, and he laugheth and he looketh on the brute beasts in their ramping lewdness. Yet such are their ways that the Music is not banished, but on every side the dances of maidens and the sounds of the lyre and the notes of the flute are ever circling; and with their hair crowned with golden bay leaves they hold glad revelry. (29)

It has long been recognised that these, together with other fragmentary descriptions found in the works of classical writers, refer to Britain, and the description is remarkably similar to that of the later May Day revels, as we shall see.

That the descriptions in both Layamon and Wace's writings are memories of a more ancient, native, probably Celtic, festival is almost certainly the case. And as John Goulstone rightly points out in his *The Summer Solstice Games* (29), the implied relationship between solsticial ritual and games in Layamon is borne out by an entry (quoted by the same writer) from the cartulary of Barnwell Priory in Cambridge for 1295 or 1296. This refers to a charter, granted to the priory in 1229, of land on which an annual fair had previously taken place, 'apparently rooted in earlier games celebrated every Midsummer eve close to what was evidently an age-old holy spring'.

> ... from the midst of that site there bubbled forth springs of clear fresh water, called at that time in English, Barnewell, the children's springs [i.e. Bairn-Well] – because once a year, on St John Baptist's Eve [Midsummer], boys and youths met there, and amused themselves in the English fashion with wrestling matches and other games, and applauded each other in singing songs and playing on musical instruments. Hence by reason of the crowds of boys and girls who met and played there, a habit grew up that on the same day a crowd of buyers and sellers should meet in the same place to do business. (29)

There is an abundance of evidence of this kind in documents of the time – descriptions of games and sports, fairs and races, held between May Day and Midsummer – which make it clear that annual fairs, in all probability connected with solsticial worship, were still in place as early as the thirteenth century (the time at which the Robin Hood ballads were circulating widely). That these games were, even then, regarded as dangerous and of pagan origin is made clear by the number of attacks mounted upon them by the Church. Thus Bishop Latimer, in a sermon delivered before King Edward VI in 1549, relates how he came to a place on his way back to London where he had given prior warning that he intended to preach there in the morning:

> Because it was a holy day, and me thought it was an holy day's work; the church stood in my way; and I took my horse and my company and went thither; I thought I should have found a great company in the church, and when I came there the church door was fast locked. I tarried there half an hour and more, and at last the key

was found; and one of the parish comes to me, and says: Sir, this is a busy day with us, we cannot hear you; it is Robin Hood's Day. The parish are gone abroad to gather for Robin Hood. I thought my rochet [Bishop's red robe] would have been regarded, though I were not; but it would not serve; it was fain to give way to Robin Hood's men.

He continues, perhaps not unreasonably, on a pained note:

It is no laughing matter, my friends, it is a weeping matter, a heavy matter, under the pretence of gathering for Robin Hood, a traitor and a thief, to put out a preacher, to have his office less esteemed, to prefer Robin Hood before the ministrations of God's word ... This realm hath been ill provided, for that it hath had such corrupt judgements in it, to prefer Robin Hood to God's word. (75)

Though we may be tempted to smile at this picture of the outraged bishop, languishing outside a locked church while his parishioners were off gathering for Robin Hood, this offers a clear enough indication of just how important the May Games, as ruled over by Robin Hood, were to the people of medieval England.

Nor were things to alter all that much in the succeeding centuries. More than two hundred years later, in 1736, the minister of the deanery of Stowe in Gloucestershire issued a tract aimed against the celebration of such games, which were evident 'relics of paganism' and no more than thinly disguised echoes of 'sacrificial worship'. (29)

What exactly was it that took place at the May Day Games that so alarmed and angered the churchmen? Accounts differ, but it is possible to find a pattern in the extant descriptions that form a coherent whole.

The May Day Revels

Just as the introduction of the Green Man into the gothic cathedrals of the Middle Ages represents the entrance – by the back door – of the old pagan force of nature into the Christian architraves, so the May Games of Robin Hood represented the entrance of a forest law into the realm of the city and the everyday. Wildness, of a kind deplored by so many

Puritan writers that it must evidently have had a strong hold, broke out everywhere once the May Pole had been erected. These poles, most often of oak, elm or birch, were brought from the forest and erected in town and village alike, where they became the focus of joyful and uninhibited games, feasting and general merriment.

'There can be no doubt,' asserted Lord Raglan in his book *The Hero* (73), 'that it [May Day] was of pagan origin – that it was, in fact, the Spring festival which was theoretically superseded by the Christian Easter. We should expect a Pagan festival to be associated with a Pagan deity, and we should not be disappointed. We have in Robin Hood a deity particularly associated with Spring and vegetation. He was the King of May, and Maid Marian was the Queen of May.'

Accounts of the May Day Games exist in plenty, and it is possible to put together a fairly complete picture from sources that show the wide distribution of the revels. In Wales, according to the folklorist Marie Trevelyan,

On the morning of May Day – that is, at the very first glimmer of dawn – the youth and maidens in nearly every parish in Wales set out to the nearest woodlands. The gay procession consisted of men with horns and other instruments, which were played, while vocalists sang the songs of May-time. When the merry part reached the woodlands each member broke a bough off a tree, and decorated the branch with flowers, unless they were already laden with May blossoms. A tall birch tree was cut down, and born on a farm wagon drawn by oxen into the village. At sunrise the young people placed the branches of May beside the doors or in the windows of their houses. This was followed by the setting up of the Maypole on the village green. The pole was decorated with nosegays and garlands of flowers, interspersed with bright coloured ribbon bows, rosettes and streamers. Then the master of ceremonies, or leader of the May dancers, would advance to the pole, and tie a gay coloured ribbon around it. He was followed by all the dancers, each one approaching the pole and tying a ribbon around it until a certain number had been tied. The dance then began, each dancer taking his or her place according to the order in which the ribbons had been arranged around the pole. The dance was continued without intermission until the party was tired, and then other dancers took their places. (89)

Three hundred years or so before this, the Puritan writer Philip Stubbs described, in jaundiced fashion, a similar scene:

They have twenty or forty yoke of oxen, every ox having a sweet nosegay of flowers tied on the tip of his horns, and these oxen draw home the maypole (this stinking idol rather) which is covered all over with flowers and herbs, bound about with strings from the top to the bottom, and sometimes painted with variable colours, with two or three hundred men, women, and children following it with great devotion. And this being reared up, with handkerchiefs and flags streaming on the top, they strew the ground about, bind green boughs about it, set up Summer bales, bowers, and arbours hard by it. And then fall they to banquet and feast, to leap and dance about it, as the heathen people did at the dedication of their idols ... (35)

A poem published in pamphlet form by the Puritan writer Thomas Hall in 1660 gives a voice to the Maypole itself, and in condemning the sport and lawlessness of the May Day Games points to the wholly necessary power of the occasion:

I am Sir May Pole, that's my name
Men, May, and Mirth give me the same.

And thus hath Flora, May, and Mirth,
Begun and cherished my birth,
Till time and means so favour'd mee,
That of a twig I waxt a tree:
Then all the people, less and more,
My height and tallness did adore.

... where 'tis noised that I am come,
My followers summoned by the drum.
I have a mighty retinue ...

Maid-Marrian and the Morris Dance ...
I tell them 'tis a time to laugh,
To give themselves free leave to quaff,
To drink their healths upon their knee,
To mix their talk with ribaldry ...

The honour of the Sabbath-day
My dancing greens have ta'en away;
Let preachers prate till they grow wood:
Where I am they can do no good. (10)

But the Maypole represented more than a last remnant of pagan superstition. It was really the Axile Tree, connecting Earth and Heaven, Sky Father and Earth Mother. The ribbons, yellow and black, represented Winter and Summer, the very energies which, represented by their champions, came together to fight for the hand of the Flower Maid. As the people of village and town danced around the pole, winding themselves in intricate mazes of dance into the very heart of Creation, they were, consciously or not, echoing a rhythm that had existed since the beginning of time. As the poet Stevenson put it in his *Twelve Months*:

Why should the priest against the May pole preach?
Alas! it is a thing out of his reach;
How he the error of the time condones,
And says, 'tis none of the celestial poles;
Whilst he (fond man!) at May-poles thus perplext,
Forgets he makes a May-game of his text.
But May shall triumph at a higher rate,
Having trees for poles, and boughs to celebrate;
And the green regiment, in brave array,
Like Kent's great waling grove, shall bring in May'. (10)

The importance of the May Day celebrations can hardly be overemphasised. Bringing in boughs clad with the new leafage of Spring was in itself a significant act, one which, in the words of Jane Harrison, 'takes little notice of death and Winter, uttering and emphasising only the desire for the joy in life and Spring'. (35)

The May King and Queen

The central figures of the May Games were the King and Queen of the May. Various suggestions have been put forward as to their origin, including the queen as a representation of the Roman goddess Flora, the deity of Spring, and the king as a late aspect of the Green Man. With the latter we need have no quarrel, since this is precisely the conclusion reached in Chapter 3. In the case of the queen, she is certainly older than Roman times. In fact, no one can say with any certainty where she, or her consort in the games, originated. It seems most likely that they derive from ancient representations of the season itself, possibly once effigies carried in procession, or in flower-bedecked oxcarts which were taken through towns and villages to be displayed in a sacred grove or stone circle. Essentially, she is the Flower Bride, echoes of whose status and origin may be seen in such figures as the Welsh Blodeuwedd (Flower Face), who was created out of flowers by the Magician-Gods Math and Gwydion. A poem attributed to the sixth-century Welsh bard Taliesin probably refers to her.

> Not of mother nor father was my creation.
> I was made from the ninefold elements –
> From fruit trees, from paradisal fruit,
> From primroses and hill-flowers,
> From the blossom of trees and bushes,
> From the roots of the earth was I made,
> From the broom and the nettle,
> From the water of the ninth wave ...
>
> (trans. Caitlín Matthews)

We shall meet this figure again in Chapter 5, when we come to our discussion of Maid Marian.

At some point, if they had not always been so, the effigies gave way to human representations, and in the time of the medieval May Day Revels, where they can be seen in the form of the white-clad, golden-crowned maiden and her lusty, green-clad lord – the very images of Robin and Marian indeed. C. A. Burland sums it up precisely when he writes:

The central figure of May Day was the May Queen. In historic and recent times she wore a white gown and garlands of flowers. She was carried in procession seated on her throne, and her position was much coveted. She had to be a girl of good character [i.e. a virgin] who was chosen by her fellows. The blessing on her was that the position made her a desirable bride, a symbol of life and love. Yet the weight of evidence is that May Queens were a revival of something almost forgotten. The ancient goddess returned to the scene by way of a procession of little girls who went around the village in their best dresses carrying miniature maypoles garlanded with flowers, and a May queen who was just a doll in a box all decorated with fresh blossoms. (13)

Even here the symbolism was precise, as it is in Ireland, where straw dolls called 'brideogs', are still placed in a basket during the May Day celebrations with the accompanying words 'Bride is in the bed'. Bride is Briged, one of the ancient tutelary goddesses of Ireland, and her recollection at this time is wholly in keeping with the celebration of May Day.

Just as we shall see in Chapter 5 that Marian came to represent the May Queen, so it has been suggested, by more than one commentator, that Robin Hood superseded the King of the May. There is abundant evidence to support this. In the churchwarden's accounts for the village of Crosscombe in Somerset for 1506, the May Day revels are named 'the Sport of Robart Hode'. Elsewhere we find the Elizabethan writer Henry Machlyn reporting how 'on the 23rd of June (1559) there was a May Game ... with giant and drums and guns, and nine worthies with speeches, and a goodly pageant with a Queen; and then Saint George and the Dragon, the Morris dance, and after, Robin Hood and Little John, and Maid Marian, and Friar Tuck, and they had speeches around about London ... '(10)

Another account is worth quoting at length, since it not only confirms the importance of Robin Hood in the celebrations of May, but also gives a very detailed picture of the way in which he would have appeared in the seventh year of the reign of King Henry VIII (1516). The quotation is from Edward Hall's *Chronicles*.

The King and the Queen [Katherine of Aragon], accompanied by many lords and ladies, rode a-Maying from Greenwich to the high ground of Shooter's Hill; and as they passed by the way, they espied a company of tall yeomen, clothed all in green, with green woods and with bows and arrows, to the number of 200. One, being the chieftain, was called Robin Hood, who required the King and all his company to stay and see his men shoot, and the king was content. Then he whistled, and all the 200 archers shot and loosed at once; and then he whistled again and they likewise shot again; their arrows whistled by craft of the [arrow] head, so that the noise was strange and great, and much pleased the king, the queen and all the company ... Then Robin Hood desired the king to come into the Greenwood, and to see how the outlaws lived. The king demanded of the queen and her ladies if they durst adventure to go into the wood with so many outlaws. Then the queen said, if it pleased him, she was content. Then the horns blew till they came to the wood under Shooters Hill, and there was an arbour made of bows, with a hall, and a great chamber, and an inner chamber, very well made and covered with flowers and sweet herbs, which the king much praised ... Then the king and queen sat down and were served with venison and wine by Robin Hood and his men ... Then the King departed and his company, and Robin Hood and his men conducted them; and as they were returning, there met with them two ladies in a rich chariot drawn by five horses ... and in the centre sat the lady May, accompanied by the lady Flora, richly apparelled; and they saluted the king with diverse goodly songs, and so brought him to Greenwich ... (75)

The presence here not only of Robin and his band of archers, but of the Queen of the May (supported by Flora) is significant in itself, as is the fact that the archers carry 'green woods'. But then, as W. E. Simeone remarks in a valuable article on 'Robin Hood and the May Day Games',

wherever the May Games were celebrated, through much of the fifteenth century, all of the sixteenth century when the outlaw reached the height of his popularity, and through most of the seventeenth century, among all classes in England and Scotland, Robin Hood unequivocally dominated the whole festival. In fact, the May Games became, during those centuries, a saint's day for the canonised outlaw. (77)

The insistence of certain scholars that Robin Hood was only associated with the May Day celebrations at a late (i.e. Elizabethan) period fails to take in the whole of the picture. If we are correct in our supposition that Robin was but the latest aspect of the age-old figure of the Green Man (see Chapter 2), then what is far more likely is that the wheel of tradition came full circle, returning Robin to his rightful place in the celebrations after a time of absence from them. This much is evident when we consider the ritual aspects underlying the May Day celebrations, each of which, in one way or another, suggests the half-glimpsed presence of Marian and Robin as Green Lady and Green Lord. As E. O. James notes,

> The representation of the May Queen and the May King as bride and bridegroom is reminiscent of the sacred marriage in the Magna Mata Festival; and as Kybele was responsible for the flowering of the fields, so the May Queen sat in an arbour wreathed with flowers, or in a porch of the church similarly adorned, like her Romano-Phrygian counterpart seated in her mountain abode and receiving floral offerings from her votaries. Her spouse the Green Man has been treated in the same manner because he has played the Attis role in the folk tradition. In short, they have both survived true to type in their essential features and the general setting of the May celebrations, in spite of the observances having now lost their earlier significance ... (46)

On the Isle of Man as late as the 1920s the festival of May Day – or, as it was called there, Laa Boaldyn – was celebrated with full ritual panoply. On May Eve the people went up onto the mountains and fired the gorse to frighten away the Faery kind. Then, next morning, on May Day itself, they welcomed in the festival with the loud blowing of horns, again with the desire of driving away any of the Faery people who might be at hand. Then the May Queen, mounted on a horse, was led into the village, attended by some twenty maidens and an equal number of boys led by a captain who formed her bodyguard. Eleanor Hull, quoting from a manuscript description of Manx customs, adds the following:

> In opposition to her [the Queen of May] is the Queen of Winter, a man dressed in woman's clothes, with woollen hood, fur tippets, and laden with the heaviest and warmest habits, one upon the other. In the same manner are her attendants dressed, and she also has a captain and troop for her defence. Being thus equipped as proper emblems, of the Beauty of Spring, and the Deformity of Winter, the two parties set forth from their respective quarters, the one preceded by violins and flutes, the other with the rough music of tongs and cleavers. Both parties march till they meet on a common, where their followers engage in a mock battle. If the forces of the Queen of Winter get the upper hand and succeed in taking the Queen of May prisoner, she has to be ransomed for a sum which will pay the expenses of the day; after which, Winter and her attendants retire to a barn to amuse themselves while the others remain on the green, dancing for a considerable time. They conclude the evening with a feast, the Queen at one table with her maids, the captain with his troop at another. There are seldom less than fifty or sixty at each board. (44)

It is easy to see that this represents the last vestiges of a fully fledged ritual depicting the struggle between the representatives of Winter and those of Summer. There is also a suggestion (supported elsewhere) that one of the underlying themes of the May Day revels was the fear of the Faery folk with whom, as we saw in Chapter 2, Robin is closely associated. The noise that often accompanied the May Day processions seems aimed specifically at scaring away the Faeries; further back in time this may have been part of a still older ceremony in which a sacrifice was made to propitiate the older gods (who themselves *became* the Faeries in later days). At an older time, this probably consisted of a human sacrifice, or of an animal token. In parts of Scotland to this day the Beltane bannock is cooked and broken into equal parts, one of which is then smeared with ash until it is black. The parts are then placed in a bag and everyone draws one forth. The person who gets the blackened piece has then to jump through a bonfire (once 'bonefire') in token of the sacrifice. In an earlier time it was perhaps thus that the willing sacrifice was chosen, and he or she burned. (In Dublin until the late nineteenth century those whose task it was to build the May Day fires used to drag a collection of bones from the boneyard to feed the flames).

The Lord of Misrule

Another central figure of the May Games was the Fool, sometimes called the Lord of Misrule. Crowned for a day, and perhaps representing the old King-for-a-Day of an older time, the Fool guided the actions of everyday mortals, and was given every courtesy, even though he represented a clownish chaos which would have put fear into the hearts and minds of ordinary folk the rest of the year. Like the King and Queen of the May, who were universally referred to as Robin and Marian where they were named at all, he ruled supreme over the area and was accorded highest honours. All three represented the wildness that was outlawed, either by necessity or prudence, throughout the rest of the year.

Phillip Stubbs is again a good source of material.

First, all the wild-heads of the parish, coventing together, choose them a Grand-Captain (of all mischief) whom they ennoble with the title 'My Lord of Misrule', and him they crown with great solemnity, and adopt for their king.

Having then selected between twenty and a hundred men to accompany him, all of whom are dressed in liveries of green and gold, the Lord of Misrule and his company then proceed 'towards the church and churchyard, their pipes piping, their drummers thundering, their stumps dancing, their bells jingling, their handkerchiefs swinging about their heads like madmen, their hobby horses and other monsters skirmishing amongst the rout.' Surprisingly, they enter the church, irrespective of whether there is a service in progress, and there they dance before the altar. After which they go out again into the churchyard where, says Stubbs, 'they have commonly their Summer Halls, their bowers, arbours and banqueting houses set up, wherein they feast, banquet and dance all that day and peradventure all the night too.'(10)

The Lord of Misrule is provided with food by the parishioners, to whom they sell 'badges' which they call 'My Lord of Misrule's Badges', and which apparently gave their owners certain protection from the merciless mockery of the lord's men. David Wiles notes: 'When we examine Stubbs' description, and relate it to the Churchwarden's account books [of costumes for the players], we find that the attributes and functions of Stubbs' Lord of Misrule in the Tudor may-games belong also to impersonators of the Greenwood outlaw.'(99)

To this day, the ceremony of the Abbots Bromley Horn Dance, which takes place in September at the other gate of the year, is unique in that the mummers enter the church and dance before the altar with much jingling of the bells tied around their legs.

In the fourteenth century in Exeter the Lord of Misrule and his men dragged people from their homes and demanded money in lieu of 'a sacrifice'. It is almost as if the original sacrificial quality of Robin Hood has been replaced by the reiving of money – even in the original ballads and before the advent of the mummers and Morris teams. That the apparently carefree nature of these 'sports' hid an older and darker theme is something we must now examine.

The Death of the Champion

There is little doubt that the May Day sports once accompanied a far more serious 'game', in which the chosen champion of Summer or Winter was beheaded. We have already seen, in Chapter 3, how the story of the Green Man and his Winter challenge to Arthur's court in the medieval poem of *Gawain and the Green Knight* tells the foundation story of the relation between the Kings of Summer and Winter and Queen of the May. That a form of this then continued, albeit in a much reduced form, into the nineteenth century is demonstrated in the journal *Folk-Lore* for 1901, where S. D. Addy collected descriptions of May Day ceremonies in the isolated village of Castleton in Derbyshire. His description, somewhat paraphrased, reads like this:

It appears that on the twentieth or 29th of May the church bell rings at 2 o'clock to call all the ringers together to make a garland of May flowers, which have been gathered by the villagers in the morning. This so-called garland is rather like a bell in shape, and as when covered with leaves and flowers it weighs about 12 stone, it naturally calls for an extremely powerful man to carry it. Robin Hood's bower may have been the same kind of thing.

The bower is made of flat lathes of wood, as for the hoops of a barrel. At the top was a circular piece of wood with a hole in it about an inch in diameter. Into this the topknot a Quane (queen?) … was inserted, made of the choicest flowers … mounted on a wooden knob. Much of the framework is filled with twigs of oak. Two men standing on barrels then lift it on to the head of the chosen King, as he is now called, though formally he was known as the Man. He is accompanied by a woman wearing a crown and called the Queen, though formally she was known as the Woman …

The king then mounts upon a horse, which he cannot guide because of his covering, and is lead about by a figure called the Ringer. Morris dancers follow and the queen brings up the rear, and they proceed through the village, pausing for the dancers to dance before every inn (it is notable, remarks Lady Raglan, the number of inns called The Green Man there are in England).

At last the procession reaches the church. The quane or topknot is removed, and the King enters the churchyard alone upon his horse, and stands under the south wall of the tower. On the tower are ringers who, using a projecting piece of masonry as a pulley, lower a rope down to the King, who fastens it into the hole left by the removal of the topknot. The garland is then drawn up to the top of the tower, where it is fastened to a pinnacle, and there remains until next year, or until it is blown away by the Winter gales. The quane is then given by the ringers to some prominent villager …

Above: 1. Robin Hood and the Bishop from a Broadside sheet printed in London for W. Onlay, *c.* 1660. (Roxborough Manuscript)

Below: 2. The title page from *The Little Gest of Robin Hood*, *c.* 1508. (Author's collection)

Above: 3. 'Morris Dancer and Maid Marian', a page from Horne's Year Book showing figures from George Tollet's window at Battley Abbey, Staffordshire. (Author's collection)

Left: 4. The Huntsman of Windsor portrayed by George Cruickshank, from *Windsor Castle* by Harrison Ainsworth. (Author's collection)

Opposite: 5. A Wodwose and a Green Man from Joseph Strutt's *Sports and Pastimes of the English People*, 1801. (Author's collection)

Left: 6. The Unicorn/Hooden Horse from the Thaxted Morris Ring, 1984. (Author's collection)

Below: 7. Jack-in-the-Green photographed by E. H. Binney (undated) from *Customs of the World* by W. Hutchinson, 1913. (Author's collection)

Opposite, top: 8. : The Major Oak in Sherwood Forest, believed by many to be the meeting place for Robin Hood and the outlaws. (Author's collection)

Opposite, bottom: 9. Robin Goodfellow as depicted by Herbert Cole in *Fairy Gold* by Ernest Rhys, 1906. (Author's collection)

A True Tale of *ROBIN HOOD.*

Or, A Brief Touch of the Life and Death of that renowned Outlaw *Robert* Earl of *Huntington*, vulgarly called *Robin Hood*, who lived and dyed in A. D. 1198. being the 9th. year of the Reign of King *Richard* the Firſt, commonly called *Richard Cœur de Lyon.*

Carefully collected out of the trueſt Writers of our Engliſh Chronicles : And publiſhed for the ſatisfaction of thoſe who deſire truth from falſhood.

By *Martin Parker.*

Printed for *J. Clark*, *W. Thackeray*, and near *Weſt-Smithfield*, 1687.

Opposite: 10. Frontispiece from *A True Tale of Robin Hood* by Martin Parker, 1687. (Author's collection)

Above right: 11. Robin and Maid Marian in their bower, as depicted by Louis Rhead in his 1916 book *Bold Robin Hood and his Outlaw Band*. (Author's collection)

Right: 12. Robin and the Peddler of Wakefield illustrated by Howard Pyle from his *The Merry Adventures of Robin Hood*, 1883. (Author's collection)

When The Sherriff Saw His earn vessels, his appetite went from 'Him

Opposite: 13. Robin serves the Sheriff of Nottingham from his own silver. Illustration by Lancelot Speed in *Tales of Romance*, edited by Andrew Lang, 1918. (Author's collection)

Above: 14. Romantic portrait of Robin by H. M. Brock from *Robin Hood and the Men of the Greenwood* by Henry Gilbert 1912. (Author's collection)

Opposite: 15. Robin
encounters King Richard
the Lionheart in disguise.
Illustration by Louis Rhead
from *Bold Robin Hood and
His Outlaw Band*, 1912.
(Author's collection)

Right: 16. Alan-a-Dale by
Louis Rhead, here presented
as a typical medieval
jongleur, from *Bold Robin
Hood and His Outlaw Band*,
1912. (Author's collection)

Above: 17. Friar Tuck carries
Robin across the river in
this illustration by Howard
Pyle from his *The Merry
Adventures of Robin Hood*,
1883. (Author's collection)

18. Robin and the Peddler of Wakefield illustrated by Howard Pyle from his *The Merry Adventures of Robin Hood*, 1883. (Author's collection)

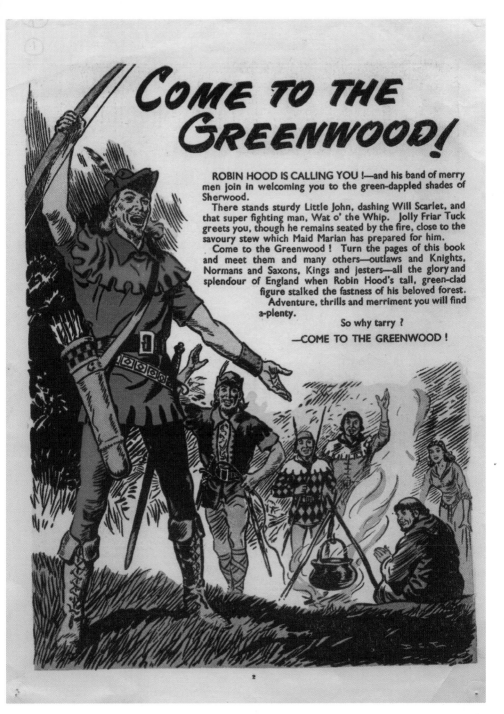

COME TO THE GREENWOOD!

ROBIN HOOD IS CALLING YOU!—and his band of merry men join in welcoming you to the green-dappled shades of Sherwood.

There stands sturdy Little John, dashing Will Scarlet, and that super fighting man, Wat o' the Whip. Jolly Friar Tuck greets you, though he remains seated by the fire, close to the savoury stew which Maid Marian has prepared for him.

Come to the Greenwood! Turn the pages of this book and meet them and many others—outlaws and Knights, Normans and Saxons, Kings and jesters—all the glory and splendour of England when Robin Hood's tall, green-clad figure stalked the fastness of his beloved forest.

Adventure, thrills and merriment you will find a-plenty.

So why tarry?

—COME TO THE GREENWOOD!

19. Robin Hood welcomes you to the Greenwood – illustration from a 1950s children's annual featuring the adventures of the famous outlaw. (Author's collection)

Above: 20. Robin Hood and Guy of Guisborne. (Author's collection)

21. Robin and Guy of Guisborne. (Author's collection)

22. 'Robin Hood's Grave' at Clifton, situated close to the Kirklees Estate in Yorkshire. Long believed to be the outlaw's final resting place. (Courtesy of cr01 under Creative Commons 2.0)

23. N. C. Wyeth's illustration from a 1917 edition of *Robin Hood*, depicting the outlaw's final act. (Author's collection)

All of this, as Lady Raglan noted in her celebrated article on the Green Man, leaves little doubt that it contains one of the last surviving echoes of a time when the king would have been sacrificed, decapitated and his head hung on a tree. It is also not without significance that many of the Green Men carved on roof bosses in medieval churches have their tongues sticking out – a not unusual feature of someone who has been hung or strangled. The image of the Green Man at Southwell Minster Chapter House, which is interpreted as a man making a hole in the Garland to look through, could equally well be someone placing a noose around his head – a feature in keeping with the idea that the sacrificed king was a willing sacrifice.

The fact that the original titles of the king and queen were 'The Man' and 'The Woman' indicates the antiquity of this whole ceremony. In Sussex as recently as forty years ago people who still practised a form of traditional native religion referred to the God and Goddess of the land as 'Im' and 'Er' [i.e. Him and Her].

The question still remains whether Robin may be seen as a type of sacrificed king. Lewis Spence certainly thought so, writing in his study of ritual games that they were closely connected with archery, and speculating that in earlier times they may have included a species of drama based on the lives of Robin, Marian, and company. He goes on:

> In my view the games of Robin Hood represented the last shadow of an enacted rite which narrated the life and adventures of a god or wood-spirit, and ended with the sacrifice of his human representative, who was dispatched by a flight of arrows ... [which] represented the rain-shower, for in all parts of the world the flint arrow-head is the emblem of rain ... (84)

Whether or not there is any truth in this remains to be seen. That the games did indeed retain the last vestiges of a more ancient ritual celebration is scarcely in doubt, nor is the belief that Robin is the inheritor of the story of the Woodland Spirit or God. Spence is right, also, about the symbolism of flint arrowheads (the elfshot of Faery tradition), and about the association of the games with archery; while Robin himself seems to have been regarded as almost the patron saint of archers. Witness Michael Drayton's description of the various devices of the English counties at the Battle of Agincourt:

> Old Nottingham, an archer clad in green,
> Under a tree with his dawn bow that stood,
> Which in a chequered flag far off was seen;
> It was the picture of old Robin Hood
>
> *The Polyolbion*

There is, unfortunately, no evidence in any of the ballads to suggest that Robin died by being shot with an arrow; however, the manner of his death as we know it is not without significance.

As we saw in Chapter 1, Robin met his death at the hands of the Prioress of Kirklees Abbey, who bled him to death while supposedly treating him for illness. This method of treatment was common during the Middle Ages, but it is also significant for our argument in that it represents a ritual mode of death. In the ballads the prioress is represented as an evil woman in league with an old enemy of Robin's, but it is much more likely that she represents a memory of the priestess whose task it was to let out the blood of the sacrificial king to fructify the earth.

Finally, in a variant version of the death ballad preserved in a fragmentary form in Bishop Percy's MSS, we learn that as Robin journeyed toward Kirklees, he met an old woman kneeling on a plank of wood over a stream. She is, apparently, banning (that is, cursing) him and he asks her why. Unfortunately, the MS is fragmentary at this point and her answer is missing. Tantalisingly, the ballad takes up the story after half a page

> ... To give to Robin Hood;
> We weepen for his dear body,
> That this day must be let blood

This suggests that a number of people are weeping for Robin's impending death, though he appears blithely unconcerned since the next verse emphasises that the prioress is his cousin and could not possibly harm him. However, it is equally likely that Robin knows that he is going to his appointed death, and does so willingly. The old woman at the ford over the stream can only be a variation of the Washer-at-the-Ford, the hag-like woman seen by Celtic warriors before a battle in which they were to die. In other words she foretells Robin's death, and he then meets a group of mourners who also know the outcome of the bloodletting. Robin is, clearly, the willing sacrifice, the King of the Wood who must die in order to give way to his successor that the seasons may continue to turn.

All this is strong enough evidence to suggest that Robin Hood was indeed synonymous with the Lord of the May, and with the sacrificed King of the Wood. This we should accept, despite the fact that the majority of the records date from comparatively late, in the fifteenth and sixteenth centuries. Of times earlier than this we can only speculate. What seems the most likely explanation is that 'Robin Hood' or 'Robin-o-the-Wood' were the May King's original, secret names, kept by those who continued celebrating the old pagan year into more recent times. With the passage of time, as the old mysteries ceased to be as important or so closely guarded, these names would have been more openly used. Thus Robin was recognised as the King of the May and Marian as his Lady – and his consort. Together they ruled over the mysterious games, which welcomed in the season of plenty and signalled an end to the harshness of Winter. They began with the bringing in of garlands and branches, which signified the bringing of the Greenwood into everyday reality, and ended with the nuptials of the Lord and Lady of the Wood, celebrated, in similar fashion, by their followers and supporters.

Once, the sacrifice of Robin (the King of the Wood) may have been part of this; but by the time of Robin Hood the Outlaw, in the thirteenth or fourteenth centuries, such things were no more than a memory, all but forgotten save in certain neglected corners of the land. The Green Man, now known as Robin Hood, still reigned supreme, as he had through the ages, but in a new form. Ever renewing like the Greenwood he represented, he could not die, only change and take on a new disguise as 'the merry outlaw of Sherwood'.

Whether or not the more ancient customs behind the May revels were widely recognised, the Church certainly knew the truth of it – as witnessed by the number of proscriptions against the May Day revels from the fourteenth century onwards. The outward innocence of the madcap sports was seen by the churchmen for what it truly was – a thinly disguised pagan celebration.

The Fate of the Games

By Tudor times the reason for the games had declined to the collection of money for the parish. Robin Hood and his troop rode from village to village, performing their play to music by a minstrel and two drummers. Although they continued in desultory fashion as late as 1607 in England and 1610 in Scotland, they were for the most part underground springs by this time, their players subject to fines or even excommunication if caught. The last embers of the Robin Hood games were dead by this time, in all save literary circles, where they continued to be referred to, in a nostalgic vein, throughout the seventeenth and eighteenth centuries.

In some places attempts were made to stop the games altogether. In Scotland they were banned in 1555, but when attempts were made to enforce the law, rioting broke out. In 1580, one Edmund Asshton wrote to a William Ffarington demanding that the May Day rites of Robin Hood be suppressed on account of the fact that they were 'lewde sports, tending to no other end but to stir up your frail natures to wantoness'. (70)

The historian Douce observed that 'during the reign of Elizabeth, the Puritans made considerable havoc among the May games by their preaching and invectives. Poor Maid Marian was assimilated to the whore of Babylon; Friar Tuck was deemed a remnant of Popery; and the Hobby Horse as a impious and Pagan superstition'. (10) In *The Anatomy of Abuses*, published in 1585, its author, Phillip Stubbs, whom we heard earlier describing the 'stinking idol' of the Maypole, inveighs against the games themselves:

> Against May, every parish, town, and village, assemble themselves together, both men, women and children, old and young ... and either going all together, or dividing themselves into companies, they go some to the woods and groves, some to the hills and mountains, some to one place, some to another, where they spend all the night in pastimes, and in the morning they return, bringing with them birch, bows, and branches of trees to deck their assemblies ... I have

heard it credibly reported ... that of forty, threescore, or a hundred maids going to the wood over night, there have scarcely the third part of them returned home again undefiled.

One gets the idea, reading between the lines, that there is more than just disgust at these heathenish practices – there is something of fear as well. What appears as unbridled lust to the puritanical mind also stands for the principle of nature set loose to roam and ravage as it wills. The freedom of spirit and joyous simplicity of life expressed in the May Day Games represented everything the Puritans desired to outlaw and proscribe. It is possible to speculate that more than one Robin-in-the-Hood walked the woods on May-Eve, and that their main objective was the deflowering of virgins!

All the repressed energies of sexuality, bawdiness and joyous love of life, suppressed by the gloomy Puritans, broke out in riotous abandon once Charles I was on the throne. In a statute dated 18 October 1633, he commanded: 'for his good people's recreation, after the end of Divine Service, his good people be not disturbed, leted, or discouraged from any lawful recreation; such as dancing, either men or women; archery for men, leaping, vaulting, or any other such harmless recreation; nor from having any May Games, Witson Ales, and Morris dances, and the setting up of May Poles, and other sports therewith used ... '(10)

All of these elements are, then, to be found in the May Day celebrations, where unofficial paganism existed alongside official Christianity. Robin Hood, the Maid Marian, Friar Tuck and the merry Morris Men preserved the last flickering light of a more ancient culture. The law of the Green Man and the Green Lady still flourished, for a time at least, in the May Games. The May Pole, connecting Earth and Heaven, wound those who danced about it into the endless dance of creation, making them one with the Earth Goddess and the Sky Father. The May King was no longer killed – in actuality at least – but his sacrifice was remembered and honoured under the smiling skies of 'Merry England' long after the true meaning of the games was forgotten.

The May Day celebrations, then, helped keep alive the secret power of what we may justly call the Robin Hood cult. Embodied in the games were all the mysteries of Robin and Marian – even though they became disparate at times – Marian and Tuck joining the Morris team while Robin remained King of the May in his own games. Ultimately they were bound by a far deeper set of laws, those that ensured the preservation of immemorial traditions in any number of ways. Robin Hood and his followers are only the bearers of a single part of the Greenwood tradition; yet in their diversity and vitality they kept alive the belief in the Green Man and the Green Lady in the land. In the end May indeed 'triumphed' as Stevenson had predicted, preserving sufficient of the old ways to keep them alive into the present time.

5

MAID MARIAN AND THE FLOWER BRIDE

> Robin's mistress dear, his loved Marian
> Was Soverign of the woods, chief lady of the game;
> Her clothes tuck'd to the knee, and dainty braided hair,
> With bow and quiver arm'd.
>> *The Polyolbion*

If Robin is the King of May then most assuredly Marian is his queen. This fact overrides any evidence to the effect that Marian is a latecomer to the Greenwood. The Green Man requires a Flower Bride, and it is as such that we shall come to recognise Marian, even if her name was only added later. But first let us deal with the few historical 'facts' that have been presented by various scholars over the years.

Marian is sometimes identified as Lady Maud or Matilda Fitzwalter (also called Maud the Fair). Stowe's *Annals* tell that King John wooed her, and that when she refused him he had her poisoned and her father banished. This story is repeated in a play of 1661 called *The Death of Robert, Earl of Huntington, Afterwards called Robin Hood of Merry Sherwood; with the lamentable tragedy of chaste Matilda, his fair Maid Marian, poysand at Dunmore by King John.*

J. W. Walker, in his 1973 book *The True History of Robin Hood* (94), quotes two entries from the Court Rolls of Wakefield Manor which refer to Robert Hood and Matilda his wife, who 'gave 12*d* to the lord of the manor for leave to take one piece of curtilage [piece of ground attached to a dwelling place] in Wrengate, near the curtilage of Robert Clement from John Pollard to hold to himself and his heirs doing the services thereon'. At the same court 'Robert Hood and his wife Matilda gave 2s for leave to take one piece of land of the lord's waste on Bichill ... of the length of 30 feet and bredth of 16 feet to hold to the aforesaid Robert and Matilda and their heirs ... '

Walker's efforts to establish Robin and Marian as historical people living in and around Wakefield in the fourteenth century deserves respect, and is interesting for the light it throws on the customs of the time, but it comes no nearer to identifying the real Robin and Marian, who as we have seen are far more elusive than this, and far older.

The interesting fact is that Matilda is referred to as Maid Marian, as if this was, again, a title. Marian can indeed be an Anglicisation of Matilda, but this seems unlikely. What seems closer to the truth is that Maid Marian was, like Robin Hood, an ancient title that was adopted by the real woman, assuming she existed at all, and that the original figure was far older.

A fifteenth-century MSS, quoted by John Brand (10), mentions Marian thus:

> At Paske [Easter] begun or Morris, and ere Pentecost our May,
> Tho' Robin Hood, Little John, Friar Tuck, and Marian deftly play

This implies that Robin and Marian, as well as Little John and Friar Tuck, were already associated with the mumming plays. But it is not until around 1500, in a text called *The Ship of Fools*, that Marian was associated with Robin Hood in a literary form. Before that her name is mentioned solely with the title of May Day Queen. From this, some investigators have seen her as a product solely of the Morris dances, where she was certainly a prominent character, as we shall see in Chapter 6. However, as David Wiles points out in his study of the later Robin Hood plays (99), the May Day Games are older than the Morris, as are the Robin Hood plays themselves, so that Maid Marian clearly belongs to an earlier date. It is more than likely that it was by this route that her name and some of her characteristics came into the sphere of the Robin

Hood legends, and there is also a suggestion that she came by way of fourteenth-century French pastourelles relating to the 'shepherd' Robin and his Marian, and in particular a play attributed to the troubadour Adam de la Halle, *Robin et Marian*, which has survived in a unique MSS of around 1283.

The story relayed by this play and its accompanying songs seems a long way from the stories of Robin and Marian in England. Here Marian is a shepherdess and Robin her bucolic swain. She is wooed by a knight whose advances she successfully resists, protesting her loyalty to Robin throughout. In the second half of the play the shepherds enact a drama of their own, appointing Robin and Marian as king and queen over their games – showing that even here the old themes of the May Day revels hold true.

Further evidence for the continued strength of the theme is provided by the Elizabethan dramatist George Peele, who seems to have had something of an understanding of the Greenwood mythos, though he wrote no play concerning Robin Hood directly. In his *Edward I* (*c.* 1593), the hero, Lleullen, when about to lose his kingdom, decides to 'become' Robin Hood. He finds men to play Little John and Friar Tuck and dubs his sweetheart Maid Marian. Declaring himself Lord of Misrule, he says that he will sell a gold chain to raise money 'to set us all in green; and we'll play the pioneers, to make us a cave and a cabin for all weathers'.

As Professor Wiles notes, 'Peele's play is clearly based upon a memory of folk practices, according to which the Summer Lord would erect a bower for as the place for his Lady or Queen'. He adds: 'One learns from Peele's play that when the Summer King or Master of Misrule went by the name of Robin Hood, his Lady or May Queen would go by the name of Maid Marian; and when two attendants were selected, these were given the names Little John and Friar Tuck.'(99)

Thus we see an ancient quartet of Robin and Marian, John and Tuck together again. But it is essentially Robin and Marian, as Summer King and Queen, or Lord and Lady of the May, who are at the centre. And at the heart of the May Day Games lies an enactment of their marriage.

The sacrifice and rising of the God, whether actual or symbolic, was enacted to ensure to passage of the seasons and the continuance of life;

the celebrations of May are linked to fertility rites. Numerous carved stones and artefacts representing male and female genitalia have been found in every part of the country. The symbolism of the Maypole itself is certainly phallic. And, as we saw in Chapter 3, the pole erected above the head of the ithyphallic Cerne Abbas giant was once the scene of unbridled festivities connected with Herne and the other horned men of ancient times.

The battle of the Summer and Winter Kings would at one time have ended in some kind of ritual consummation (real or symbolic) between the victorious Summer King and his bride. Hence we may see in Marian a late example of a kind of fertility goddess, of the kind represented by the Sheila-na-Gigs carved on church porches in both Britain and Ireland. These figures, who display their genitalia, are recognised to have been connected to pre-Christian fertility rites. The fact that those which have survived are found on churches may well be for the same reason that foliate heads are found there – the Church wanted to show that it had absorbed (and therefore conquered) pagan beliefs. Placing them in full view on the walls and pillars of their stone forests was as good a way as any of demonstrating this. (8)

As already remarked, the May Day celebrations were notoriously licentious. The allowance to cast off domesticity and unite with the Greenwood came on Beltane eve, when any girl might go to the forest and sleep with whom she wished. It was usual for most to come back again and form a lasting, domestic relationship. Marian does not. She exemplifies the Queen of the May, who remains in the Wildwood with Robin as her consort. The birth of Robin himself, according to the ballad quoted in Chapter 1, may have been the result of a Wildwood (Beltane) assignation. It is consistent with the births of heroes who are conceived on virtuous women by unknown, outlaw men.

In a play by Braithwaite called *Strappando for the Devil* (1615) we read:

> As for his blood,
> He says he can derive't from Robin Hood
> And his May-Marian, and I thinke he may,
> For's mother plaid May-Marian t'other day. (10)

The result of May Day frolicking in the woods – merry meet weddings under the Greenwood trees – may well account for the fact, as Robert Graves surmises, that the most popular names in England still echo those of Little John (Jackson, Jacobson, etc.) and Robin Hood (Hudson, Hodson, Hod, etc.).

For Graves also Robin and Marian are to be equated with the figures of the wizard Merlin and his nemesis Nimue, who likewise fled the world for the sanctuary of the woods and lived an idyllic life there. Nimue and her variant selves, including Merlin's sister Ganeida and his wife Gwenddydd, were all types of Flower Bride. It is time that we looked more closely at this figure, who offers a more precise point of origin for Marian as Queen of the May.

The Rape of the Flower Bride

A central aspect in any proper understanding of Marian's part in the May Day celebrations is the ancient theme known as the rape of the Flower Bride. We have already touched upon this in Chapter 3, where we saw how the struggle of the Winter and Summer champions for the hand of the Spring Maid evolved, over a long period, into certain characteristics of the May Day Games. We also saw, in the passage quoted in the previous chapter, how in the time of Henry VIII the pastime of 'maying' was still being practised. An earlier account, from Thomas Malory's fifteenth-century romance *Le Morte d'Arthur*, shows the true significance of the event.

> It befell in the month of May, Queen Guenever called unto her knights of the Table Round; and she gave them warning that early upon the morrow she would ride a-Maying in the woods and fields beside Westminster. And I warn you that there be none of you but that he be well horsed, and that ye all be clothed in green ... and I shall bring with me ten ladies, and every knight shall have a lady behind him ... And so upon the morn they took their horses with the Queen, and rode a-Maying in woods and meadows as it pleased them, in great joy and delights ... (58)

Into the midst of this idyllic scene erupts the knight Meleagraunce, who has loved Guenever from afar for years. He ambushes the party and carries off the queen, imprisoning her in his tower, from which Lancelot shortly frees her after hand-to-hand combat with Meleagraunce.

The true significance of this is clear enough. The story is about the rape of the May Queen. It is also one of the best-documented themes in Arthurian literature. The earliest version, which also happens to be the oldest surviving example of an Arthurian story, appears carved in stone on the archivolt of Modena Cathedral in Italy. The first written version is contained in the twelfth-century *Life of Gildas* by Cradoc of Llancarven (100). This tells how Guenevere was stolen away by Melwas (an earlier version of Meleagraunce), King of the Summer country, and inured in the citadel of Glastonbury, to which site Arthur came with an army in search of her, laying siege to the place.

> When he saw this, the abbot of Glastonia, attended by the clergy and Gildas the Wise, stepped in between the contending armies, and in a peaceable manner advised his king, Melwas, to restore the ravished lady. Accordingly, she who was to be restored, was restored in peace and good will.

This episode has long been recognised as deriving from a much earlier story, a mythic pattern with which we are now very familiar, in which Arthur, as the Winter King, fights Melwas, King of the Summer Lands, for the hand of Gwenhwyfar, the Spring Maiden. It is a theme that appears again and again in Arthurian literature, including the passage quoted above from Malory's great book, where later on the rapist is replaced yet again by Mordred, Arthur's son by his half-sister Morgause, who seeks to become king by forcing Guinevere to marry him. It appears again, even more clearly, in the following episode from 'The Story of Culhwch and Olwen' in the Welsh *Mabinogion* (32).

> Creiddylad the daughter of Lludd Llaw Ereint, and Gwythyr the son of Greidawl were betrothed. And before she had become his bride, Gwyn ap Nudd came and carried her away by force; and Gwythyr the son of Greidawl gathered his host together, and went to fight with Gwynn ap Nudd. But Gwynn overcame him ... When Arthur heard of this, he went to the North, and summoned Gwynn ap Nudd before him ... and made peace between ... [him] ... and Gwythyr

the son of Greidawl. And this was the peace that was made: that the maiden should remain in her father's house, without advantage to either of them, and that Gwynn ap Nudd and Gwythyr son of Greidawl should fight for her every first of May, from thenceforth until the day of doom, and that which ever of them should then be conqueror should have the maiden.

Clearly, there can be no final overall winner 'until doomsday', because the two adversaries are not ordinary men but the representatives of Winter and Summer. (Interestingly, Gwynn ap Nudd, who is a Faery being, is said to live beneath Glastonbury Tor, where in the later story Melwas imprisons Gwenhwyfar.)

That this struggle remained a well-founded tradition over hundreds of years is indicated by the following account (similar to that already quoted in Chapter 3) from Welsh folkloric tradition, concerning a mock combat which was still taking place well into the nineteenth century.

An aged Welshman described the battle as conducted in South Wales in the following way: 'When I was a boy, two companies of men and youths were formed. One had for its captain a man dressed in a long coat much trimmed with fur, and on his head a rough fur cap. He carried a stout stick of blackthorn and a kind of shield, on which were studded tufts of wool to represent snow. His companions wore caps and waistcoats of fur decorated with balls of white wool. These men were very bold, and in songs and verse proclaimed the virtues of Winter, who was their captain. The other company had for its leader a captain representing Summer. This man was dressed in a kind of white smock decorated with garlands of flowers and gay ribbons. On his head he wore a broad-brimmed hat trimmed with flowers and ribbons. In his hand he carried a willow-wand wreathed with spring flowers and tied with ribbons. All these men marched in procession, with their captain on horseback leading them, to an appropriate place ... There a mock encounter took place, the Winter company flinging straw and dry wood at their opponents, who used as their weapons birch branches, willow-wands, and young ferns. A good deal of horse-play went on, but finally Summer gained the mastery over

Winter. Then the victorious captain representing Summer selected a May King and the people nominated a May Queen, who were crowned and conducted into the village. The remainder of the day was give up to feasting, dancing, games of all kinds, and, later still, drinking. Revelry continued through the night until the next morning.'(89)

Here the elements of the ancient story and its part in the May Day revels leap into focus. The struggle of the Lords of Summer and Winter for the Spring Maiden, whether she is called Creiddylad, Gwenhwyfar or Marian, is the same – an enactment of the spiritual dimension underlying the natural turning of the seasons. As Jane Harrison puts it in her book *Ancient Art & Ritual* (35):

> The intense emotion towards the weather, which breaks out into these magical agones or 'contests' is not very easy to realise. The weather to us now a days for the most part damps a day's pleasuring or raises the price of fruit and vegetables. But our main supplies come to us from other lands and other weathers, and we find it hard to think ourselves back into the state when a bad harvest meant starvation. The intensely practical attitude of man toward the seasons, the way that many of these magical dramatic ceremonies rose straight out of the emotion towards the food-supply would perhaps never be fully realised but for the study of … food producing ceremonies …

The need to ensure the safe continuance of the seasonal round was always in the mind of our ancestors. It was from such fears and shadows that myths of the sacrificed god arose, and with it the embodiment of the principles of nature such as the Green Man and the struggle for the Flower Bride.

A whole panoply of stories from Celtic and Arthurian tradition could be called upon to add their voices to this theme: Trystan and Esyllt, Owein and Luned, Arawn and Hafgan, Merlin and Nimue. (61) It may be argued that there is no surviving story of Robin fighting for the hand of Marian, but this need not deter us from seeing the ages-old pattern which underlies the medieval ballads. Indeed, if we look for a moment at the ballad of 'Robin Hood and Guy of Gisborne' we may detect more than a hint of a lost tale in which Gisborne was the challenger and Robin the defender.

The most extraordinary detail in this otherwise ordinary ballad is Gisborne's dress. He wears clothing made from horse skin – indeed, in one illustration to a nineteenth-century children's book he is even depicted as wearing a horse's head, complete with the ears. We know that the horse was sacred to the Celts, as well as to the aboriginal people of Britain, who left carved representations in the chalk hillsides which may still be seen today.

In the mummers' plays, to which we shall turn in the next chapter, we find the character of the 'Oss or Hobby Horse, a sinister, androgynous trickster figure whose actions recall those of the Green Knight and the King of Winter. Though it can only be speculation, it is not difficult to see Robin's traditional adversary in the figure of Sir Guy, an older and more primal figure whose origins perhaps date back to the horse cults of Britain and Ireland. Nor may we ignore the fact that when the combat between the two is over – just as in the Robin Hood play discussed below – Robin puts on the clothing of his defeated foe, still another instance of a symbolic exchange between the Lords of Winter and Summer.

Marian and the Brown Girl

There is something about Marian that causes everyone to fall in love with her. This is all part of the quality expressed by the May Queen herself – her freshness and loveliness, decked out in white with may blossom in her hair, seated in her bower surrounded by her attendants. But there is something more – like Robin, Marian expresses a kind of freedom that is all but lost to us in the twenty-first century. Marian is a free woman in an age when women were far from free – the stories which tell of the nobly born Lady Matilda who flees her Norman suitor to live in the Wildwood with the greatest outlaw of all time has a ring to it to which we can still respond. A famous early medieval poem, 'The Maid of the Moor', expresses this perfectly.

> Maiden in the moor lay,
> In the moor lay,

Seven nights full,
Seven nights full,
Maiden in the moor lay,
In the moor lay
Seven nights full and a day.

Well was her meat;
What was her meat?
The primrose and the violet,
The primrose and the violet,
Well was her meat;
What was her meat?
The primrose and the violet.

Well was her drink;
What was her drink?
The chill water of the wellspring,
The chill water of the wellspring
Well was her drink;
What was her drink?
The chill water of the wellspring.

Well was her bower;
What was her bower?
The red rose and the lily flower,
The red rose and the lily flower,
Well was her bower;
What was her bower?
The red rose and the lily flower.

(Author's trans.)

If this is not a description of Marian, the May Queen, in her flower-bedecked bower, it is hard to see what else it could be.

Robin and the Bull

A curious tradition recorded in Staffordshire adds a new thread to the story of Robin's marriage – and brings the ancient theme of the sacrificed king into sharper prominence.

The tradition concerns the custom of bull-running, which took place at Tutbury Castle, the home of John of Gaunt, from around 1374. At this time there existed a private Court of Minstrels with its own duly appointed 'king', who ruled for a year and gave judgements in matters of dispute between his 'subjects'. Every year, in August, a bull was given to the minstrels, which they then proceeded to madden by cutting off its horns, cropping its ears and tail and smearing it all over with soap, prior to blowing pepper up its nose. It was then released and the first person to cut away part of its hair while it was still in Staffordshire took this cutting to the market cross to prove his deed and the minstrels then received the bull as a prize.

This is astonishingly like customs recorded of the Celts, to whom cattle were sacred beasts, and it recalls particularly the famous 'Hunting of the Trwch Twryth' by Arthur and his warriors in 'Culhwch and Olwen', where the hero had to seize the comb and scissors stuck behind the ears of the giant boar in order to win the hand of Olwen.

Robin's association with this curious tradition is recorded in a ballad called 'A New Ballad of Bold Robin Hood, Shewing his birth, breeding, valour, and marriage at Titbury Bull-Running'. In this he meets Clorinda, the Queen of the Shepherds, and falls in love with her. On asking if she will marry him she replies:

> It may not be so, gentle sir,
> For I must be at Titbury Feast;
> And if Robin Hood will go hither with me,
> I'll make him the most welcome guest.

Robin agrees and the two, together with Little John, make their way to Tutbury, taking a freshly killed buck as an offering. On the way they encounter a gang of eight ruffians who are soon sent about their business. Robin and Clorinda continue to the feast and are duly married.

This is clearly a late ballad, and Clorinda has been substituted for Marian, but the underlying themes are still clear enough to see. At the feast where the bull is to be baited and then killed, Robin marries his queen. But it is not hard to see the pattern beneath this simple tale. The bull is a surrogate, killed in lieu of the Green King, who instead is wedded to the Lady of the Beasts, the Shepherdess, for whose hand he has to fight just as the Summer King fights the Winter King for the hand of the Spring Maiden. Nor should we forget the roles played out by Robin and Marian in Adam de la Halle's pastourelle discussed above, where both protagonists are shepherds.

It was themes such as these, told in ballad and oral tradition, which provided the stories for a new dramatic form, to which we must now turn for the next stage of our quest.

The Plays of Robin Hood

We cannot go any further in our investigation without turning to the subject of the various Robin Hood plays that were performed throughout the countries of England and Scotland from the fifteenth to the seventeenth centuries. These plays did much to keep alive the stories, and themselves subsumed many of the themes and characters of the May Day revels and the Morris dances and mummers. They presented the characters of Robin, Marian, Little John, Will Scarlet and the Sheriff of Nottingham in familiar settings. A typical example is 'The Play of Robin Hood, very proper to be played in May games', printed around 1562. It begins with Robin introducing himself and the Merry Men to the spectators:

> ROBIN: Now stand ye forth my merry men all
> And hark what I shall say.
> Of an adventure I shall you tell,
> The which befell this other day.
> As I went by the high way with
> A stout Friar I met,
> And a quarterstaff in his hand,
> Lightly to me he leapt
> And still he bade me stand ... (99)

The story then proceeds to follow more or less the lines of Robin's classic meeting with Tuck, their combat and the matter of the Friar's well-trained dogs, which can catch arrows in their mouths (see Chapter 6). There is much knockabout farce, which sets the tone of the rest of the Robin

Hood plays that have survived. Indeed, one could say that the central theme of them all is combat, and this, as we shall see, is an important factor in itself.

The fragmentary text of one such play, dated *c.* 1475, has been reconstructed plausibly by David Wiles. It deals with a combat between Robin and an unnamed knight, evidently one of the Sheriff's men. Robin is the victor after a number of trials of strength including archery, stone-throwing, wrestling and fighting with swords. Having slain the knight, Robin cuts off his head and wraps it in his own green hood – an astonishing piece of symbolic verification of the origin of the Robin myths.

Let the text speak for itself:

> Now that I have the mastery here,
> Off will I smite this sorry head.
> This knight's clothes will I wear,
> And in my hood his head will bare. (99, author's trans.)

The dialogue – such as it is – reminds one strongly of another such contest, this time between the Arthurian hero Gawain and the fearsome Green Knight. As we saw in Chapter 3, the figure of the Green Knight is a reminder of a much earlier story, in which the Knight of Summer replaces the Green King of Winter. As Dr Wiles remarks, 'the beheading of the Knight by the green outlaw must have ritual origins of the same kind'. (99) He points out also that Robin dons the apparel of the slain knight, thus proving, in traditional manner, that he is now the Lord of Summer.

In the second part of the play the action shifts to a scene in which Little John and Friar Tuck are having a friendly archery contest. They do not see the approach of the Sheriff, who captures them all, including Robin, and imprisons them. Having got the outlaws where he wants them, the Sheriff returns to gloat, but Robin and his men have loosened their bonds, and when the Sheriff opens the door they spring out and after a short scuffle throw the Sheriff and his men into the prison in their place.

The theme is again of contest and substitution. First Robin and the Outlaws are inside, then they break out and the Sheriff is forced to take their place. Once again it is Dr Wiles who points to the underlying meaning of the scene.

The central action is the emergence of the green men from their prison cage, and the locking away of their opponents. The gates [of the prison] must once have been a representation of death – a version of Hell-mouth – and the escape of Robin and his outlaws symbolises the emergence of Spring. (99)

In this way was so much ancient symbolism preserved. Nor was it really hidden from open view, as the vitriolic nature of Puritan attacks against the Robin Hood plays in the sixteenth century makes clear. The strength of feeling which could be evinced by the plays is shown in this diatribe, probably penned by one Sir Richard Morrison in 1560, addressed to King Henry VIII:

In Summer commonly upon the holy days in most places of your realm, there are plays of Robin Hood, Maid Marian, Friar Tuck, wherein besides the lewdness and ribaldry that there is opened to the people, disobedience also to your officers is taught, whilst these good bloods go about to take from the Sheriff of Nottingham one that for offending the laws should have suffered execution. How much better is it that those plays should be forbidden and deleted and others devised to set forth and declare lively before the peoples eyes the abomination and wickedness of the bishop of Rome, monks, friars, nuns, and such like, to declare and open to them the obedience that your subjects by god's and man's laws owe unto your majesty. (19)

A further account of the plays associates them with a group of people traditionally found on the edges of society – the gypsies. This is not the place to go into the complex history of these people, who prefer the name Rom or Romany to the term gypsy, which traditionally derives from the word Egyptian – giving rise to some unlikely derivations. The account in question comes from a book written by Father Richard Augustine, who was researching the geology of the Saintclaire family, lords of Rosslyn, a few miles from Edinburgh (*Genealogy of the Saintclaires of Rosslyn*, 1835). According to Fr Augustine, Sir William Sinclair, a late sixteenth-century holder of the title, saved an 'Egyptian' from the gallows. Subsequently, every year gypsies came to perform folk plays at Rosslyn. They were made welcome and housed in two towers of the castle, which were known as Robin Hood and Little John, making it clear that the subject of the plays was almost certainly the Outlaw of Sherwood. Given that at the time the law commanded all gypsies to be whipped, branded on the cheek or ear, or to have the right ear cut off, this is a remarkable story. The connection has remained in the memory of contemporary Rom, who recently sent representatives to the castle in search of Robin Hood.[1]

The Morris dances and the Robin Hood plays developed along quite different lines, having begun more or less in the same way (and at the same time). Both grew out of folk-memories of older, ritual acts, preserved in this way against the encroachment of Christianity. Certainly, from the fourteenth century onwards, they gave a home to the characters of Robin and the Merry Men, while adding to the band both Marian and Friar Tuck. Indeed, to such an extent were the two traditions married that many of the mumming plays began to be solely about Robin Hood and are even referred to as such in contemporary records.

Robin is essentially a figure who belongs to the Springtime, to May in its full flowering. The plays are Spring plays equivalent to the Winter dramas featuring St George. This balance between the two ends of the year is itself important. The Winter festival concerns itself with the death of the dragon, and with the later torture and sacrifice of St George. The Spring plays of Robin Hood have to do with the setting free of the natural world from the bondage of Winter. Robin is really a Springtime aspect of the Green Man – he who holds the land in thrall and breaks free of his more ancient, darker aspects in Spring, adopting the lighter aspect of the Green Jack. His marriage to Marian, the May Queen, is a wholehearted celebration of creativity, of burgeoning sexuality and the creative urgency of nature itself.

But it is to the mumming plays and their offshoots that we must turn for the best evidence of the roles adopted by Robin, Marian, Little John and Tuck in the times which followed the decline of the May Day Games. As is often the case, these later dramas preserve details from a much

---

1 I am grateful to David Elkington for drawing my attention to this.

earlier time, including the enactment of the Corn God's death and rebirth, and the symbolic wedding of the May King and Queen.

Marian and the Mummers

The first recorded mumming play took place before Henry VII in 1494. David Wiles, an expert on the Robin Hood plays, suggests that 'to a large extent it served to replace the Robin Hood game' (19) which had reached its peak of popularity just before this time (*c.* 1460). However Church records from a period between 1499 and 1530 give evidence of money laid out for the putting on of what is sometimes referred to as 'a king game', and at others 'a Robin Hood game', from which we may deduce that these were interchangeable and probably refers to the same thing. Since the Robin Hood games derive directly from the May Day revels, it is easy to see that these strands blended together to form something that was, at the same time, both new and old.

Despite this, the exact relationship between the Morris dance and the Robin Hood plays remains obscure. But one point is of interest. We are used to seeing modern Morris men dressed in white with a variety of coloured ribbons for decoration; however, originally the Morris colours were primarily green, which suggests not only a connection with Robin Hood, but also with the colour of the Faery race.

The history of mumming and Morris dancing in this country is fraught with suppositions, often unfounded, which makes it difficult to say with any certainty when or where they originated. We shall be examining the history of the Morris and its relationship to Robin in the next chapter; for the moment it is sufficient to quote Cecil Sharp, the acknowledged master of the subject and largely responsible for the revival of Morris dancing in Britain. The Morris dance, he states, together with the mummers play and the Sword Dance, are all aspects of 'the seasonal pagan observances prevalent amongst primitive communities, and associated ... with the fertilisation of all living things, animal and vegetable. The central act of the ceremony was the slaughter or a sacred animal to provide a solemn sacramental feast ... the object of the sacrifice of the holy animals and at the subsequent feast was to cement the bond between the god and the members of the clan.' (51)

This is clear enough. The dancers represent the death of the god and his rising again – symbolism carried over into the rites of corn-gods everywhere. Looking at the nature of the Morris dance, as well as the Sword Dance, we can see the roles of Robin as Green Man and sacrificed King and Marian as Green Goddess and Queen of May clearly set forth. The symbolism of the Sword Dance, with its six-pointed star formed from swords, placed over the head of the victim with the cry of 'a nut! a nut!' – for which read 'a knot!', the endless knot which also appears on Gawain's shield in the story of his fight with the Green Knight – all this points to the fact that Robin and Marian took on the roles of the chief players in a ritual as ancient as the land itself. The struggle between Winter and Summer, the sacrifice of the Green God of vegetation – both these themes are clearly represented here.

That the mumming plays were themselves the last vestiges of much older sacred dramas is evidenced by the fact that the very word 'mumming' derives from German *mumme* or Danish *mom*, both of which have the meaning 'to keep silent' or, as we might still say today, 'to keep mum'. In the early Middle Ages mummers made silent pilgrimage to a noble lord or overseer to ask for favours or money. Later, as we shall see, this became rowdier, combining the sacredness of the original mumming ceremony with the wilder nature of the May Day sports.

Yet another curious aspect of Maid Marian's part in the history of the Morris is that she is frequently played by a man. A wonderful description of this exists in an anonymous play, *Pasquill and Marforius*, which dates from 1589.

> Martin himself is the Mayd Marian, trimly dressed up in a cast gown, and a kerchief of Dame Lawson's, his face handsomely muffled with a diaper napkin to cover his beard, and a great nosegay of flowers in his hand of the principlerst flowers I could gather. (10)

This ancient androgynous character dates back to the trickster figures that are known worldwide, and presents a different set of characteristics to those generally associated with Marian. That s/he is also connected to the Hobby Horse of the Morris dancers will be demonstrated in Chapter 6.

All of this points to a much older figure than the Maid Marian of the fifteenth to seventeenth centuries. Thus in a 1506 record of the costume bought for the person playing the part of Marian, she is simply referred to as 'the Lady', while in several records of the Morris or Robin Hood dances, the curious term 'mowren' appears applied to the character of Marian. David Wiles suggests that 'it is tempting to see this ... as a prototype of the Elizabethan Marian'. He quotes a sixteenth-century account that describes Queen Elizabeth watching a rustic dance that included 'a lively morisdans, according to the ancient manner: six dauncerz, mawd-marion, and the fool'. Wiles derives the word 'mowren' from 'moor' – a Saracen – as both 'Morris' and 'morisco' (a type of Morris dancer) have been suggested to originate; but there is still another possibility.

Given the variable nature of spelling at the time, it is possible indeed that mowren is a corruption of Marian or indeed of Maid Marian, but it is possible also that we have a veiled, half-forgotten reference to a 'mow-wren' – someone who 'showed' the wren – or who expressively enacted the killing of the wren.

This can only be speculative, but it is worth considering in the light of the traditions surrounding the ceremonial killing of the wren, 'the king of all birds'. This strange and rather barbaric ceremony was still being enacted all over Ireland until recent times, when 'the Wren Boys' travelled about the countryside showing the corpse of the dead bird tied to a bush. It had been previously hunted to death along the hedgerows on St Stephen's Day (26 December) by bands of excited villagers. Somehow the bird, which was considered unlucky, had come to represent the killing of the King, as a surrogate for the older sacrifice of the King of the Wood himself – i.e. Robin Hood (see also Chapter 6). If Marian's ancient role in the drama of the King's death was as a mourner, someone who displayed the body of her dead consort, then this would not be out of place. The theatrical term 'to mope and mow' was applied to the Fool (female or man/woman) who danced rather than spoke.

Wiles also suggests that if the Moorish derivation of the Morris or morisco is correct, then the male dancers accompanying the figure of the Sultan in various Morris plays might well have given rise to a man/woman figure called the 'May Moren' in his/her 'morenys' coat. This whirling, dancing personage could well have become associated with the May Queen Marian of earlier times. (99) However, as we shall see, there is at least one other suggestion, to be discussed later in the next chapter, which indicates an older and more surprising origin.

Tollett, in his depiction of the Morris dancers on the window he designed for Bettley Hall, Cheshire in the seventeenth century, describes 'the celebrated Maid Marian, who, as Queen of May, has a golden crown on her head, and in her left hand a red pink, as emblem of Summer. Her vesture is fashionable in the highest degree ... Her coif is purple, her surcote blue, her cuffs white, the skirts of her robe yellow, the sleeves of a carnation colour, and her stomacher red, with a yellow lace in cross bars ... '(10)

This in turn sounds like an attempt to create a woman dressed in all the colours of Spring, not unlike the figure of the Flower Bride described above.

There were apparently seven original members of the mummers' team, judging from the number of costumes purchased for them in villages up and down the land. One may speculate that they represented the key figures of the Robin Hood story:

1. Robin Hood
2. Maid Marian
3. Little John
4. Friar Tuck
5. Will Scarlet
6. Much the Miller's Son
7. The Sheriff of Nottingham

It is not hard to picture the scene. 'Robin Hood', mounted on a horse and clad in green, leads a motley crew, some dressed as particular characters from the stories – Maid Marian, Friar Tuck, Little John being as ever the most popular – the rest colourfully clad in green and yellow or general motley. This merry band travelled from village to village within each individual parish, collecting money – sometimes with cheerful menaces! – and receiving ale, wine and food for their pains. There was undoubtedly much drunkenness, and enough heads were broken to spell an inevitable ending to these cheerful revels in a few years. This was really the last flowering of the ritual element in the Robin Hood story. The true nature of the games was beginning to be forgotten, the only surviving links with the past being details like the green and yellow liveries of the people playing the parts, and the presents of money!

It was a far cry from the original Robin Hood, maybe, but something of the spirit of an earlier time still prevailed, for the importance of the plays was also bound up with the fact that they were devised and celebrated by the people themselves. Robin had always been a people's hero (hence the curious film of his adventures made in Russia a few years ago) and here as elsewhere his name was synonymous with freedom of expression and a wildness that was unbridled and unfettered by daily cares or circumstances.

Robert and Matilda

Once Robin and Marian had been brought together in the Morris dances and plays, the subsequent development of their story continued apace. In the distant echoes of the marriage of the Green Man and his lady, later balladeers saw a romantic tale from which they could wring many sorrowful and moving variations.

One such story, of later and somewhat doubtful provenance, recalls the meeting and marriage of 'Robert' and 'Matilda'. These are simply the Normanised names of Robin and Marian, but the story preserves something of the freshness and innocence of the earliest ballads, and of the love between these two.

> A bonny fine maid of worth degree,
> Matilda called by name,
> Did live in the North, of excellent worth,
> For she was a gallant dame.

> For favour of face, and beauty most rare,
> Queen Helen she did excel:
> Few could surpass this country lass
> That did in the county dwell.

> As Robert was ranging in the Earl's wood
> He espied this pretty maid,
> Her gait it was graceful, her body was straight,
> And her countenance free from pride.

Her eyebrows were black, and so was her hair,
And her skin was a smooth as glass.
Her visage spake wisdom and modesty too.
Said Robin, Oh! what a fine lass.

Her gown was of cloth as green as the grass,
And her buskin did reach to the knee;
The cloth was homespun, but for colour and make
It might have befitted a queen.

But when she chanced him to see,
She turned away her head;
Oh! fear me not thou pretty maid,
And do not fly from me.

Then to her he doffed his cap,
And to her bended low.
Said Robin, Fair Lady, oh whither away?
And she made him answer, To kill a fine buck.

Said Robin, Lady Fair, wander with me
A little to yonder green bower,
Then set down to rest you, and you shall be sure
Of a brace or a leash in an hour.

And as they were going to the green bower,
Two hundred good bucks they espied;
She chose out the fattest that was in the herd,
And she shot him through side and side.

By the faith of my body, said bold Robin Hood
I never saw woman like thee;
And coms't thou from east or from west,
Thou need'st not beg ven'son from me.

Where dost thou dwell my pretty maid?
I prithee tell to me:
And wither goest thou pretty maid?
May I be thy true love?

Said she, Oh! tell me your name, gentle sir?
And he said, t'is bold Robin Hood. My lady,
Wil't thou answer me a question?
Said Matilda, Any that you may ask.

Said Robin, A question that every true man
Asks of a woman once in her life.
And how sweet it would be,
If thou would'st be my wife.

This ring my mother gave to me,
It was her own betrothal ring;
She prayed me when with all my heart
I loved a maid, to pass it down her finger.

Will you have it? Will you wear it?
She blusht at the thought, yet after a pause,
Said, Yes, sir, and with my whole heart,
Thy true love will I be ...

Then let us be married as soon as we can;
So to the holy chapel they did them betake,
Sir Roger the Priest bade them join hands,
With a ring he joined them in marriage full fast.

In loving content together they lived
For many long years in the North country.
For the people that live in the North can tell
Of Marian and bold Robin Hood. (94)

A related version of this ballad, included in Ritson's collection, tells how
Robin left Marian and went to the woods. She followed him, dressed as a

man; when they met, not recognising each other, they fought until Robin cried hold and asked if the bold fellow with whom he struggled would join his band. Recognising her lover's voice, Marian revealed herself and they fell into each other's arms.

The Greenwood wedding of Robin and Marian may be celebrated here by 'Sir Roger the Priest', but it still echoes the last dying account of an older marriage, that of the Summer King and his Spring Lady, whose continuing presence in the forest ensured the well-being of the land and its people.

6

MUMMERS, THE MORRIS AND THE MERRY MEN

With a noise and a din,
Comes the Morris-dancer in,
With fine linen shirt, but a buckram skin.
Oh, he treads out such a peale
From his pair of legs of veal,
The quarters are idols to him.

Witt's Recreations, 1640

The Pagan Morris

The phenomenon known as the Morris dance, despite being much written about and commented upon, remains something of a mystery. Involving a team of varying numbers of men (or in more recent times, women), who carry sticks or kerchiefs and dance a broad variety of complex steps to the accompaniment of fiddle or accordion, the Morris is preserved in various forms to the present time, though its origins are still vague. Even the derivation of the name has never been agreed upon. 'Morisco,' says one early authority, 'a Moor; also a dance, so called, wherein there are usually five men, and a boy dressed in a girl's habit, whom they call the Maid Marian, or perhaps Morian, from the Italian Morione, a head-piece, because her head was wont to be gaily trimmed up [sic]. Common people call it a Morris-dance.' (10)

Aside from the nonsensical suggestion about Marian's name, this derivation of Morris, frequently repeated since the eighteenth century, has been recently brought into question. Douglas Kennedy, the late director of the English Folk-Song and Dance Society, in his book *England's Dances* (51), suggests that the confusion arose from the tradition of the Morris teams blacking up their faces, which gave rise to an association with the Moors and possibly even the renaming of an older dance. 'A still simpler explanation,' Kennedy continues, 'is that the word "Moorish" was used in the sense of "Pagan", and that the Morris was a pagan dance.' This seems eminently sensible in the light of the evidence already presented for the age and derivation of the May Day traditions. (However, another suggestion is outlined below.)

The presence of another character – the Hobby Horse or 'Oss – seems to confirm this. The 'Oss undoubtedly derives from pagan times, possibly from the very earliest era of human occupation, and from the first stirrings of the shamanic tradition in these islands. At present you can see the 'Oss at many Morris or mummer performances. It is usually a man dressed in a strange costume that includes a horse-skull mask, a wide hooped skirt and sometimes a hobbyhorse stick with mask or skull attached. The sole purpose of this strange and sometimes sinister character is to play tricks and chase people about – especially young women, whom he covers with his wide skirt. He also makes jokes and gestures that are generally of a sexual nature, so that it is not difficult to recognise both a type of the ancient Trickster, whose like can be found in many parts of the world, and of a potent fertility figure whose presence is wholly in keeping with the mythology of Robin Hood.

Francis Douce, a nineteenth-century investigator of the origins of the Morris, recalls that 'it has been supposed that the Morris-dance was first brought into England in the time of Edward the Third, when John of Gaunt returned from Spain ... but it is much more probable that we had it from our Gallic neighbours, or even from the Flemings. Few, if any, vestiges of it can be traced beyond the time of Henry the Seventh, about which time, and particularly that of Henry the Eighth, the churchwarden's accounts in several parishes affords materials that throw much light on the subject ... ' (*A Dissertation on the Ancient English Morris Dance*, 1807) (10)

The accounts referred to concern themselves with money allocated to various players for their costumes, which include those for Robin Hood, Maid Marian, and Friar Tuck – all consistent participants in the Morris.

As to the suggestion that the Morris originated in Europe, this is somewhat supported by the description of a dance that is still current in Romania. Here the dancers are called 'Calusari', a name that is often translated as 'Faeries' (though it means literally 'Little Horses', a term not unconnected, perhaps, with the 'Oss). Their remarkable dance, which is clearly shamanic in content, consists of a kind of contest between the 'Faeries' themselves and 'the Animal-Men'. The former are beautifully dressed in ribbons and bells, which glitter in the sun; the latter are roughly clad in animal skins and carry a short (phallic?) maypole, garlanded with wild garlic. From the early morning the whole team goes through a kind of initiation rite, involving each and every man being beaten with staves. A ring is then formed by the 'Faeries' in which a symbolic wedding ceremony takes place, occasionally interrupted by the 'Animal-Men', who attempt to thrust their way into the house. Finally women whose children are sick bring them out and the 'Faeries' dance around them and over them. The whole day ends up in a general dance in which the whole village joins – those girls who manage to touch one of the dancers being assured of fertility and a happy marriage. (51)

This is clearly a very ancient ceremony, and there are sufficient similarities with the Morris to suggest a connection. The dance in which the symbolic wedding is performed, interrupted by the 'Animal Men', points to a shamanic tradition in which the shaman would have performed a healing dance representing the invasion of spirits into his charmed circle. These would then be driven out and the sick person – adult or child – be healed.

One of the oldest and best-established celebrations involving Morris dancers takes place at Helstone in Cornwall on 8 May every year. It has been celebrated in much the same way for several hundred years (the exact date of its beginning is uncertain). Called the Furry-Day (or more recently the Floral Day) – a name which has given rise to considerable speculation as to its meaning and derivation – it preserves one of the most powerful traditions of any relating to Robin Hood.

The following description comes from *The Gentleman's Magazine* for June 1790.

In the morning, very early, some troublesome rogues go round the streets with drums, or other noisy instruments, disturbing their sober neighbours, and singing parts of a song [in which there is mention] of going to the green wood to bring home 'the Summer and the May-O'. And, accordingly, hawthorn flowering branches are worn in the hats. The commonality make it a general holiday; and if they find any person at work, make him ride on a pole, carried on men's shoulders, to the river, over which he is to leap in a wide place, if he can; if he cannot he must leap in, for leap he must, or pay money ... About the middle of the day they collect together, to dance hand-in-hand round the streets, to the sound of a fiddle, playing a particular tune, which they continue to do until it is dark. This they call a 'faddy'. In the afternoon [they] go to some farmhouse in the neighbourhood to drink tea, sillabub, etc, and return in a morris dance to the town, where they form a faddy, and dance through the street till it is dark, claiming a right of going into anyone's house, in at one door, and out at the other. (10)

This sounds, on the face of it, much like the May Day Games we discussed in Chapter 4. But there are some interesting variations. What, for instance, are we to make of the enforced leaping over a pole laid across the river? This sounds very much like the classic meeting place and contest between both Robin and Little John, or Robin and Friar Tuck (see below). When we come to the song referred to in this account, we find something even more interesting. It is said to be of considerable antiquity – though this again is uncertain. Its words are significant:

> Robin Hood and Little John.
> They both are gone to the fair,
> And we'll go to the merry green wood,
> To see what they do there.
> For we were up as soon as any day
> For to fetch the Summer home,
> The Summer and the May – O,
> For the Summer now is come!
> Where are those Spaniards
> That make so great a boast?
> They shall eat the grey goose feather,

And we will eat the roast.
As for the brave St. George,
St George he was a knight;
Of all the knights of Christendom
St Georgie is the right.
God bless aunt Mary Moses,
And all her powers and might,
And send us peace in merry England,
Both day and night! (10)

The first part of this song is clear enough. Robin and John have gone to the Greenwood to fetch home the Summer, i.e. they have gone to bring home the bride of the May – Maid Marian herself. The second half refers to the Spanish Armada of 1588, and helps us to date the song in this form to the time of Elizabeth I. (Interestingly, the reference to eating 'the grey goose feather' suggests that bowmen are involved.) St George of course features largely in the Morris dances and mumming plays. Aunt Mary Moses is less clearly defined – though it is interesting in the light of Robin and Marian's connection with the Virgin Mary (see below) that she bears this name.

A later version of the song, still sung in this form today, has the refrain:

Hal an Tow, Jolly rumbelow
We were up, long before the day – O
To welcome in the Summer,
To welcome in the day – O

Various suggestions have been put forward as to the meaning of 'Hal an Tow', but the most likely one is that it is simply a corruption of 'heel and toe' and refers to the dance step.

As for the name of the ceremony, 'Furry Dance' has been said to derive from 'Flora's Dance', in which case it possibly dates from Roman times, when celebrations in honour of the Goddess Flora, the deity of Spring or Summer, may have taken place in Britain. However, a more obvious derivation suggests itself – that the dancers of Helstone are really dancing a 'Faery Dance' (like the Faeries of Rumania), following literally in the footsteps of the otherworldly dancers whose feet left so many well-trodden rings throughout the countryside, and who may still be doing so – in a more elaborate fashion – through the so-called 'Crop Circle' rings which have been appearing all over the country in the last few years.

Either way the connection with Robin is distinct enough to suggest a further link between the May Day celebrations, the Morris and the mummers, who seem to have done so much to preserve the more ancient traditions of the Hooded Man.

Certainly Robin himself, along with Little John, Friar Tuck and Maid Marian, were among the leading characters in the Morris plays. If, as we are to suppose with those quoted here, that the Morris is of ancient provenance, then it must follow either that the characters are themselves ancient or that they are adopted from such archetypal beings. An examination of some of the leading characters in the Robin Hood mythos shows this to be true.

Bold Outlaws All

No complete list of the Merry Men exists, and despite Margaret Murray's statement that Robin was always accompanied by thirteen companions (thus tying them to the number of people generally found in a witchcraft coven) the number in fact varies from seven to 150, never being the same twice. By putting together all the references from the various ballads we arrive at the following:

Maid Marian
Little John
Friar Tuck
Will Scarlet
Alan-a-Dale
Much the Miller's Son
Gilbert of the White Hand
George-a-Green
William of Goldsborough
Right-Hitting Brand
Reynold

Some of these are almost unknown, but it will be noticed at once that these number eleven and not twelve. Even if there were twelve – thus making, with Robin, the mystical thirteen – nowhere in any of the ballad sources is there a reference to Robin's band being of this number. Many of the outlaws named above do not appear in the same story, so that in fact, apart from Marian, Tuck, Little John and Will Scarlet, they often appear only in one ballad. The notion that, together with Robin, they were a band of thirteen, in keeping with other heroic groups and with the supposed witch's coven, is therefore unlikely.

This being said, however, an examination of the various characters of the outlaws does suggest some other, more intriguing, parallels. If we begin by looking at what we know of the more familiar members of the merry band, we shall see some interesting details begin to emerge.

John the Little

The first mention of Little John is in Fordun's *Chronicle* of 1341, where 'Robertus Hode and Littill Johanne' are described as wild outlaws living in England. In the *Gest* John is the first named of Robin's band:

> And Robin Hood in Barnsdale stood,
> And leaned him to a tree,
> And by him stood Little John,
> A good yeoman was he.

John is always the first among Robin's followers; he is brave, strong and eminently resourceful, while his skills with the bow are almost as legendary as Robin's. Joseph Ritson, quoting an earlier authority, says:

> Tradition informs us that in one of Robin Hood's peregrinations, he, attended by his trusty mate Little John, went to dine [at Whitby Abbey] with the Abbot Richard, who, having herd them often famed for their great dexterity in shooting with the long bow, begged them after dinner to show him a specimen thereof; when, to oblige the Abbot, they went up to the top of the abbey, when each of them shot an arrow, which fell not far from Whitby-laths, but on the contrary side of the lane; and in memorial therefore a pillar was set up by the Abbot in the place where each of the arrows was found ... that field where the pillar for Robin Hood's arrow stands being still called Robin Hood's field, and the other ... still preserving

the name of John's field. Their distance from Whitby Abbey is more than a measured mile ... (*The History of Whitby*, 1779)

However, the main detail, which is always stressed, is Little John's size, which may or may not have given rise to his name. Some authorities would have it that he was called John Litel, and that the reversal of the name was a pun made by Robin himself after the famous meeting on the bridge described in the seventeenth-century ballad 'Robin Hood and Little John'. In the same work he is described thus:

> Tho' he was call'd Little, his limbs they were large,
> And his stature was seven foot high;
> When ever he came, they quak'd at his name,
> For soon he would make them to fly. (75)

Even sober commentators like Jim Lees have admitted that the legends of Little John suggest he was once a giant, and this would make him a good companion to Much the Miller's Son (see below) who may also have been of more than normal size. It has also been pointed out that the name may indeed be a joke, and that John is no larger than any of the band. That he could even be a small man, as his name would suggest, is hardly ever considered. Lees, in his book *The Quest for Robin Hood* (56), quotes a letter from a lady living in the neighbourhood of Hathersage who mentions an old family belief that John's name was really 'John of the Little Wood', an interesting possibility which strengthens the belief that Little John was once a forest spirit, who naturally became one of the Merry Men.

It is also significant that the famous first encounter between Robin and John takes place at the ford over a river. In almost every instance where this occurs in mythology or folklore, the guardian of the river is a spirit or otherworldly character. The same story is told of Friar Tuck (see below) and in each case the outcome is the same: after their battle, both men join Robin's band. According to very ancient tradition, when one champion defeats another he takes the place of the defeated – in this instance, when Robin is defeated, the winners become 'Merry Men'.

Nor should we forget the *Little Gest* in which the Sheriff, having been captured by the outlaws, is made to put on their green garb and spends the night as one of their company. In the morning he is constrained to take the oath of friendship that all must make on joining the Merry Men – so he in fact becomes one of them. As he departs in anger and chagrin he is said, significantly, to be 'full of green wood'!

There is a persistent rumour that associates Little John with Ireland. The Tudor writer Richard Stanihurst (1547–1618) relates how there is a hillock near Ostmantown Green (on the outskirts of Dublin) named 'Little John's Shot', the naming of which came about after the death of Robin Hood, when Little John fled to Ireland. On his arrival in Dublin news of the famous outlaw spread quickly and he was asked to demonstrate his skill with the bow. This he did, standing on the middle of the bridge over the Liffy and shooting a single arrow to the hillock which ever after bore his name. The story is much like that of the contest between Robin and the man mentioned above – but it is interesting that even here John stands on a bridge over a river to make his shot!

Little John has been frequently described as coming from the village of Hathersage in Derbyshire, while J. W. Walker in his *True History of Robin Hood* (1944) makes the identification even more specific. John was, he maintains, 'the second son of George Little, a farm labourer of Mansfield, and was brought up as a nail maker by trade which he followed for some time, until his wonderful strength determined him to try his fortune elsewhere'. This is in keeping with another persistent belief that John's real name was Naylor, which is indeed still a family name in modern-day Hathersage. However, it seems more likely that John is a supernatural companion rather than a real man, and no evidence has so far been produced to identify him finally, any more than has been found for Robin himself.

Margaret Murray suggested his identification with the Basque oak-spirit Janicot, while according to Peter Vansittart in *Worlds and Underworlds* (91) 'Little John is said to have lead the Wild Hunt'. This leads the same author to describe John as 'a Wood God' in another book, a factor that would certainly make him an ideal companion for Robin.

Stories abound of his giant bones being discovered at places as far afield as Morayshire in Scotland (John is believed to have died in Scotland according to more than one account), at Thorpe Salvin near Worksop and at Wincle in Cheshire. However, the most persistent belief is that he is buried at Hathersage, where his grave is still to be seen. It measures thirteen feet, and bones of unusual size were discovered there in 1784. Dire fate came to those who ordered the grave opened and those who did the digging. The trouble ceased when the bones were returned to their resting place. The present grave markers are set thirteen feet and four inches apart, and were erected by the Ancient Order of Foresters in 1929.

John remained Robin's faithful friend and supporter to the end. It is he who buries his leader, who hides the body in the depths of Sherwood. A fragmentary song sums up their relationship:

> Robin Hood, Robin Hood,
> Is in the mickle wood;
> Little John, Little John,
> He to the town has gone.

> Robin Hood, Robin Hood,
> Is telling his beads,
> All in the Greenwood,
> Among the green weeds.

> Little John, Little, John,
> If he comes no more,
> Robin Hood, Robin Hood,
> He will fret full sore. (36)

The Merry Friar

The first recorded mention of Friar Tuck is in the *Calendar of Rolls* for 1417, where a certain cleric from Lindfield in Sussex is mentioned as having assumed the name on becoming an outlaw. He does not appear at all in the earlier ballads, the first account of his appearance being in a 1475 fragment of 'Robin Hood and Guy of Guisborne' found in Bishop Percey's Folio. He next appears, in the guise with which he is most familiar, in 'Robin Hood and the Curtall Friar', a ballad that dates from around 1610. In this we have the familiar episode of Robin's meeting with Tuck.

According to the ballad, one day, as the outlaws are playing games of skill in the forest, Will Scathlock remarks that there is a certain 'curtall friar' at nearby Fountains Abbey who is so skilled with a sword and bow that he could beat any of the Merry Men. Robin at once swears that he will not eat until he has met the remarkable friar, and putting on his helmet of steel and taking his bow in his hand he makes his way to Fountains Dale, where he sees the friar walking by the side of a river. Robin demands that the friar carry him across the water, which he does, and then in turn Robin carries him across to the other side. A second time Robin insists that he be carried over, and this time, midway across the water, the friar throws him in. A great fight ensues, in which neither can gain the upper hand. Finally Robin blows his hunting horn and at once a hundred outlaws with bows bent appear. Surrounded, the remarkable friar whistles three times and a pack of dogs appears. As the outlaws loose their bows, the dogs catch the arrows in their mouths. At last Little John intervenes, and with great skill shoots ten of the dogs, at which point the friar begs mercy and agrees to pay a ransom every Sunday throughout the year. The ballad ends:

> This curtal friar had kept Fountains Dale,
> Seven long years and more,
> There was neither knight, lord, nor earl,
> Could make him yield before. (56)

This is a curious story. The friar owns a pack of hounds, which he has trained to catch arrows in their mouths! He wears a steel cap and carries a sword – strange objects for a man of the cloth to own. Then, there are inconsistencies. If he is really from Fountains Abbey then he is a monk rather than a friar and would have belonged to the Cistercian order. If he came from Fountain Dale, which is in Nottinghamshire at a place then called Broadmarsh and only later Fountaindale, then he would have been a Franciscan friar. Unlike monks, who stayed in one place for most of their lives, friars were wandering preachers (also called mendicants) who travelled through the country and generally had no fixed or permanent abode. They first began preaching in England in 1221 – twenty years before the supposed death of Robin Hood. There were three such orders: Franciscans, who wore grey robes; Carmelites, who wore white; and Dominicans, who wore black. Tuck is usually portrayed as wearing russet or brown robes, so that he may belong to none of these. Indeed he displays more of the characteristics of a hermit, one of those strange characters who crop up so often in the medieval Grail romances, offering advice and wisdom to the wandering Knights of the Round Table.

The other element which is present in the ballad, as indeed it is in almost every subsequent story in which the good friar features, is his association with (even guardianship of) water, in this case the river at Fountains Dale. Guardians of riverbanks have ever been associated with otherworldly characters, and there are numerous folktales in which the Devil is made to give rides across the water in just the same way as Tuck does with Robin. In local tradition Tuck's cell stood at Copmanhurst in the woods of Fountain Dale on the banks of the little River Rain in Yorkshire. Is it possible that, behind the fat and smiling visage of the curtal friar, we may catch a glimpse of an earlier, pagan character – perhaps a being as tricky as Robin Goodfellow, who also, incidentally, plays the water-crossing trick on unwary humans? Evidence appears to support such a seemingly unlikely premise. Nor should we forget the curious echo of the Green Knight from the Gawain poem, who, like Tuck, guarded a valley against all comers.

A famous stained-glass window from Betley Old Hall in Staffordshire, painted around 1620, depicts a group of people dancing, including a merry monk. This has traditionally been identified as Tuck. He has a full clerical tonsure, a chaplet of white and red beads in his right hand; his corded girdle and red-brown habit suggest he is a Franciscan, or one of the Grey Friars. His stockings are red, and he has a red girdle ornamented with a golden twist, and a golden tassel. At his girdle hangs a wallet for provisions – the only revenue that mendicant friars were permitted in the Middle Ages – for which reason they were also referred to as Walletters, or Budget-bearers. The meaning of the term 'curtall' is still debated; according to some authorities the word refers to the cord with which the friars bound their habits while working, or from their curtal (or cur) hunting dogs – an interesting suggestion in the light of the friar's pack of highly trained dogs.

John Brand suggested that 'from the occurrence of the name on other occasions, there is good reason for supposing that [the name Tuck] was a sort of generic appellation for any friar, and that it originated from the dress of the order, which was tucked or folded at the waist by means of a cord or girdle. Thus Chaucer in his Prologue to the *Canterbury Tales*, says of the Reve: "Tucked he was, as is a friar about...", and he describes one of the friars in the "Sumener's Tale": "with scrip and tipped staff, tucked he."'

Another suggested origin for Tuck is Friar Rush – known as Bruder Rausch in Germany. The origin of this character, like so many folk heroes, is uncertain. The main source for his story is a sixteenth-century chapbook, which appears to have been adapted from an earlier Danish story. The text presented is of a curious nature, a kind of amalgam of satire and fairytale with a strong tinge of morality play and a dash of broad humour. In the beginning the Friar seems more like a kind of minor devil, sent from hell on a mission to plague gluttonous and lascivious friars. But as the story progresses his character changes to become more like that of a mischievous spirit. He has been compared – rightly, I think – to Robin Goodfellow, and the latter part of the story is much like that of the 'Merry Pranks' (see Chapter 2). This makes him a more than worthy companion of Robin Hood, and it is fascinating to speculate that we may have here a distant memory of a story in which the two impish sprites, Robin and Rush, played tricks on the clumsy, ignorant human-folk. As for whether this amounts to an influence on the character of Friar Tuck, readers must make up their own minds. Certainly, however, there is an impish quality about the developing character of Tuck which is not out of keeping with a more otherworldly origin, while his established guardianship of the riverbank adds to the idea that he may once have been a very different figure than the rotund friar of Sherwood.

In one of the Robin Hood plays, written around 1475, Tuck introduces himself thus:

> *Deus hic, deus hic*, god be here –
> Is not this a holy word for a friar?
> God save all this company.
> But am I not a jolly friar,
> For I can shoot both far and near,
> And handle the buckler,
> And this quarter staff also?
> If I meet with a gentleman or yeoman
> I am not afraid to look him upon,
> Nor boldly with him to carp;

If he speak any words to me
He shall have stripes two or three
That shall make his body smart ... (99)

We have already seen the importance of the mummer's plays in the story of Robin Hood. The presence of Tuck in this fragmentary play suggests that this is the most likely method by which he entered the mythos in the first place. The mummers' plays were such an important aspect of the May Day Games that it is more than likely that it is at this junction that he effectively joins the outlaw band. Here he is Marian's constant companion, as the May Queen's chaplain, and it is even possible that he may thus not have originally been associated with Robin at all but rather accompanied Marian into the merry band. There were, however, a number of 'Mock Abbots' in the May Games, and Robin is certainly associated with these – so that we have there another possible thread in Tuck's development.

By the late 1500s he seems to have assumed a somewhat lecherous character, possibly because he is a friar who dances with the May Queen. He also seems to have had an independent dance in the mumming drama, as evidenced by records of his travelling alone from Kingston to Croydon in 1536 accompanied only by a piper. He might have been 'filling in' for another character, of course, but more likely this was a solo performance, emphasising Tuck's importance as an independent figure.

The Man of Scarlet

Much less is known about the outlaw known variously as Will Scarlet, Shacklock, Scadlock, Scarlock, etc. From quite early on in the ballad history he is represented as the first among the Merry Men after Little John, and he appears in many of the ballads as well as in the *Gest*. The Sloane MSS *Life of Robin Hood*, a transcript of which will be found at the end of this book, gives us a little more, telling how Robin met Scarlet one day

as he walked solitary and like a man forlorn, because a maid to whom he was affianced was taken from him by the violence of her friends, and given to another that was old and wealthy, whereon Robin, understanding when the marriage-day should be, came to the church as a beggar, and having his own company not far off, which came in so soon as they heard the sound of his horn, he took the bride by force from him that would have married her, and caused the priest to wed her and Scarlocke together.

The exact same story is told in another ballad, but of Allan-a-Dale the minstrel rather than Scarlet, the most likely reason being that Allan seems to have habitually worn red, so that the two have become confused. He may also be the same 'Will Stutly' mentioned in the ballad of 'The Rescuing of Will Stutly', where we read that on hearing of Will's capture by the Sheriff of Nottingham, Robin vowed to rescue him. The verse following reads:

> He clothed himself in scarlet red,
> His men were all in green;
> A finer show, throughout the world,
> In no place could be seen. (57)

This is intriguing, since it apparently refers to Robin himself. Why should he put on 'scarlet red' before setting out to rescue Will? It may be that we are looking here at a mystery of the blood, which, since Robin himself carries the sacred blood of the land in his veins, may suggest that Will Stutly does also, and that they are therefore related.

Another suggestion is that Scarlet is in fact Robin's 'cousin' Young Gamwell. This is based upon the statement made by the character himself in a broadsheet ballad of 1650, 'Robin Hood Newly Revived' in which he says he is 'his [Robin's] own sister's son' and adds that 'in Maxfield was I bred and born, my name is young Gamwell'. While in a late (*c.* 1846) variation on the ballad 'The Bold Pedlar and Robin Hood', Robin himself says, 'You are my own sister's son, what nearer cousins can we be?' In the same ballad he is given the name Gambol Gold, which seems like a corruption of Gamwell. (23)

Who then is this Gamwell? According to the seventeenth-century ballad 'Robin Hood and the Prince of Aragon', he may have been someone quite different to the usual idea we have of the outlaw. In this, admittedly late, ballad Robin is a champion of Christendom against the Moors (not so impossible if one recalls the rumour that he joined the Crusades). The Prince of Aragon has sworn to take a certain princess as his prize – or else spoil the land – unless three champions can be found to fight against him and two giants whose services he has acquired. Robin Hood, Little John and Will Scarlet accept the challenge, which takes place, interestingly enough, on Midsummer's Day, 24 June, in the presence of the King. Of course Robin and his men are victorious, and slay all three 'infidels', at which point the outlaws, who have been disguised, reveal their identity and ask for the King's pardon. This is granted, but the King then points out that by rights one of the three should marry the princess. They submit themselves to her judgement and she chooses Will Scarlet, who later discovers his father at the court and proves to have noble blood.

This is a far cry from the rough, hot-tempered outlaw of Sherwood. But there is enough evidence to suggest that Scarlet may have been of noble descent, as was Robin himself. Perhaps there was once a more fully fleshed-out story attached to him under the name of Gamwell?

The possibility exists that he is to be identified with the hero of a fourteenth-century poem called 'The Tale of Gamelyn' (48), which tells a familiar story of the son whose father dies while he is in infancy and who spends many years fighting his brother for the possession of lands and inheritance, ending up for a time in the forest, where he joins an outlaw band whose 'King', though unnamed, might well be an early representation of Robin Hood. Finally, after many adventures, Gamelyn, who certainly shares Scarlet's strength and fiery temper, wins back his lands and earns a pardon to live out his years in peace.

Following this line of reasoning it is possible that this character may be the same as 'Gandelyn' in the medieval lyric 'Robin and Gandelyn' published by Ritson in his *Ancient Songs* of 1790, and included by Child in his collection. Despite the statement by Dobson and Taylor (29) that 'by no stretch of the imagination can the Robyn of this lyric be properly identified with the Robin Hood of the other ballads', there is indeed a link which not only suggests that they are one and the same, but adds a further detail to our general argument that Robin is a mythical rather than a historical figure.

The ballad is worth giving in full, in my own free rendition:

> I heard the singing of a clerk
> All at the fair wood's side
> Of good Robyn and Gandelyn –
> No better friends betide.
>
> Robyn lieth in the green wood bounden...

Strong were those two fellows
And Bowmen good and gracious;
Then went into the wood
To get them meat,
If God he would it send them.

Robyn lieth in the green wood bounden...

All day went those two fellows
But meat they found them none
Till it again were evening,
When they would both go home.

Robyn lieth in the green wood bounden...

Then half a hundred fallow deer
Came within their path,
And markings had they none.
By dear God, good Robyn said
Now shall we have a one.

Robyn lieth in the green wood bounden...

Robyn bent his jolly bow
And in it set an arrow;
The fattest deer of all
He meant to cleave in two.

Robyn lieth in the green wood bounden...

The deer was not yet flayed,
Nor half out of its hide
When came an arrow from the West
That felled poor Robyn's pride.

Robyn lieth in the green wood bounden....

Gandelyn looked both East and West
He looked on every side –
Now who has slain my master just,
Now who has done this deed.
Nor shall I leave the good green wood
Till I see his sides to bleed.

Robyn lieth in the green wood bounden...

Gandelyn looked both East and West
And sought him under the sun,
Until he saw a little boy
That was named Wrennock of Donne.

Robyn lieth in the green wood bounden...

A good bow in his hand he held,
An arrow strung therein,
And four and twenty good arrows
Trussed in a bundle too.
Beware, beware, stout Gandelyn
Lest he you too shall kill.

Robyn lieth in the green wood bounden...

Beware, beware stout Gandelyn
Lest he of you get plenty
Ever on for another Gandelyn said,
Ill-fortune to he who flies.

Robyn lieth in the green wood bounden...

Whereat shall our mark be?
Said stout Gandelyn:
At each other's heart,
Answered Wrennock again.

Robyn lieth in the green wood bounden...

Wrennock shot a full good shot
And shot he not too high,
but through the fork of Gandelyn's breeches
it touched neither thigh.

Robyn lieth in the green wood bounden...

Now hast thou shot at me before
All thus to Wrennock said he;
And by the might of Our Lady
Still better shall I be.

Robyn lieth in the green wood bounden...

Gendelyn bent his good long bow
And set therein an arrow –
He shot that Wrennock in the breast
And cleft his heart in two.

Robyn lieth in the green wood bounden...

Now shalt thou never boast
Neither at ale nor wine
that thou hast slain good Robyn
Or his knave Gandelyn.

Robyn lieth in the green wood bounden ...

What are we to make of this? Robert Graves, with typical ingenuity, suggests that it reflects the annual hunting of the wren at Midwinter in revenge for the murder of the robin at Midsummer (see Chapter 5). Certainly the name Wren-nock would seem to bear this out, and if we are right in thinking that Robin is a Year King, then there is certainly some grounds for taking Graves' suggestion seriously. If so, then it would seem that Gandelyn, or Gamwell, or Gambol, Robin's cousin, might well be one whose task it was to dispatch the King – in which case the nickname

'Scarlet' takes on an entirely new meaning. The haunting refrain 'Robyn lieth in the green wood bounden...' certainly suggests a deeper meaning than the surface of this song, suggesting that Robin was somehow held fast with the forest.

The ballad appears to allude to the Midwinter custom of 'the hunting of the Wren', which, as we have seen, was still enacted, complete with wren sacrifice, in Ireland until early this century. The wren in Celtic tradition is 'the King of all birds', having gained its title by a ruse. The eagle claimed to be king of all birds and promised to prove this by flying higher than all others. Unbeknownst to him, the wren had crept onto his back and so flew the higher. The ballad also speaks of the sleight of hand needed to shoot 'through Gandalyn's breeches'. This steady-handed shot is curiously similar to that of the Celtic hero Llew Llaw Gyffes who receives his name 'the Lion with Steady Hand' because of his feat of shooting of a wren between the sinew of the leg and the bone! (32)

The contest is clearly both a seasonal and a ritual one, and though we are partly in the realm of speculation, the true identity of Will Scarlet may be inferred from this.

The Miller's Son

Much (or 'Mitch') the Miller's son is another of the regularly named members of the Merry Men. His name contains something of a pun, which may also point to his archetypal identity. The name Much is derived from Old English *mycel, muchel* or, in modern dialect, muckle, meaning 'great' – so he is really the Great Miller or the Miller's great son, titles more appropriate to a deity than a simple miller.

If Much is really a big man (bigger than 'Little' John) then he may even have been, at one time, a giant. The *Little Gest* describes him as having 'not an inch upon his body/that was not worth that of a whole man' and elsewhere he is said to have carried Little John himself – no small feat if John was really seven feet tall. The gormless figure, whose mighty strength is greater than other men's but who is often presented as less mentally agile than they, appears often in folk tradition. We have only to look at any of the stories featuring Jack the Giant Killer to see this.

In medieval tradition the Miller was an unpopular figure since he was appointed by the feudal lord to mill all grain, charging his own rate of exchange for this service. A miller who champions other folk's rights is as strange a companion for Robin as Matthew the tax collector was to Jesus. However, mythologically speaking, the figure of the Miller is an important one, especially in Celtic and Scandinavian tradition.

The mill is seen as an edifice in which all things are finely ground, for which reason it often appears in otherworldly scenarios as the Mill of Heaven, where the very stars themselves are ground out and in which the divine elements of Creation are refined. (76) Thus in the Celtic story of 'The Voyage of Maelduin' in which the hero visits a number of archetypal islands, we find one in which the voyagers encounter the surly custodian of the mill of Innbir the Senant. Half the corn for the whole of Ireland was ground there – provided by those who begrudged each other or acted ungenerously towards one another. Maelduin and his men saw a long line of such people, burdened down with their sacks, and quickly left the place. (60)

As with all of these figures we are seeing the last echoes of a once established tradition. It may be hard to discern Much the Miller's son as a primeval giant, or a demi-god turning the mill-wheels of the gods, but so often are these ancient racial memories buried in names or roles in the later stories and ballads of the Middle Ages that we would be unwise to dismiss them.

Mary's Men

Having looked in detail at the individual members of the outlaw band, what conclusions can we reach? We have seen that both John and Tuck are guardians of river crossings – an ancient and important role which is much in keeping with ancient traditions. Much, as a Miller, is one of the guardians of the Quern of the Heavens, and Scarlet may have been a nobleman or more anciently a ritual assassin.

If we look at some other famous bands of heroes, both in literature and folklore, we find that it is usual for notable leaders like Arthur or Charlemagne to be accompanied by a host of unusually talented people who each in their own way disguise the presence of older and more primal figures. Thus in the medieval Welsh story 'Culhwch & Olwen' (37) we find a list of Arthur's warriors which includes men who can hear an ant scratching itself several miles distant, or see for miles from the top of a tree, or stretch up to the height of a mountain.

This kind of heroic band is characterised in folklore by the story type called 'Six Go Through the World', which concerns the adventures of a hero or heroine who acquires the help of six extraordinary people, each possessing a particular talent that enables him or her to succeed in the tasks appointed by an adversary. That Robin should be in the company of such remarkable characters – albeit heavily disguised as human adventurers – should not surprise us. It merely goes to prove, even more solidly, the theory expressed throughout this book – that Robin Hood is a mythic, folkloric character, who takes his place among other mythic, folkloric characters, such as the Merry Men are shown to have once been.

Robin himself is said to have had a particular devotion to the Virgin Mary, and herein lies a clue to the nature of the Merry Men themselves, which Robert Graves first noted in his seminal book *The White Goddess*. The Merry Men, he thinks, were really 'Mary's Men', the followers of Mary, a curious turn of affairs brought about by some possibly deliberate confusion between the words 'Mary', 'Marian' and 'Morris'. This last word, according to Graves, was first written 'Maris', thus equating with *Stella Maris*, Star of the Sea, one of the many symbolic names for Mary – the earliest spelling of whose name in England was – Marian! Furthermore, the name is a good deal closer to 'Merry' than the OED would have us suppose. With a poet's subtle understanding of the true meaning of words, Graves proposes that the 'Merry Men', once 'Mary's Men', share this title with the Morris teams – deriving their importance from the fact that they were the followers of the cult of Mary – not necessarily the Virgin, but either the Magdalene or Mary of Egypt, both of whom had a considerable, if unorthodox, following in the Middle Ages.

The fusion of Marian with Mary may seem quite untenable, yet when Thomas the Rhymer encounters the Faery Queen in the Scots Border ballad he cries out:

> All hail thou mighty Queen of heaven
> For thy like on earth I n'er did see.'
> Oh no, oh no, true Thomas, she said,
> That name does not belong to me.
> I'm but the Queen of Fair Elfland … (17)

If we are right to believe that Marian was always the name of the May Queen – and therefore of the Green God's consort (see Chapter 5) – then to suggest that her followers (as well as Robin's) were actually 'Mary's Men' seems less out of the way. Robin's own particular devotion is thus still to 'Mary', which would have been interpreted as the Virgin by medieval authors but which probably refers to an earlier figure – Marian or May, the consort of the Green Man.

ENVOI

IN THE HEART OF
THE FOREST

Come in, my scraps of Lincoln green; come in,
my slips of green wood. You're much wanted here!
...
Come in, my jolly minions of the moon,
My straggling hazel-boughs!
...
Come in, my Dian's foresters, and drown us
With may, with blossoming may.
...
Welcome, welcome, good friends of Huntingdon,
Or Robin Hood, by whatsoever name
You best may love him ...

Alfred Noyes, Robin Hood

The Mythic Pattern

All of the criss-crossing paths we have taken through the entanglement of folklore, myth and primordial tradition which make up the Robin Hood mythos would be scarcely worth the effort if it were not for the continuing power of the stories themselves. These are at very least the expression of a continuing need – the need to encounter the greenness and the wildness that exists at the heart of the world, and which is all around us if we make the effort to see it. In the Robin Hood mythos it is the forest, the Wildwood – that mysterious place where almost anything can happen – and does. It is the same mythic forest in which Shakespeare's lovers wander, the magic wood of Broceliande, where the heroes of the Arthurian myths encounter most of their most daunting trials, and it is the wood in which Dante wakes one day, 'mid way through this life', to find himself at the beginning of a great adventure. It is the home of Puck, of Robin Goodfellow, of the Faery race and of Herne the Hunter. It is full of tests and trials for those who walk there unwarily – and who may have more than their purses stolen by lurking outlaws!

There is a deep and very ancient ritual pattern which can still be glimpsed in the roles assumed by Robin – from Green King in Winter to the Robin or Green Jack in Spring, to the Puck in Summer and Robin Goodfellow in Autumn. It may be expressed in diagrammatic form as pictured opposite:

Marian similarly conforms to four shadowy aspects: Green Lady in Winter, Maid Marian in Spring, the Huntress or Warrior Maiden in Summer and Long Meg or Margery (an ancient folklore name sometimes applied to her) in Autumn.

It is in these mythic patterns, discernible within the stories and legends at every point, that the true meaning and identity of Robin Hood lies. Through the ballads of the thirteenth and fourteenth centuries we have traced distant memories of the Year King, ruling for twelve months, then going willingly to his death to be replaced by another. We have seen how the folklore traditions of Britain preserved such ancient beliefs and recognised them again in the form of Robin, Marian and the Merry Men. We have traced the faint echoes of other primal heroes in the form of the bold outlaw band, and we have seen how in the sixteenth and seventeenth centuries the plays of Robin Hood, the May Day and the mumming dances celebrated in every village and town across the country subsumed the characters of Robin and his band into their hearts, keeping the myth-haunted tales alive for another age.

Despite the efforts of numerous explorers there is really no adequate evidence to associate Robin Hood with a specific historical personage or period before the emergence of the ballad as a literary genre in the thirteenth and fourteenth centuries. We may suppose that oral tales of the Outlaw of Sherwood were circulating before that time (just as, earlier than that, there were traditions relating to the Green Man) and that these became fused with those of Robin-i-the-Hood.

A whole concatenation of events thus came together to create the character of Robin Hood the outlaw and champion of the people. The time was right for the social injustice of landowners toward their tenants to become the setting for the ballads – even if we discount for the moment the natural animosity that existed between Saxon and Norman. The ancient pre-Christian traditions still flourishing in parts of the country made it inevitable that the figure of the Green Man should reappear in a new guise which could be openly discussed and whose stories became popular on the lips of a hundred ballad-makers. The many folk traditions (including those surrounding the May Day Games and the Morris dances) themselves preserved elements that passed through the channel of the Robin Hood myths and emerged with new characteristics acquired from the ballad characters.

The complex relationship between the myths of the Green Man, the ballads of Robin Hood and the folk traditions relating to May Day have been outlined at length in this book. Readers must decide for themselves whether they stand up and whether they have succeeded in calling forth the

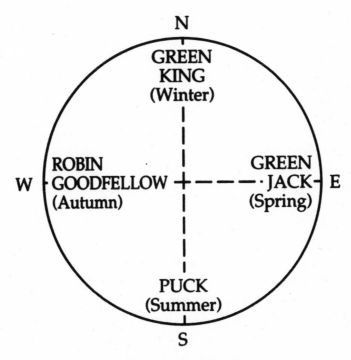

The Circle of the Year.

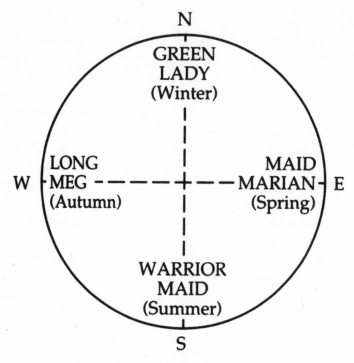

N
GREEN
LADY
(Winter)

W ⊦MEG ─ ─ ─ ─ ─ ┼ ─ ─ MARIAN⊣ E
LONG   MAID
(Autumn)   (Spring)

WARRIOR
MAID
(Summer)
S

The Aspects of Maid Marian

real Robin Hood. I remain convinced that he originated in the character and tradition of the Green Man, and that he only gradually developed into the Outlaw of Sherwood, shedding certain characteristics and gaining others, until he is, on the face of it, a far cry from his origins. Historical outlaws, whether named after him or not, certainly added to the reality of the stories, giving them a more personal and local setting that continued to grow in the telling. The story continued in the May Day Games and Robin Hood plays of the sixteenth and seventeenth centuries, which still bear traces harking back hundreds, and even thousands of years to another time and another culture, where the Green Man was honoured as the most powerful force in the cosmos, the spirit of Nature itself.

That this belief has continued in a number of ways up to and into the present is borne out by the number of popular reworkings of the Robin Hood stories that have appeared over the last few years alone. Thus we have seen the phenomenally successful TV series *Robin of Sherwood*, devised by Richard Carpenter, which took the mythology firmly into the present while glancing over its shoulder at some of the earliest arcs of the mythos. Kevin Costner's portrayal of Robin in the movie *Prince of Thieves* (1991) harks back to Douglas Fairbanks' earlier swashbuckling portrayal, and though the *raison d'être* of the movie is adventure, even here the ending, in which Robin and Marian are married in the shadow of the Greenwood, holds a powerful evocation of the magical, May-time mystery of the old stories. Soon to grace both the small and big screen are no less than seven new films and TV series in production – very clear proof, if any is needed, of the continuing resonance of the Green Lord of Sherwood.

AFTERWORD

THE GREEN WOMAN

My first contact with the legends of Robin Hood was through watching the TV series *Robin of Sherwood* in 1975. When Herne the Hunter appeared I was moved to tears. He represented an ancient guardianship of the land, which I have always perceived as being watched over by spiritual guardians.

The stories of Robin, Marian and the Merry Men have always represented liberation from injustice and oppression. The Normans, who are represented as Robin's chief adversaries, were frequently cruel and arrogant, having the power of life and death over their Saxon serfs. Women in general and Saxon women in particular lost much of their independence under the Norman system of inheritance and marriage. The later Middle Ages were the most misogynistic in European history. It is not surprising that Marian, in her aspect of Flower Bride representing the feminine side of nature, lacks substance in the Robin Hood mythos.

In the media too she is generally represented as a powerless figure, denied access to any feminine spiritual power. In several of the more recent retellings of the legends she seeks sanctuary in the Greenwood from the demands of an arranged marriage, but shows no sign of understanding the deeper mysteries of the natural world. For example, in the *Robin of Sherwood* series, Robin has Herne, to whom he turns in time of trouble; to whom did Marian go for inner support, I began to wonder?

While Green Men were sprouting forth oak leaves over the cathedrals of Europe, the tiny numbers of female foliate heads which have come to light are all associated with legends which repeat this pattern. The three women carved on the tomb of St Frideswide in Christchurch Cathedral, Oxford, depict the saint and her two companions, who were forced to flee to a woodland sanctuary (believed to be in the area of nearby Binsey) to escape the amorous advances of a seventh-century Saxon king. It is interesting that these heads are surrounded by wildflower foliage, rather than the oak-ringed head, presumably representing the king, which once also adorned the tomb, though it has since been removed. For me, this tomb will always be a representation in stone of an attempted rape of the Flower Bride.

Earlier in this book John has shown how 'Marian' is a product of a dualistic mythology of loss and restoration through the battle of the 'dark' forces of Winter and the 'light' forces of Summer for the body and soul of the Flower Maid. What a dangerous belief on which to build! It is never mentioned in these stories that, for those who are ravaged, the Wasteland never fully heals. If Marian represents the female aspect of the land, and society continues to see the land as something over which wars are fought, or which is possessed, owned, lost and recaptured, her fate will naturally be depicted in that way. The core of this mythology is rotten.

The potent pre-historic Mistress of the Animals – of which Marian is but a later aspect – is thus diminished to a nubile virgin huntress, who does not have the strength to protect herself from becoming the prey. This ever-maidenly image is largely a product of classical Greek thinking. When 'civilization' of this kind means abandoning a more primitive, woodland-based hunting-and-gathering existence, the primal, fertile chaos of the forests becomes something to conquer and control.

The interplay between civilization and wildness is depicted in a number of beautiful medieval tapestries depicting wildmen and women. These mostly originated in the area now occupied by Germany and Switzerland – once heavily forested. Wildwomen had a happier life than the Flower Brides. They rode deer, stroked unicorns, mated with wildmen and bore wild children – all in a landscape of innocence and primal beauty.

An illustration exists which shows a rare Wildwood version of the 'Adoration of the Magi' in which a queenly wildwoman sits amid a landscape of trees and flowers, nursing her two wild children. To one side a wildman brings her the lion of Summer; from the other comes one bearing the stag of Winter. A third figure brings a horn of plenty. The picture seems to represent a reconciliation of wildness with the continuing cycles of nature.

The link between the three 'Magi' and the Green Woman is possibly St Helen, Helena or Elen, who is said to have discovered the heads of the original three kings in Jerusalem. In Yorkshire, where many of the Robin Hood legends originate, there are many place-names associated with Helen. This is in part due to the story that the semi-legendary St Helen was said to have lived in York with her Roman husband Constantine Chlorus in the fourth century AD. Her 'life' is full of pagan hunting imagery. Near York, once part of the forest mentioned in the legends, are St Helen's Ford and St Helen's Well, Tadcaster; St Helen's Well, Heston (which has three submerged Celtic heads); St Helen's Church, Healaugh, and St Helen's Church, Bilton, both of which proliferate with primitive carvings of Green Men and Sheila-na-Gigs. These latter seem to be the female companions of Green Men, and the two are often found together. They are possibly a medieval manifestation of the goddess of life and death, a reflection of the feminine power of the land itself.

St Helen seems to have a special affinity with Sheila-na-Gigs. The oldest carving of this kind in England is in St Helens, Austerfield, in Yorkshire; another is in Hellifield, a mile from St Helen's Well, Eshton; and the only one with an inscription, 'Elui', was found a few miles from Colchester, long believed to be St Helen's 'home town'.

St Helen was also very important to the Knights Templar. This order was founded in 1119 with the primary intention of guarding all pilgrims to the Holy Land. This is because of an interesting piece of symbology. St Helen *was* said to have discovered the 'True Cross,' or 'Tree of Life',

  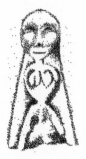

the actual cross on which Christ died, in Jerusalem. The head of Adam, the primal Christian ancestor, and those of the three kings, were also said to have been discovered at the same spot. Helena's son Constantine built the first Christian church, the Holy Sepulchre, on this site. It was considered to be the *omphalos*, the centre of the Christian world, and all Templar churches were based on its circular shape. York was the only place, apart from London, to have a Templar Grand Master, because it originally held the treasury of the Order. Thus, Robin and his men are often seen as intercepting gold on its way to York along the Great North Road.

I have spent the past ten years trying to answer the question that came to mind as I first watched *Robin of Sherwood* – who is the female equivalent of Herne the Hunter? The answer for me has to be the Green Woman, the antlered goddess or huntress, the Mistress of the Animals.

There is nothing complicated about contacting the Green Woman. In essence she is the primal life force that flows through healthy trees, woods and gardens. She is present in all weathers, and in all seasons. Her regeneration is the key to the healing of the earth.

Chesca Potter, 1993

THE SONG OF THE GREEN

The Green Man flares in my head
like a song of seasons
and Robin is come to the Green again
singing:
> O, I am in
> the Greenwood
> alone, so alone.

The May King dances in my head
like a bough in blossom
and a trumpet blows in the woodland
singing:
> O. I am in
> the Wildwood
> deep, so deep.

The Faery-King dances on the green
like a Summer blessing
and I am transformed
in green and gold
singing:
> O, I dance
> In Faeryland
> forever and ever.

John Matthews
Oxford, 1992–2016

APPENDIX 1

GAZETTEER OF PLACES ASSOCIATED WITH ROBIN HOOD AND HIS MERRY MEN

Just as with the other great national hero, King Arthur, sites bearing the name of Robin Hood (and indeed of Marian and the Merry Men) litter the countryside. Though most of them are clearly fictitious, they illustrate the importance and popularity of the outlaws among the common people of the country. This is by no means a complete list, as such would extend far beyond the range of this book, but I have included the most famous and recognisable places to encourage modern seekers to follow the path of the Green King. The numerous 'Wells' and 'Butts' baring Robin's name are largely excluded, but again I have retained all of those that are of more than passing interest. A butt was a site where archery took place. Even the briefest glance at these sites make it clear that the northern Midlands, especially Yorkshire and Nottinghamshire, are key places on the map of Robin Hood's Britain.

Berkshire
ROBIN HOOD'S ARBOR/BOWER: A prehistoric earthwork near Maidenhead Thicket, described as 'Robin Hood's Bower' in the late seventeenth century. A local historian named Thomas Hearne suggested that Robin once frequented the Chiltern Hills.

Cumberland
ROBIN HOODS BUTTES: A field near Eskdale Wood, Farlam, two miles south-east of Brampton. The name is recorded as early as 1598.

ROBIN HOOD'S CHAIR: A natural outcrop of rock near Ennerdale Water, the westernmost lake in the Lake District National Park. Like many other heroes Robin is frequently named in natural features of the land.

Derbyshire

HATHERSAGE: Supposed birthplace of Little John. In the parish churchyard lies the grave traditionally associated with the great outlaw. Measuring nearly 14 feet, with a Victorian headstone, it is said to have been opened in 1798 and a thighbone thirty-two inches in length was discovered. What happened to it, or indeed the rest of the body, remains unknown. A cottage which once stood nearby is supposed to be where John died, but this can be traced back no further than 1652. Two and a half miles south-east lies LITTLE JOHN'S WELL, while a second well, associated with Robin, is just half a mile further at Longshaw Lodge.

ROBIN HOOD: An actual hamlet named after the outlaw, some six miles west of Chesterfield. It may have taken its name from a Robin Hood Inn, which is marked on the 1840 Ordnance Survey Map of the area but no longer exists.

ROBIN HOOD'S CAVE: Just a mile and a half to the north of Hathersage, this cave is hidden among the crags of Stanage Edge.

ROBIN HOOD'S CHAIR: F. J. Child, in his collection of the Robin Hood ballads, mentions that 'a rude natural rock in Hope Dale is his chair'.

ROBIN HOOD'S CROFT: Again only a few miles north-west of Hathersage lies an old sheep shelter and field in the shadow of Lead Hill. Local tradition cites it as being the site of Robin's home.

ROBIN HOOD CROSS: Three miles west of Hathersage, this wayside cross stands on the moorland a mile east of Bradwell, in the parish of Hazlebadge. The base of the cross still survives and is named as 'Robin Crosse' in 1319, and 'The Robin Crosse' in 1640. The age of the cross makes it one of the older sites named after the outlaw.

ROBIN HOOD'S MOSS: Eleven miles north-west of Sheffield, this is a stretch of bleak moorland overlooking the Derwent Dams. Its association with Robin Hood is lost in the mists of local legend.

ROBIN HOOD'S PICKING RODS: Two stone pillars resting in a stone socket which stand on Ludworth Moor, about two and a half miles south-west of Glossop. These curiously named markers are first listed under this name in the Ordnance Survey Map for 1842. There is no known legend associating them with the Outlaw.

ROBIN HOOD'S STOOP: A boundary stone on Offerton Moor, a mile and a half to the south-west of Hathersage. Local tradition says this marks the site of another famous long shot – into Hathersage churchyard, more than 2,000 yards away.

ROBIN HOOD'S STRIDE: Measured, it is said, by two stones amid a clutch of fractured rocks on Hartle Moor, some three miles south of Bakewell, these suggest that Robin must, at one time, have been considered almost a giant.

Lancashire

ROBIN HOOD: Another hamlet named after the outlaw, lying at a crossroads one mile south of Wrightington and five miles north-west of Wigan. The ascription seems to go no further than the eighteenth century.

ROBIN HOOD'S BED: Like many heroes Robin gets places named after him where he is said to have stayed or slept. Here, five miles north-east of Rochdale, the prominent ridge of Blackstone Edge in the Pennines has acquired such a name – though when is unknown.

ROBIN HOOD'S HOUSE: A ruined farm lying at the edge of Widdop Moor, this seems only to date from the nineteenth century.

Leicestershire

LITTLE JOHN HILL: Six miles north-west of Leicester. This small hill in the southern part of Charnwood Forest is named after the outlaw. No tradition exists as to why.

LITTLE JOHN'S STONE: Leicester. According to an eighteenth-century history of Nottinghamshire edited by W. Thoroton, 'near the Abbey of Leicester, stands an upright ponderous forest stone, which goes by the name of Little John's Stone; but for what reason none can tell'.

London

A surprisingly large number of streets in the capital city are named after Robin Hood – testifying again to his continuing popularity. Most date from the seventeenth century and are no longer to be found.

ROBIN HOOD LANE, Poplar (still extant).
ROBIN HOOD YARD, off Leather Lane, immediately North of Holborn (still extant).
ROBIN HOOD COURT, Cordwainer Ward.
ROBIN HOOD COURT, Cripplegate Ward Without.
ROBIN HOOD COURT, Cheap Ward and Cripplegate Ward Within.
ROBIN HOOD COURT, Farringdon Ward Within.
ROBIN HOOD COURT, Queenhithe Ward.

Northamptonshire
ROBIN HOOD AND LITTLE JOHN STONES: Three miles west of Peterborough two weathered stones stand in Castor Field near Gunwade Ferry. *The Natural History of Northamptonshire* published in 1712 says they mark the spot where Robin and Little John fired arrows from nearby Alwalton Church-Yard. As with most such places the shot is beyond that of any normal archer.

Northumberland
ROBIN HOOD'S ROCK: Three and a half miles north of Dunstanburgh is a small rock approximately 500 yards from the Northumberland coast. Traditionally known as Robin Wood's Rock, this is a common seventeenth- or eighteenth-century alternative for Hood.

Nottinghamshire
NOTTINGHAM: The place most closely associated with Robin Hood from the fifteenth century onwards includes a number of memorials, including Maid Marian Way, the frescoes in the cupola of the Council House (1927–9) and statues on Castle Green sculpted by James Woodford in 1949. Of the many Robin Hood place names in Nottingham, the oldest (now disused) include **ROBIN HOOD'S ACRE** and **ROBIN HOOD'S CLOSE.**

ROBIN HOOD'S WELL: Mentioned in the civil records for 1500. It was also known as St Anne's Well as early as the sixteenth century, as there are references to a 'Seynt Anne Well' in 1551, and a 'Robyn Hood Well alias Saynt Anne Well' in 1596. Situated at the foot of a hill two miles north-east of the town centre, it was one of the most famous places associated with the Robin Hood mythos. In the seventeenth and eighteenth centuries it was still possible to see Robin's chair, bow, arrows, cap and slippers.

FOUNTAIN DALE: Three miles south-east of Mansfield, this wooded area, one of the few areas of Sherwood Forest still standing, has been identified with the 'Fountains Dale' where the Curtal Friar of the ballad lived 'seven long years or more'. This association seems to date no further back in time than the nineteenth century as it appears for the first time on a map of 1826.

FRIAR TUCK'S WELL: Three miles south-east of Mansfield, this well is to the east of Fountain Dale.

MAJOR OAK: Located close to the village of Edwinstowe, in the heart of Sherwood Forest, this mighty tree is widely believed to have been used by the Merry Men as a place of refuge. However, dendrologists have contradicted this claim by estimating the tree's true age to be around 800 years, which would make it little more than a sapling in Robin's time. This has not stopped generations of children playing at Robin Hood and the Sherriff in and around the tree. It is so vast and ancient that its boughs are currently held up with wooden props. Most historians today agree that it only became associated with the outlaws after the publication of John Major's *History of Greater Britain, Both England and Scotland*, in 1521.

ROBIN HOOD'S CAVE: Two miles north of Ollerton lies a cave overlooking the River Maun in Walesby parish. The earliest mention is on a map from 1805.

ROBIN HOOD'S GRAVE: Seven miles north of Mansfield this may have acquired its connection with Robin Hood by accident since its earliest mention is from the 1840s, where it is called simply Robin's Grave.

ROBIN HOOD HILL: Four miles west of Southwell, and one mile north of the village of Oxton, this appears to be a prehistoric tumulus.

ROBIN HOOD'S HILLS: Four miles south-west of Mansfield. A group of small hills forming a natural amphitheatre in Sherwood Forest closely associated with a neighbouring Robin Hood's Chair and Robin Hood's Cave. The name is recorded in 1775 but may be part of the eruption of names that began in the 1700s. It may be no older.

ROBIN HOOD'S LARDER: Three miles west of Ollerton. One of two great and ancient trees in Sherwood Forest associated with Robin Hood. Traditionally he is said to have hung venison he and his men had poached. Another name for the tree was 'The Shambles', a title derived from areas in towns when butchery took place. The tree collapsed in 1958. A more famous tree, the Major Oak, long associated with Robin, stands about a mile to the east.

ROBIN HOOD'S STABLE: A rough cave cut into sandstone one mile north of Papplewick and seven north of Nottingham.

ROBIN HOOD'S WELL: Seven miles north-west of Nottingham itself, the well lies in High Park Wood, just north of Beauvale Priory in the parish of Greasley.

SHERWOOD FOREST: Lying just north of Nottingham, this has become the most well known of all medieval English forests through its connection with the Robin Hood stories and ballads. The Lincoln Cathedral Manuscript, which includes the first dated Robin Hood song (*c.* 1420), makes an explicit reference to the outlaw – 'Robyn hode in scherewode stod.' Soon after in 1460 a monk of Witham Priory included in his *Chronicle* that 'around this time, according to popular opinion, a certain outlaw named Robin Hood, with his accomplices, infested Sherwood and other law-abiding areas of England with continuous robberies'. The name *Sciryuda,* meaning Shirewood, appears in a local charter dated to as early as 958. Now a 450-acre county park, it was once much larger in extent, before parts were developed for farmland and dwellings. Though much of it has been deforested, there are still parts of the original woodland where one may capture the sense of what it must have been like in Robin Hood's day.

Somerset

ROBIN HOOD'S BUTTS: Six miles south of Taunton. Three Iron Age long barrows sited close to Otterford and the Chard and Wellington roads have been known by this name since the nineteenth century.

ROBIN HOOD'S BUTTS: Five more long barrows on Brown Down, a mile south of those listed above, are also connected by the name of Robin Hood.

Surrey

ROBIN HOOD'S BUTTS: Two hills, now known as Budburrow and Rowbury Hills, to the north-east of Compton Village near Godalming. The great antiquary John Aubrey referred to them by the alternative name in 1673.

Richmond Park and Environs

The association of Robin with Richmond Deer Park possibly arises from the Robin Hood plays and May Day Games put on there for the entertainment of Henry VIII. A number of places in the areas bear witness to this:

ROBINHOOD WALK: Recorded as 'Robynhood Walke' in the reign of Henry and as 'Robyn-hodes Walke' in 1548.

ROBINHOOD GATE: The south-eastern gate into the park, at the northern end of Kingston Vale. Recorded in 1785.

ROBIN HOOD WAY: Two miles north-east of Kingston-on-Thames on the part of the Kingston Bypass to the west of Wimbledon Common.

Warwickshire

ROBINHOOD'S FARM: According to the Ordinance Survey map for the area from 1830, this was the name of a farm lying some ten miles south of Birmingham near Tamworth in the hundred of Kineton.

LOXLEY: Three miles south-east of Stratford-upon-Avon, this village was claimed as Robin's birthplace by J. R. Planche in his book *A Ramble With Robin Hood*. Planche followed Stukeley's attempt to make Robin Hood a descendant of the Fitzooths, with Robert Fitzodo, lord of the manor of Loxley in the late twelfth century, identified as the great outlaw. (For Loxley in West Yorkshire see below.)

Westmorland

ROBIN HOOD: Called 'Robin Hood's Wood' in the 1859 Ordnance Survey map, one of the hills on Shap Fells had become Robin Hood by 1865.

ROBIN HOOD'S GRAVE: A cairn on the summit of Crosby Ravensworth Fell is marked as the grave of Robin Hood on the 1859 Ordnance Survey map. There seems to be no local tradition in support of this.

Wiltshire

ROBIN HOOD BALL: A Neolithic tumulus at Netheravon in Elstub Hundred, twelve miles south of Marlborough, is listed as 'Robin Wood Ball' on a topographical map of Wiltshire dated 1773.

ROBIN HOOD'S BOWER: Two miles south of Warminster lies a circular earthwork in Southleigh Wood. Though there seems to be no local folklore this name has stuck since the 1800s.

Yorkshire, North Riding

ROBIN HOOD'S BAY: One of the oldest place names associated with Robin Hood. In correspondence between the Count of Flanders and King Edward I from the years 1324 to 1346 it is referred to as Robin Oed's Bay, a name which could be either a corruption of Robin's name or to have been named after the Outlaw.

ROBIN HOOD'S BUTTS: Two miles south of Robin Hood's Bay stand three tumuli, approximately a mile from the shore and 775 feet above sea level, south of the beacon at Stoupe Brow. They probably get their name from Robin Hood's Bay, and are no older than the eighteenth century.

ROBIN HOOD'S HOWL: A mile west of Kirkbymoorside, a hole or hollow on the southern escarpment of the North Yorkshire Moors seems to have acquired this colourful title in the nineteenth century; the wind whistling through it probably gave it its name, but the association with Robin Hood is obscure. Perhaps the howl is an echo of Robin's famous horn?

ROBIN HOOD AND LITTLE JOHN INN: Castleton. Perhaps the most famous of the many inns named after Robin. The story goes that Robin and Little John met here for the last time, but though an inscription on the lintel over the door dates the building to 1761 no mention of it has been found in local records before this time, making the association doubtful.

ROBIN HOOD'S TOWER: Richmond Castle. This is an eleventh-century tower projecting from the curtain wall of the castle. It seems to have been named this only since the fifteenth century.

WHITBY: Two fields immediately west of Whitby Laithes were recorded in 1713 as ROBIN HOOD'S CLOSE and LITTLE JOHN'S CLOSE. The reason for this is probably two stone monoliths that once stood at the side of the two fields. According to the sixteenth-century *Cartularium Abbathiae de Whiteby*, one bore the name of Robin and the other Little John and were said to mark the spot at which arrows shot by Robin and John from the top of Whitby Abbey reached the ground. This would have been a shot well over the ability of any normal archer and the lateness of the reference make it unlikely. Local folklore has suggested that the stones one marked the graves of Robin and John, but this seems to have no source beyond the twentieth century.

Yorkshire, West Riding

So much ink has been spent to claim Robin Hood for this county rather than NOTTINGHAMSHIRE with a variety of evidence, good and bad, that it has become a matter of personal choice as to which is correct. Below are listed the specific sites most closely associated with Robin for the longest period of time.

BARNSDALE: Lying just six miles north of Doncaster, this forest has been claimed as the real Sherwood. The famous traveller John Leyland (1503–52) wrote in his nine volumes of notes known as his *Itinerary*, 'The wooddi and famose forest of Barnesdale, wher they say Robyn Hudde lyvid like an owtlaw.' It covers an area approximately four to five miles north to south and east to west between the River Went and the villages of Skelbrooke and Hampole. Local tradition lists the following as being closely associated with Robin.

ST MARY MAGDALENE, CAMPSALL: According to John Paul Davis in his book *Robin Hood the Unknown Templar* (Peter Owen, 2009), the Church of St Mary Magdalen at Campsall in South Yorkshire could be the site of the chapel dedicated to Mary Magdalene described in the *Gest*:

> I made a chapel in Bernysdale,
> That seemly is to see,
> It is of Mary Magdaleyne,
> And thereto wolde I be.

Davis indicates that this is only church dedicated to Mary Magdalene within reach of Barnsdale Forest. The church was built in the late eleventh century by Robert de Lacy, but local legend to this day suggests that Robin Hood and Maid Marian were married at the church.

ALL SAINTS CHURCH, KIRKBY: In Song 28 of the *Polyobion*, written by the seventeenth-century poet Michael Drayton, the poet states that the great outlaw died at Kirkby, a mere three miles from the site of the Sayles Plantation (see below) where the outlaws are said to have robbed a significant number of travellers. If the historians who believe that Robin was active in the area of the Went Valley and Wentbridge, near the modern town of Pontefract, are to be believed, this is a feasible site for the events at the end of Robin's life. A priory hospital was at one time connected to All Saints' Church, and the the Tudor historian Richard Grafton was convinced that the prioress who murdered Robin was in charge of the infirmary, and that she buried the outlaw beside the road, so that 'common strangers and travelers, knowing and seeing him there buried, might more safely and without fear take their journeys that way, which they durst not do in the life of the said outlaws'.

SAYLES PLANTATION: South-east of the modern Wentbridge Viaduct, this is supposedly the place where Little John is commanded to walk to at the beginning of the *Gest*. Nowadays Wentbridge is a village in the City of Wakefield district of West Yorkshire. It lies around three miles south-east of Pontefract, close to the A1 motorway. During the medieval age Wentbridge was sometimes locally referred to by the name of Barnsdale because it was the predominant settlement in the forest. Wentbridge is mentioned ballad of *Robin Hood and the Potter*, which reads, 'He met them both at Went-breg.' Nineteenth-century antiquary Joseph Hunter was the first to identify the site.

LITTLE JOHN'S WELL: One mile north-west of the village of Hampole lies a stone well just off the Doncaster–Wakefield Road to the west of Barnsdale. It appears as 'Little John's Cave and Well' in an 1838 tithe award, and as 'Little John's Well' on the 1840 Ordnance Survey map. A plaque still bears his name.

LOXLEY: Three miles north-west of Sheffield, this is the second Loxley mentioned in the records. According to the nineteenth-century antiquarian Joseph Hunter: 'the fairest pretensions to be the Locksley of our ballads, where was born the redoubtable Robin Hood. The remains of a house in which it was pretended he was born were formerly pointed out in a small wood (Bar Wood) ... and a well near called Robin Hood's Well' (*Hallamshire*, 1819).

ROBIN HOOD'S GRAVE, KIRKLEES: A short distance from the A664, between Brighouse and Mirfield, on a secluded part of the Kirklees estate, lies the supposed grave of the great Outlaw. It is close the ruins of the Cistercian nunnery Kirklees Priory, where according to legend the outlaw is supposed to have met his death. The inscription on the grave reads,

Hear underneath dis laitl stean
Laz robert earl of Huntingtun
Ne'er arcir ver as hie sa geud
An pipl kauld im robin heud
Sick [such] utlawz as he an iz men
Vil england nivr si agen
Obiit 24 kal: Dekembris, 1247

Both the date and origin of this inscription are generally considered to be spurious, but there is no gainsaying the atmosphere of the place.

ROBIN HOOD HILL AND HOUSE: A mile and a half south of Huddersfield, at Berry Brow near Almondbury, a hill and house bear Robin's name.

ROBIN HOOD'S WELL: Six miles north of Doncaster, on the eastern side of the Great North Road, this well is more or less at the centre of Barnsdale forest. It is near the site of a 'Stone of Robin Hood' recorded in a charter of 1422. In the seventeenth and eighteenth centuries it was one of the most famous stopping places on the highway. The well house was designed by the famous landscape gardener Sir John Vanbrough (1664–1726) for the Earl of Carlisle.

ROBIN HOOD'S WELL: Another well is sited a mile and a half north of Threshfield, in Wharfedale. It has been recorded as 'Robin Hood's Beck and Well' since the nineteenth century.

ROBIN HOOD'S WELL: This third well lies in the grounds of Fountains Abbey, and is associated with the fight between Robin Hood and Friar Tuck, as recorded in the ballad 'Robin Hood and the Curtal Friar'. This connection seems only to date from the eighteenth century.

WENTBRIDGE: A village in the City of Wakefield district of West Yorkshire. During the medieval period Wentbridge was sometimes locally referred to by the name of Barnsdale because it was the predominant settlement in the forest. Wentbridge is mentioned in an early ballad, 'Robin Hood and the Potter', which reads, '"Y mete hem bot at Went breg," syde Lyttyl John.' And, while Wentbridge is not directly named in the *Gest*, the poem does appear to make a cryptic reference to the locality by depicting a poor knight explaining to Robin Hood that he 'went at a bridge' where there was wrestling.

APPENDIX 2

THE LIFE OF ROBIN HOOD

The following document, from a manuscript contained in the British Museum Library (MS Sloane 780 folios 46–48) is included here for the sake of interest. It was probably written down around 1600 by an anonymous author who had seen or heard the best-known of the ballads and was probably familiar with John Major's *History of Greater Britain*. It is printed here in the edition prepared by William J. Thomas for his *Early English Prose Romances* (1890), updated by myself. In turning the seventeenth-century English into modern prose I have striven to keep the wording of the original as far as possible, with the occasional exception for the sake of clarity. I have not hesitated to silently re-punctuate the text, which is otherwise clumsy and misleading. Missing words are indicated by [...]

The text throws considerable light on the way in which Robin was regarded at the beginning of the seventeenth century, and is a useful account of the 'history' attributed to the outlaw from the sixteenth century onward and which has become the default storyline for most versions written since.

***

Robin Hood was borne at Locksley in Yorkshire, or according to others in Nottinghamshire in the days of Henry II, about the year 1260, but lived till the latter end of Richard I. He was of [noble] parentage, but so riotous that he lost or sold his patrimony and for debt became an outlaw, there joining to him many stout fellows of like disposition, amongst whom one called Little John was principal, or next to him. They hunted about Barnsdale forest, Clopton Park, and such other places; they used most of all shooting [archery], wherein they excelled all the men of the land, though as occasion required, they had also other weapons.

One of his first exploits was the going abroad into a forest, and bearing with him a bow of exceeding great strength. [There] he fell in to company with certain rangers or woodmen, who fell to quarreling with him as making show to use such a bow as no man was able to shoot withal. Whereupon Robin replied that he had two better than that at Locksley, and the one he bear with him now was a birding bow. At length the contention grew so hot that there was a wager laid about the killing of a deer a great distance off, for performance whereof, Robin was ordered to lay his head to a certain sum of money, of the advantage of which rash speech the other(s) presently took.

So the mark being found out by one of them, they were both determined to make his heart faint and hand unsteady as he was about to shoot, urging him with the loss of his head if he missed the mark. Notwithstanding Robin killed the deer, and gave every man his money again save to him who at the point of shooting so upbraided him with danger to lose his head, for that very day he said they would drink together. Thereupon the others could not stomach the matter, and from quarrelling they grew to fighting with him, but Robin getting him somewhat away from them, with shooting dispatched them and so fled away, betaking himself to live in the woods by such booty as he could get.

His company increased to an hundred and a half, and in those days whether they were favored, howsoever they were considered, invincible. And whosesoever he heard of that were of unusual strength and hardiness, he would disguise himself in rags and [...] go like a beggar to become acquainted with them. And, after he had tried them with fighting, never give them over till he had used means to draw [them] to live after his fashion. Among such men he procured the Pinder of Wakefield to become one of his company and a friar called Muchel [?Tuck], though some say he was another kind of religious man, for the order of friars was not yet sprung up.

Scarlock he induced upon this occasion, one day meeting him as he walked solitary and like a man forlorn, because a maid to whom he was affianced was taken from him by the violence of her friends, and given to another who was old and wealthy. Whereupon Robin, understanding when the marriage day should be, came to the church as a beggar, having his company not far off, who came in so soon as they heard the sound of his horn. Taking the bride by force from him who was in hand to have married her, he caused the priest to wed her and Scarlock together.

Amongst others who greatly friended him was Sir Richard of Lee, a knight of Lancashire, lord of [... rso] castle. Upon this occasion it was the manner of Robin and his retinue to live by thieving and robbing though yet he were somewhat religiously affected, and not without superstition, but of all saints he most honored the Virgin Mary, so [that] if any for her sake asked ought of him, he would perform it if possibly he could, neither would he suffer any that belonged unto him to violate women or men, or any of the husbandry. All their attempts were chiefly against fat prelates and religious persons and house friars, and he is commended of John Mayor for the prince of all thieves and robbers etc.

Now once it happened that he sent Little John, Scarlock and Tuck to the Sailes upon Watling Street to get some booty they wanted. When any prey came to their hands to lead them into the wood, and to their habitation, as if they would get some hospitality, but after they had eaten would make them pay dearly for their vitals by stripping them of such things as they had.

So they dealt with Sir Richard Lee, leading him to their men, who made him the best cheer they had, and when Sir Richard would have departed only with giving thanks, Robin told him it was not his manner to dine anywhere but that he paid for such things as he took, and so should others do to him ere they parted. And it was, as he said, no good man's way to refuse such doing.

The knight told him he had but 10 shillings which should have born his charges at Blyth or Doncaster, and if he had none he fared full well with him at the time to be put from it, only he promised, as he should be able, to requite his courtesy with the like.

Robin, not so contented, caused him to be searched and found no more but what the knight had told him of, whereupon he commended his true dealing and enquired further touching the cause of his sadness and bareness. The knight told him of his state and ancestry and how his son and heir, falling at variance with a knight in Lancashire, slew him in the field, for which, and some other such like exploits, being in danger to lose his life, the knight, to secure his deliverance, had been at great charges and even lastly driven to pawn his castle and living to the abbot of St Mary's at York for £400. And the chief justice so dealt with the abbot for his state or investment therein, that being like to forfeit his living for lack of money to redeem it at the day appointed, he despaired now of all recovery. Robin, pitying his case, gave him 400 marks, which was out of such booty as they had, and goods and surety for payment again in a twelvemonth was [sworn by] Our Lady.

They also furnished him with apparel out of which he was worn quite, and therefore for very shame meant shortly to have passed over the seas to spend the rest of his life as a mournful pilgrim in going to Jerusalem; but being now enlightened he despaired just as his day appointed to the abbot came near.

Where the chiefs of the shire conversed, accounting all the knight's lands saved to themselves, and set the knight to try their charity, [he] made show as if he wanted money to pay the debt, and when he found no token of compassion, [gave them] the money and recovered his land. For with that payment he offered to farm the abbot thereby.

Now ere the twelvemonth was expired Sir Richard paid the 400 marks and a hundred sheaf of good arrows which he meant to bestow on Robin Hood, and encountering on the way certain people who were wrestling for a great wager, he stood still to see the event of the matter, so there he prevailed. But the other pretending it was rather because he was but poor and alone accorded among they [who sought] to oppose him with wrongs, the knight took his place and rescued him and at parting gave him 5 marks.

Now it befell, that near to Nottingham all the chiefest archers had appointed a day of shooting for some great wager, the Sheriff himself being appointed to see the game. Now that sheriff was a fell adversary to Robin and his company, and he again no less maligned. Therefore, to see all matter, Little John was sent in disguise to go shoot amongst them, where he sped him so well the sheriff judged him to be the best archer, and so importuned him to be his man that Little John went home with him in the name of Raynold Greenleaf, and telling him he was born in Holdernes.

So Little John watched all advantages to do his master some mischief, and understanding where he used to go hunting, by some means procured that Robin Hood and his retinue should be in readiness thereabout. So one day the sheriff and all his people had gone a-hunting, and Little John of purpose kept behind and lay a-bed as somewhat sick. Later he got up and enquired for his dinner of the steward who with curse words denied him victuals till his master were come home. Whereupon little John beat him down and entered the buttery. The cook, being a very stout fellow, fought with him a long time, but at length accorded to go with him to the forest. So they two rifled the house, took away all the sheriff's treasure and best things and conveyed it to Robin Hood.

Then Little John repaired to the sheriff, who in his heat [...] took him for one of his company, whereupon Little John told him he had seen the goodliest heard of deer that was in the forest not far off – seven score in a company, which he could bring him to. The sheriff, glad to hear of so strange a matter, went with him till he came where Robin Hood and his company were. They led him to their habitation [...] and there served him with his own plate and other things that Little John and the cook had brought away. So that night they made him lie on the ground like their own men, wrapped in a green mantel, and the next day sent him away, after they had taken an oath from him never to pursue them but do the best he could to serve them. But the sheriff afterward made no more account of the oath than was meet.

After this Little John, Scarlock, and others were sent forth to meet with some company, [and] if they were poor to help them with some such things as they had, [or] if rich to handle them as they saw on occasion. So upon the way, near Barnsdale, they met with two black monks well horsed and accompanied with fifty persons. Now because Robin then held [Our] Lady in great reverence when any booty came to their hand, they would say the Lady sent them there.

Wherefore when Little John saw the company he merrily used such persuasion to his fellows, encouraging them to the encounter. Coming to the monks he told them that though they were but three, they durst never see their meinie again, but if they brought them to diner with him; and who the monks served, Little John begged to speak reproachfully for making his men stay for diner so long. Whereupon the monks enquired for his name, and Little John told him it was Robin Hood. The monk angrily replied he was an arrant thief, of whom he never heard good. Little John replied as contumaciously, saying he was a yeoman of the forest and bade him to diner. So the [dispute] grew from words to strokes till they had killed all but one or two and they led perforce to their men, who saluted the lowly. But the monk, being stout hearted, did not the like to his; then Robin blew his horn, and his retinue came in, and they all went to dinner. And after this Robin asked him of what abbey he was, who told him he was of St Mary.

Now it was the same to whose abbot the knight ought to pay the 400 marks that Robin lent him to redeem his lands. Perceiving this, Robin began to jest. He declared that Our Lady had not sent him yet his pay, which she was surety for betwixt the knight and him. Have no care, said little John, you need not to say. This monk hath brought it I dare well sware, for he is of her abbey.

So Robin called for wine and drank to him, and prayed him to let him see if he had brought him the money. The monk swore he had never heard speech of such a covenant before, but Robin bare him down. He dissembled saying he knew both Christ and his Mother were so just. And [Robin], since the monk was their servant and messenger, must needs have it, and therefore thanked him for coming so at this day. The monk still denying, Robin asked how much money he had about him. But twenty marks, said the monk. Then said Robin, if we find more we will take it as of Our Lady's sending, but will not of that which is thy own spending money. So Little John was sent to search his bags, and found about 800 marks, which lie he related to his men, telling him withal how Our Lady had doubled his payment. Yea, I told thee, monk, said Robin, what a trusty woman she is, so he called for wine and drank to the monk, bidding him commend him to Our Lady, and if she had need of Robin Hood, she should find him thankful for so liberal a dealing.

Then they searched the lode of another horse, wherefore the monk told him it was no courtesy to bid a man to drink and beat and bind him. And it is no manner, said Robin, to leave but a little behind, So the monk made haste to be gone, and said he might have dined as good [and as] cheap at Blyth or Doncaster. And Robyn called to him as he was going, and bad him greet well his abbot and the rest of their convent, and wish them to send him such a monk each day to dine.

Then shortly came the knight to keep his day and after salutations was about to pay him his money, for his courtesy [....] but Robin gave it him again, telling him how Our Lady had sent him more by the abbey's cellarer, and it were to him a shame to be twice paid. But the bows and arrows he accepted for which he gave him at parting another 400 marks.

Now the sheriff proclaimed a day of shooting for the silver arrow, whereto Robin boldly with all his train repaired, appointing but six of his company to shoot with him; all the rest to stand appointed to him. So Little John, Robin, Tuck, Scarlock, Gilbert, and Reynold shot, but Robin won the prize from all, whereupon the sheriff and his company began to quarrel, and fought so long till Robin and his accomplices had destroyed the sheriff's train for the most part.

In the conflict Little John was sore wounded with an arrow in the knee, and being not able to go requested his men to slay him, and not suffer him to come into the sheriff's hands. [But Robin] avouched he would not lose him for all England, wherefore Tuck was appointed to bare him away on his back, and with much labour, and oft resting, he brought him to Sir Richard Lee's castle, whence also after the broil repaired Robin himself and the rest of his company, where they were gladly received and defended the castle who utterly refused to yield any there till he knew the king's mind.

The sheriff went to London, and informed the king of all the matter, who dispatched the sheriff back to levy a power of men in the county, telling him that a fortnight after he himself would be at Nottingham to determine of the matter. In the meanwhile Little John being cured of his hurt, they all got them to the forest again.

When the Sheriff heard thereof he was much aggrieved and sought by all means to apprehend Sir Richard Lee for defending them, and watching his time all unawares, he surprised him with a power of men as he was at hawking, and went to put him in the ward at Nottingham and hang him. Wherefore the knight's Lady rode in all haste to Robin, and gave him intelligence of her Lord's distress – who in all haste pursued the sheriff and overtaking him at Nottingham with an arrow slew him and [cut] off his head after enquiring what message he brought from the king, objecting to the breach of promise he had made to them in the forest after they overthrew the sheriff. [He then] returned and loosed the [knight] out of his bonds, and furnishing him with weapons, took him with them to the forest, intending to use what means they could to procure [of] the king a pardon.

The King presently came to Nottingham with a great retinue, and understanding the matter seized the knight's living into his hands and surveying all the forests in Lancashire he came to Ploutu [?] Park, and finding all the deer destroyed he was greatly wroth, seeking about for Robin Hood and making proclamation that whoso could bring him Sir Richard Lee's head should have all his land.

So the king stayed about Nottingham half a year, and could not hear of Robin, till being advised what hard feelings he bare against all religious, he got him into a monk's weeds, and with a small company went as a traveller on the way where he thought Robin made abode. [Robin] took hold of the king's horse, making show as he took him for an abbot, and began to enquire after some spending, but the king excused the matter, telling him how he had lain at Nottingham at great charges a fortnight, and had left him but 40 marks. But Robin took them, and having divided it amongst his men, gave the king part again, who seemed to take it in good part, and then pulled out. The king [...] told him how he did greet him well, and charged him to come to Nottingham. Whereupon Robin kneeled down and thanked the abbot, for he pretended to think him none other for bringing such a message to him, and [that] he loved [him] most dearly of all men, told him that for his labor he should dine with him.

So being brought to the place of their abode, Robin blew his horn and all his company came, obedient to their master. The king marvelled and Robin perceiving did himself with his best men instruct the king, welcoming him for the king's sake as he said. Then he showed him the course of their lives in the sky, and that he might inform the king thereof, and supposed this penalty to him that shot one of the garlands that the abbot, should give him a good buffet, and for the nonce made himself to forfeit. And when the abbot refused to strike him, saying it fell not for his order, Robin would not cease till he made him smite him soundly so that he fell to the ground when Robin commanded him [...]

Afterwards Robin explained how he knew it was the king, and together with Sir Richard and his men, kneeled down and asked forgiveness, which the king granted, upon condition he would [come] before him at the court. So Robin arrayed the king and his company in mantels of Lincoln green, and went to Nottingham, the king seeming also to be one of the outlaws. [Robin and] the king were shooting together for buffets, and Robin oft boxed with the king, and people suspecting they should be all destroyed by Robin and his company, ran away, till the king revealed himself and comforted them. And each one was fain [that] there should be a great feast for all people, and Sir Richard Lee had his lands restored, for which Robin gave the king humble thanks.

Then Robin dwelt in the court a year, till with lavish spending he had nothing left to maintain himself and his men, and therefore all were departed from him but Little John and Scarlock. And on a time seeing youngsters shooting, it come to his mind how he was alienated from the exercise, for which he was very aggrieved and cast in his mind how to get away. Wherefore he devised to tell the king how he had erected a chapel in Barnsdale of Mary Magdalen, and been sore troubled in dreaming about it, and therefore craved liberty to go [on] pilgrimage there, barefoot.

So the king gave him a week of respite for going and coming, but Robin being come there remembered his old ways and never returned back to the court.

After which time he continued the course of life about twenty years, till distempered with cold and age he had great pain in his limbs, his blood being corrupted. Therefore to be eased of his pain by letting blood, he repaired to the prioress of Kirklees, which some say was his aunt, a woman very skillful in physic and surgery, who perceiving him to be Robin Hood, and knowing how fell an enemy he was to the religious, took revenge of him for her own house and all other, by letting him bleed to death. And she buried him under a great stone by the highway's side.

It is also said, how one Sir Roger of Doncaster, bearing a grudge towards Robin for some injury, incited the prioress, with whom he was very familiar, in such way to dispatch him, and then all his company was soon dispersed. The place of Little John's burial is to this day celebrated for the yielding of excellent whetstones.

APPENDIX 3

THE BALLADS OF ROBIN HOOD

Introduction

This collection includes most if not all of the major ballads, ranging from the twelfth to the seventeenth centuries, featuring Robin Hood and the Merry Men – the main source for the myths of the hero. They are not great literature, but they are full of the voices of the English folk who made them and who sang them, and kept the stories of Robin alive. They are given here without glosses, but most of the unusual words can be looked up or will be found in the brief glossary at the end of the collection. The best resource for all things Robin Hood is *The Robin Hood Project* at The Robins Library in Rochester University. Visit them at http://www.rochester.edu/robinhood. Their ongoing digital project will eventually hold most of not all references to Robin Hood from its beginnings to the present. The inclusion of …. or [ ] refer either to missing words or lines, or to suggested additions. Spelling and punctuation varies hugely due to the variety of periods involved and the preferences of earlier editors. I have chosen for the most part to leave this unchanged, for the sake of the tone and nature of each ballad.

The collection is by no means definitive, and I must pay tribute to the great collectors on whose work this is firmly based. Without the skills of Joseph Ritson, Francis Child and their ilk, this would not have been possible.

A List of the Ballads
Robyn and Gandeleyn
Robin Hood and the Monk
Robin Hood and the Potter
Robin Hood and Guy of Gisborne
Robin Hood's Death
Adam Bell, Clym of the Clough and William of Cloudesly
Robyn Hode and the Potter
Robin Hood and the Beggar
A True Tale of Robin Hood by Martin Parker
Robin Hood's Birth, Breeding, Valour, and Marriage
Robin Hood's Progress to Nottingham
The Jolly Pinder of Wakefield, with Robin Hood, Scarlet and John
Robin Hood and the Bishop
Robin Hood and the Butcher
Robin Hood and the Tinker
Robin Hood and Allin 'A' Dale
Robin Hood and the Shepherd
Robin Hood and the Curtall Fryer
Robin Hood and the Stranger
Robin Hood and Queen Katherine
Robin Hood's Chase
Robin Hood's Golden Prize
Robin Hood's Rescuing Will Stutly
The Noble Fisher-Man or, Robin Hood's Preferment
Robin Hood's Delight
Robin Hood and the Beggar (2)
Little John and the Four Beggars
Robin Hood and the Ranger – True Friendship after a Fierce Fight
Robin Hood and Little John
Robin Hood and the Bishop of Hereford
Robin Hood Rescuing the Widow's Three Sons from the Sheriff
Robin Hood and Maid Marian
The King's Disguise and Friendship with Robin Hood
Robin Hood and the Golden Arrow
Robin Hood and the Valiant Knight
The Death of Robin Hood (Variant Version)

Robin and Gandeleyn

I heard a carping of a clerk
All at yon woodes end,
Of good Robin and Gandeleyn,
Was there none other thing.

Strong thieves wern tho children none,
But bowmen good and hend;
They wenten to wood to getten them
   flesh
If God would it them send.

All day wenten tho children two,
And flesh founden they none,
Till it were again even,
The children would gone home.

Half a hundred of fat fallow deer
They comen ayon,
And all they wern fair and fat enow,
But marked was there none.
'By dear God,' said good Robin,
'Hereof we shall have one.'

Robin bent his jolly bow,
Therein he set a flo,
The fattest deer of all.
The heart he cleft a-two.

He had not the deer i-flaw
Ne half out of the hide,

There came a shrewd arrow out of the
west
That felled Robert's pride.

Gandeleyn looked him east and west,
'Who hath my master slain?
Who hath done this deed?
Shall I never out of Greenwood go
Till I see his sides bleed.'

Gandeleyn looked him east and west,
And sought under the sun;
He saw a little boy.
They clepen Wrennok of Donne.

A good bow in his hand,
A broad arrow therein,
And four and twenty good arrows
Trussed in a thrum.
'Beware thee, ware thee, Gandeleyn,
Hereof thou shalt have some.

'Beware thee, ware thee, Gandeleyn,
Hereof thou gettest plenty.'
'Ever one for another,' said Gandeleyn;
'Misaunter have they shall flee.

'Whereat shall our mark be?'
Saide Gandeleyn.
'Everich at otheres heart,'
Said Wrennok again.

'Who shall give the first shot?'
Saide Gandeleyn.
'And I shall give thee one before,'
Said Wrennok again.

Wrennok shot a full good shot,
And he shot not too high;
Through the sanchothes of his breek,
It touched neither thigh.

'Now hast thou given me one before';
All thus to Wrennok said he;
'And through the might of our Lady
A better I shall give thee.'

Gandeleyn bent his good bow,
And set therein a flo;
He shot through his green kirtle,
His heart he cleft on two.

'Now shalt thou never yelp, Wrennok,
At ale ne at wine,
That thou hast slaw good Robin
And his knave Gandeleyn.

'Now shalt thou never yelp, Wrennok,
At wine ne at ale,
That thou hast slaw good Robin
And Gandeleyn his knave.'

Robin Hood and the Monk

In Summer, when the shaws be sheen
And leaves be large and long,
It is full merry in fair forest
To hear the fowles song,

To see the deer draw to the dale,
And leave the hilles hee,
And shadow them in the leaves green,
Under the Greenwood tree.

It befel on Whitsuntide,
Early in a May morning,
The sun up fair can shine,
And the briddes merry can sing.

'This is a merry morning,' said Little John,
'By him that died on tree;
A more merry man than I am one
Lives not in Christiante.

'Pluck up thy heart, my dear master,'
Little John can say,
'And think it is a full fair time
In a morning of May.'

'Yea, one thing grieves me,' said
    Robin,
'And does my heart much woe;
That I may not no solemn day
To mass nor matins go.

'It is a fortnight and more,' said he,
'Syn I my Saviour see;
To-day will I to Nottingham,
With the might of mild Marie.'

Then spake Much the milner son,
Ever more well him betide!
'Take twelve of thy wight yeomen,
Well weapon'd by thy side.

Such one would thyselfe slon,
That twelve dare not abide.'

'Of all my merry men,' said Robin,
'By my faith I will none have,
But Little John shall bear my bow,
Till that me list to draw.'

'Thou shall bear thine own,' said
    Little John,
'Master, and I will bear mine,
And we will shoot a penny,' said
    Little John,
'Under the Greenwood lyne.'

'I will not shoot a penny,' said Robin
    Hood,
'In faith, Little John, with thee,
But ever for one as thou shootes,' said
    Robin,
'In faith I hold thee three.'

Thus shot they forth, these yeomen
    two,
Both at bush and broom,
Till Little John won of his master
Five shillings to hose and shoon.

A ferly strife fell them between,
As they went by the way,
Little John said he had won five
    shillings
And Robin Hood said shortly nay.

With that Robin Hood lied Little
    John,
And smote him with his hand;

Little John waxed wroth therewith,
And pulled out his bright brand.

'Were thou not my master,' said Little
    John,
'Thou shouldest by it full sore;
Get thee a man where thou wilt,
For thou gettest me no more.'

Then Robin goes to Nottingham,
Himself mourning alone,
And Little John to merry Sherwood,
The paths he knew ilkone.

When Robin came to Nottingham,
Certainly withouten layn,
He prayed to God and mild Mary
To bring him out safe again.

He goes into Saint Mary church,
And kneeled down before the rood;
All that ever were the church within,
Beheld well Robin Hood.

Beside him stood a great-headed
    monk,
I pray to God woe he be!
Full soon he knew good Robin,
As soon as he him see.

Out at the door he ran,
Full soon and anon;
All the gates of Nottingham,
He made to be sparred everychone.

'Rise up,' he said, 'thou proud sheriff,
Busk thee, and make thee bown;

I have spied the kinges felon,
For sooth he is in this town.

'I have spied the false felon,
As he standes at his mass;
It is long of thee,' said the monk,
'And ever he fro us pass.

'This traitor name is Robin Hood,
Under the Greenwood lynd;
He robbed me once of a hundred
   pound,
It shall never out of my mind.'

Up then rose this proud sheriff,
And radly made him yare;
Many was the mother son,
To the kirk with him can fare.

In at the doors they throly thrast,
With staves full good wone;
'Alas, alas!' said Robin Hood,
'Now miss I Little John.'

But Robin took out a two-hand sword
That hanged down by his knee;
Thereas the sheriff and his men stood
   thickest,
Thitherward would he.

Thrice throughout them he ran then
For sooth as I you say,
And wounded many a mother son,
And twelve he slew that day.

His sword upon the sheriff head
Certainly he brake in two;

'The smith that thee made,' said
   Robin,
'I pray God work him woe.'

'For now am I weaponless,' said
   Robin,
'Alas! against my will;
But if I may flee these traitors fro,
I wot they will me kill.'

Robin into the churche ran,
Throughout them everilkone,
   ...
   ...

Some fell in swooning as they were
   dead,
And lay still as any stone;
None of them were in their mind
But only Little John.

'Let be your rule,' said Little John,
'For his love that died on tree;
Ye that should be doughty men;
It is great shame to see.

'Our master has been hard bestood,
And yet scaped away;
Pluck up your hearts and leave this
   moan,
And hearken what I shall say.

'He has served Our Lady many a day,
And yet will, securly;
Therefore I trust her specially
No wicked death shall he die.

'Therefore be glad,' said Little John,
'And let this mourning be;
And I shall be the monkes guide,
With the might of mild Marie.'

......
'We will go but we two;
And I meet him,' said Little John,

...

'Look that ye keep well our tristel-tree,
Under the leaves smale,
And spare none of this venison
That goes in this vale.'

Forth then went these yeomen two,
Little John and Much on fere,
And looked on Much emes house,
The highway lay full near.

Little John stood at a window in the
    morning,
And looked forth at a stage;
He was ware where the monk came
    riding,
And with him a little page.

'By my faith,' said Little John to
    Much,
'I can thee tell tidinges good;
I see where the monke comes riding,
I know him by his wide hood.'

They went into the way, these yeomen
    both,
As curteis men and hend;

They spyrred tidinges at the monk,
As they had been his friende.

'Fro whence come ye?' said Little
    John,
'Tell us tidinges, I you pray,
Of a false outlaw, called Robin Hood,
Was taken yesterday.

'He robbed me and my fellows both
Of twenty mark in certain;
If that false outlaw be taken;
For sooth we would be fain.'

'So did he me,' said the monk,
'Of a hundred pound and more;
I laid first hand him upon,
Ye may thank me therefore.'

'I pray God thank you,' said Little
    John,
'And we will when we may;
We will go with you, with your leave,
And bring you on your way.

'For Robin Hood has many a wild
    fellow,
I tell you in certain;
If they wist you rode this way,
In faith ye should be slain.'

As they went talking by the way,
The monk and Little John,
John took the monkes horse by the
    head,
Full soon and anon.

John took the monkes horse by the
head,
Forsooth as I you say;
So did Much the little page,
For he should not scape away.

By the gullet of the hood
John pulled the monke down;
John was nothing of him agast,
He let him fall on his crown.

Little John was sore aggrieved,
And drew out his sword on high;
This monke saw he should be dead,
Loud mercy can he cry.

'He was my master,' said Little John,
'That thou hast brought in bale;
Shall thou never come at our king,
For to tell him tale.'

John smote off the monkes head,
No longer would he dwell;
So did Much the little page,
For fear lest he would tell.

There they buried them both,
In neither moss nor ling,
And Little John and Much in fere
Bare the letters to our king.

...

He kneeled down upon his knee:
'God you save, my liege lord,
Jesus you save and see!

'God you save, my liege king!'
To speak John was full bold;
He gave him the letters in his hand,
The king did it unfold.

The king read the letters anon,
And said, 'So mote I the,
There was never yeoman in merry
England
I longed so sore to see.

'Where is the monk that these should
have brought?'
Our king can say:
'By my troth,' said Little John,
'He died after the way.'

The king gave Much and Little John
Twenty pound in certain,
And made them yeomen of the crown,
And bade them go again.

He gave John the seal in hand,
The sheriff for to bear,
To bring Robin him to,
And no man do him dere.

John took his leave at our king,
The sooth as I you say;
The next way to Nottingham
To take, he yede the way.

When John came to Nottingham
The gates were sparred each one;John
called up the porter,
He answered soon anon.

'What is the cause,' said Little John,
'Thou sparres the gates so fast?'
'Because of Robin Hood,' said the porter,
'In deep prison is cast.

'John and Much and Will Scathlock,
For sooth as I you say,
They slew our men upon our walles,
And sauten us every day.'

Little John spyrred after the sheriff,
And soon he him found;
He opened the kinges privy seal
And gave him in his hond.

When the sheriff saw the kinges seal,
He did off his hood anon;
'Where is the monk that bare the
    letters?'
He said to Little John.

'He is so fain of him,' said Little John,
'For sooth as I you say,
He has made him abbot of
    Westminster,
A lord of that abbay.'

The sheriff made John good cheer,
And gave him wine of the best;
At night they went to their bed,
And every man to his rest.

When the sheriff was on sleep,
Drunken of wine and ale,
Little John and Much for sooth
Took the way unto the jail.

Little John called up the jailor;
And bade him rise anon;
He said Robin Hood had broken
    prison,
And out of it was gone.

The porter rose anon certain,
As soon as he heard John call;
Little John was ready with a sword,
And bare him to the wall.

'Now will I be porter,' said Little
    John,
'And take the keys in hond';
He took the way to Robin Hood,
And soon he him unbound.

He gave him a good sword in his hand,
His head therewith for to keep,
And thereas the wall was lowest
Anon down can they leap.

By that the cock began to crow,
The day began to spring;
The sheriff found the jailor dead,
The comyn bell made he ring.

He made a cry throughout all the
    town,
Whether he be yeoman or knave,
That could bring him Robin Hood,
His warison he should have.

'For I dare never,' said the sheriff,
'Come before our king;
For if I do, I wot certain
For sooth he will me hing.'

The sheriff made to seek Nottingham,
Both by street and sty,
And Robin was in merry Sherwood,
As light as leaf on lynd.

Then bespake good Little John,
To Robin Hood can he say,
'I have done thee a good turn for an evil;
Quite thee when thou may.

'I have done thee a good turn,' said
    Little John,
'For sooth as I you say;
I have brought thee under green wood
    lyne;
Farewell, and have good day.'

'Nay, by my troth,' said Robin Hood,
'So shall it never be:
I make thee master,' said Robin Hood,
'Of all my men and me.'

'Nay, by my troth,' said Little John,
'So shall it never be;
But let me be a fellow,' said Little John,
'No nother keep I be.'

Thus John gat Robin Hood out of prison,
Certain withouten layn;
When his men saw him whole and
    sound,
For sooth they were full fain.

They filled in wine, and made them glad,
Under the leaves smale,
And gat pasties of venison,
That goode was with ale.

Then worde came to our king
How Robin Hood was gone,
And how the sheriff of Nottingham
Durst never look him upon.

Then bespake our comely king,
In an anger hee:
'Little John has beguiled the sheriff,
In faith so has he me.

'Little John has beguiled us both,
And that full well I see;
Or else the sheriff of Nottingham
High hanged should he be.

'I made them yeomen of the crown,
And gave them fee with my hand;
I gave them grith,' said our king;
'Throughout all merry England.

'I gave them grith,' then said our king;
'I say, so mote I the,
Forsooth such a yeoman as he is one
In all England are not three.

'He is true to his master,' said our
    king;
'I say, by sweet Saint John,
He loves better Robin Hood
Than he does us each one.

'Robin Hood is ever bound to him,
Both in street and stall;
Speak no more of this matter,' said
    our king;
'But John has beguiled us all.'

Thus ends the talking of the monk,
And Robin Hood i-wis;
God, that is ever a crowned king,
Bring us all to his bliss

Robin Hood and the Potter

In Summer, when the leaves spring,
The blossoms on every bough,
So merry doth the birdes sing
In woodes merry now.

Hearken, good yeomen,
Comely, courteous, and good;
One of the best that ever bare bow,
His name was Robin Hood.

Robin Hood was the yeoman's name,
That was both courteous and free;
For the love of Our Lady
All women worshipped he.

But as the good yeoman stood on a
    day,
Among his merry meyne,
He was ware of a proud potter
Came driving over the lee.

'Yonder cometh a proud potter,' said
    Robin,
'That long hath haunted this way;
He was never so courteous a man
One penny of pavage to pay.'

'I met him but at Wentbridge,' said
    Little John,
'And therefore evil mote he thee!

Such three strokes he me gave,
That by my sides cleft they.

'I lay forty shillings,' said Little John,
'To pay it this same day,
There is not a man among us all
A wed shall make him lay.'

'Here is forty shillings,' said Robin,
'More, and thou dare say,
That I shall make that proud potter,
A wed to me shall he lay.'

There this money they laid,
They toke it a yeoman to keep.
Robin before the potter he breyde
And bade him stand still.

Hands upon his horse he laid,
And bade the potter stand full still;
The potter shortly to him said,
'Fellow, what is thy will?'

'All this three year and more, potter,'
    he said,
'Thou hast haunted this way,
Yet were thou never so courteous a
    man
One penny of pavage to pay.'

'What is thy name,' said the potter,
''Fore pavage thou ask of me?'
'Robin Hood is my name,
A wed shall thou leave me.'

'Wed will I none leave,' said the potter,
'Nor pavage will I none pay;
Away thy hand fro my horse!
I will thee tene else, by my fay.'

The potter to his cart he went,
He was not to seek;
A good two-hand staff he hent,
Before Robin he leaped.

Robin out with a sword bent,
A buckler in his hand;
The potter to Robin he went
And said, 'Fellow, let my horse go.'

Together then went these two yeomen,
It was a good sight to see;
Thereof low Robin his men,
There they stood under a tree.

Little John to his fellows said,
'Yon potter will stiffly stand':
The potter, with an ackward stroke,
Smote the buckler out of his hand.

And ere Robin might get it again
His buckler at his feet,
The potter in the neck him took,
To the ground soon he yede.

That saw Robin his men
As they stood under a bough;

'Let us help our master,' said Little John,
'Yonder potter else will him slo.'

These yeomen went with a breyde,
To their master they came.
Little John to his master said
'Who hath the wager won?'

'Shall I have your forty shillings,' said
    Little John,
'Or ye, master, shall have mine?'
'If they were a hundred,' said Robin,
'In faith, they been all thine.'

'It is full little courtesy,' said the
    potter,
'As I have heard wise men say,
If a poor yeoman come driving on the
    way
To let him of his journey.'

'By my troth, thou says sooth,' said
    Robin,
'Thou says good yeomanry;
And thou drive forth every day,
Thou shalt never be let for me.

'I will pray thee, good potter,
A fellowship will thou have?
Give me thy clothing, and thou shalt
    have mine;
I will go to Nottingham.'

'I grant thereto,' said the potter;
'Thou shalt find me a fellow good;
But thou can sell my pottes well,
Come again as thou yode.'

'Nay, by my troth,' said Robin,
'And then I beshrew my head,
If I bring any pottes again,
And any wife will them chepe.'

Then spake Little John,
And all his fellows hend;
'Master, be well ware of the sheriff of
   Nottingham,
For he is little our friend.'

'Heyt war howt,' said Robin;
'Fellows, let me alone;
Through the help of Our Lady,
To Nottingham will I gone.'

Robin went to Nottingham,
These pottes for to sell;
The potter abode with Robin's men,
There he fared not ill.

Though Robin drove on his way,
So merry over the land:
Here is more, and after is to say
The best is behind.

When Robin came to Nottingham,
The sooth if I should say,
He set up his horse anon,
And gave him oats and hay.

In the midst of the town,
There he showed his ware;
'Pottes, pottes,' he gan cry full soon,
'Have hansel for the mare!'

Full often against the sheriff's gate
Showed he his chaffare;
Wives and widows about him drew
And cheped fast of his ware.

Yet, 'Pottes, great chepe!' cried Robin,
'I love evil thus to stand.'
And all that saw him sell
Said he had be no potter long.

The pottes that were worth pence five,
He sold them for pence three;
Privily said man and wife,
'Yonder potter shall never thee.'

Thus Robin sold full fast,
Till he had pottes but five;
Up he them took off his car
And sent them to the sheriff's wife.

Thereof she was full fain;
'Gramercy, sir,' then said she;
'When ye come to this country again
I shall buy of thy pottes, so mote I thee.'

'Ye shall have of the best,' said Robin,
And sware by the Trinity;
Full courteously she gan him call,
'Come dine with the sheriff and me.'

'God amercy,' said Robin,
'Your bidding shall be done.'
A maiden in the pottes gan bear,
Robin and the sheriff wife followed
   anon.

When Robin into the hall came,
The sheriff soon he met;
The potter could of courtesy,
And soon the sheriff he gret.

'Lo, sir, what this potter hath give you
    and me;
Five pottes small and great!'
'He is full welcome,' said the sheriff,
'Let us wash, and go to meat.'

As they sat at their meat,
With a noble cheer,
Two of the sheriff's men gan speak
Of a great wager;

Of a shooting was good and fine,
Was made the other day,
Of forty shillings, the sooth to say,
Who should this wager win.

Still then sat this proud potter,
Thus then thought he;
'As I am a true Christian man,
This shooting will I see.'

When they had fared of the best,
With bread, and ale, and wine,
To the butts they made them prest,
With bows and bolts full fine.

The sheriff's men shot full fast,
As archers that were good;
There came none near nigh the mark
By half a good archer's bow.

Still then stood the proud potter,
Thus then said he;
'And I had a bow, by the rood,
One shot should ye see.'

'Thou shall have a bow,' said the sheriff,
'The best that thou will choose of three;
Thou seemest a stalwart and a strong,
Assay[ed] shall thou be.'

The sheriff commanded a yeoman that
    stood them by,
After bows to wend;
The best bow that the yeoman brought,

Robin set on a string.
'Now shall I wot and thou be good,
And pull it up to thine ear.'
'So God me help,' said the proud potter,
'This is but right weak gear.'

To a quiver Robin went,
A good bolt out he took;
So nigh unto the mark he went,
He failed not a foot.

All they shot about again,
The sheriff's men and he;
Of the mark he would not fail,
He cleft the prick in three.

The sheriff's men thought great shame
The potter the mastery won;
The sheriff laughed and made good
    game,
And said, 'Potter, thou art a man.

...

...

'Thou art worthy to bear a bow
In what place that thou go.'

'In my cart I have a bow,
Forsooth,' he said, 'and that a good;
In my cart is the bow
That gave me Robin Hood.'

'Knowest thou Robin Hood?' said the
    sheriff;
'Potter, I pray thee tell thou me.'
'A hundred turn I have shot with him,
Under his trystell-tree.'

'I had liefer nor a hundred pound,'
    said the sheriff,
And sware by the Trinity,
' ...
That the false outlaw stood by me.'

'And ye will do after my rede,' said
    the potter,
'And boldly go with me,
And tomorrow, ere we eat bread,
Robin Hood will we see.'

'I will quite thee,' quoth the sheriff,
'I swear by God of might.'
Shooting they left and home they went,
Their supper was ready dight.

Upon the morrow, when it was day,
He busked him forth to ride;
The potter his cart forth gan ray,
And would not leave behind.

He took leave of the sherriff's wife,
And thanked her of all thing:
'Dame, for my love and you will this
    wear,
I give you here a gold ring.'

'Gramercy,' said the wife,
'Sir, God yield it thee.'
The sheriff's heart was never so light,
The fair forest to see.

And when he came into the forest,
Under the leaves green,
Birdes there sang on boughes prest,
It was great joy to see.

'Here it is merry to be,' said Robin,
'For a man that had ought to spend;
By my horn I shall awit
If Robin Hood be here.'

Robin set his horn to his mouth,
And blew a blast that was full good;
That heard his men that there stood,
Far down in the wood.

'I hear my master blow,' said Little
    John,
...
...
They ran as they were wood.

When they to their master came,
Little John would not spare;
'Master, how have you fare in
    Nottingham?
How have you sold your ware?'

'Yea, by my troth, Little John,
Look thou take no care;
I have brought the sheriff of Nottingham,
For all our chaffare.'

'He is full welcome,' said Little John,
'This tiding is full good.'
The sheriff had liefer nor a hundred
    pound
He had never seen Robin Hood.

'Had I wist that before,
At Nottingham when we were,
Thou should not come in fair forest
Of all this thousand year.'

'That wot I well,' said Robin,
'I thank God that ye be here;
Therefore shall ye leave your horse
    with us
And all your other gear.'

'That fend I god's forbode,' quoth the
    sheriff,
So to loose my good;
  ...
  ...

'Hither ye came on horse full high,
And home shall ye go on foot;
And greet well thy wife at home,
The woman is full good.

'I shall her send a white palfrey,
It ambleth, by my fay,
  ...
  ...

'I shall her send a white palfrey,
It ambleth as the wind;
Nere for the love of your wife,
Of more sorrow should you sing!'

Thus parted Robin Hood and the
    sheriff;
To Nottingham he took the way;
His wife fair welcomed him home,
And to him gan she say:

'Sir, how have you fared in green
    forest?
Have ye brought Robin home?'
'Dame, the devil speed him, both body
    and bone;
I have had a full great scorn.

'Of all the good that I have led to
    green wood,
He hath take it fro me;
All but this fair palfrey,
That he hath sent to thee.'

With that she took up a loud laughing,
And sware by him that died on tree,
'Now have you paid for all the pottes
That Robin gave to me.

'Now ye be come home to Nottingham,
Ye shall have good enow.'
Now speak we of Robin Hood,
And of the potter under the green
    bough.

'Potter, what was thy pottes worth
To Nottingham that I led with me?'

'They were worth two nobles,' said he,
'So mote I thrive or thee;

...

...
So could I have had for them
And I had there be.'

'Thou shalt have ten pound,' said Robin,
'Of money fair and free;

And ever when thou comest to green
    wood,
Welcome, potter, to me.'

Thus parted Robin, the sheriff, and
    the potter,
Underneath the green wood tree;
God have mercy on Robin Hood's soul,
And save all good yeomanry!

Robin Hood and Guy of Gisborne

When Shaws been sheen, and shradds
    full fair,
And leaves both large and long,
It is merry, walking in the fair forest,
To hear the small bird's song.

The woodweel sang, and would not
    cease,
Amongst the leaves o' lyne,
And it is by two wight yeomen,
By dear God, that I mean.

'Methought they did me beat and bind,
And took my bow me fro;
If I be Robin alive in this land,
I'll be wroken on both them two.'

'Swevens are swift, master,' quoth
    John,
'As the wind that blows o'er a hill;
For if it be never so loud this night,
Tomorrow it may be still.'

'Busk ye, bown ye, my merry men all,
For John shall go with me;
For I'll go seek yond wight yeomen
In Greenwood where they be.'

They cast on their gown of green,
A shooting gone are they,
Until they came to the merry
    Greenwood,
Where they had gladdest be;
There were they 'ware of a wight
    yeoman,
His body leaned to a tree.

A sword and a dagger he wore by his side,
Had been many a man's bane,
And he was clad in his capul-hide,
Top and tail and mane.

'Stand you still, master,' quoth Little John,
'Under this trusty tree,
And I will go to yond wight yeoman,
To know his meaning truly.'

'Ah, John, by me thou sets
   no store,
And that's a ferly thing;
How oft send I my men before,
And tarry myself behind?

'It is no cunning a knave to ken,
And a man but hear him speak;
And it were not for bursting of my
   bow,
John, I would thy head break.'

But often words they breeden bale;
That parted Robin and John;
John is gone to Barnesdale,

The gates he knows each one.
And when he came to Barnesdale,
Great heaviness there he had;
He found two of his fellows
Were slain both in a slade,

And Scarlet afoot flying was,
Over stocks and stone,
For the sheriff with seven score men
Fast after him is gone.

'Yet one shot I'll shoot,' says Little
   John,
'With Christ his might and main;
I'll make yond fellow that flies so fast
To be both glad and fain.'

John bent up a good yew bow,
And fettled him to shoot;
The bow was made of a tender bough,
And fell down to his foot.

'Woe worth thee, wicked wood,' said
   Little John,
'That e'er thou grew on a tree!
For this day thou art my bale,
My boot when thou should be.'

This shot it was but loosely shot,
The arrow flew in vain,
And it met one of the sheriff's men;
Good William a Trent was slain.

It had been better for William a Trent
To hang upon a gallow
Than for to lie in the Greenwood,
There slain with an arrow.

And it is said, when men be met,
Six can do more than three:
And they have ta'en Little John,
And bound him fast to a tree.

'Thou shalt be drawn by dale and
   down,
And hanged high on a hill.'
'But thou may fail,' quoth Little John,
'If it be Christ's own will.'

Let us leave talking of Little John,
For he is bound fast to a tree,
And talk of Guy and Robin Hood
In the Greenwood where they be;

How these two yeomen together they
   met,
Under the leaves of lyne,
To see what merchandise they made
Even at that same time.

'Good morrow, good fellow,' quoth
   Sir Guy;
'Good morrow, good fellow,' quoth he;
'Methinks by this bow thou bears in
   thy hand,
A good archer thou seems to be.

'I am wilful of my way,' quoth Sir
   Guy,
'And of my morning tide.'
'I'll lead thee through the wood,'
   quoth Robin,
'Good fellow, I'll be thy guide.'

'I seek an outlaw,' quoth Sir Guy,
'Men call him Robin Hood;
I had rather meet with him upon a
   day
Than forty pound of gold.'

'If you two met, it would be seen
   whether were better
Afore ye did part away;
Let us some other pastime find,
Good fellow, I thee pray.

'Let us some other masteries make,
And we will walk in the woods even;
We may chance meet with Robin Hood
At some unset steven.'

They cut them down the Summer
   shroggs
Which grew both under a briar,
And set them three score rood in
   twain,
To shoot the pricks full near.

'Lead on, good fellow,' said Sir Guy,
'Lead on, I do bid thee.'
'Nay by my faith,' quoth Robin
   Hood,
'The leader thou shalt be.'

The first good shot that Robin led,
Did not shoot an inch the prick fro;
Guy was an archer good enough,
But he could ne'er shoot so.

The second shot Sir Guy shot,
He shot within the garland;
But Robin Hood shot it better
   than he,
For he clove the good prick-wand.

'God's blessing on thy heart!' says
   Guy,
'Good fellow, thy shooting is good;
For an thy heart be as good as thy
   hands,
Thou were better than Robin Hood.

'Tell me thy name, good fellow,' quoth
   Guy,
Under the leaves of lyne:
'Nay, by my faith,' quoth good Robin,
'Till thou have told me thine.'

'I dwell by dale and down,' quoth
   Guy,
'And I have done many a curst turn;
And he that calls me by my right
   name
Calls me Guy of good Gisborne.'

'My dwelling is in the wood,' says
  Robin;
'By thee I set right nought;
My name is Robin Hood of
  Barnesdale,
A fellow thou hast long sought.'

He that had neither been kith nor kin
Might have seen a full fair sight,
To see how together these yeomen
  went,
With blades both brown and bright;

To have seen how these yeomen
  together fought
Two hours of a Summer's day;
It, was neither Guy nor Robin Hood
That fettled them to fly away.

Robin was reckless on a root,
And stumbled at that tide,
And Guy was quick and nimble withal,
And hit him o'er the left side.

'Ah, dear Lady!' said Robin Hood,
'Thou art both mother and may!
I think it was never man's destiny
To die before his day.'

Robin thought on Our Lady dear,
And soon leapt up again,
And thus he came with an awkward
  stroke;
Good Sir Guy he has slain.

He took Sir Guy's head by the hair,
And sticked it on his bow's end:

'Thou hast been traitor all thy life,
Which thing must have an end.'

Robin pulled forth an Irish knife,
And nicked Sir Guy in the face,
That he was never on a woman born
Could tell who Sir Guy was.

Says, 'Lie there, lie there, good Sir
  Guy,
And with me be not wroth;
If thou have had the worse strokes at
  my hand,
Thou shalt have the better cloth.'

Robin did off his gown of green,
Sir Guy he did it throw;
And he put on that capul-hide
That clad him top to toe.

'The bow, the arrows, and little
  horn,
And with me now I'll bear;
For now I will go to Barnesdale,
To see how my men do fare.'

Robin set Guy's horn to his mouth,
A loud blast in it he did blow;
That beheard the sheriff of
  Nottingham,
As he leaned under a low.

'Hearken! hearken!' said the sheriff,
'I heard no tidings but good;
For yonder I hear Sir Guy's horn
  blow,
For he hath slain Robin Hood.'

'For yonder I hear Sir Guy's horn
  blow,
It blows so well in tide,
For yonder comes that wighty
  yeoman,
Clad in his capul-hide.

'Come hither, thou good Sir Guy,
Ask of me what thou wilt have':
'I'll none of thy gold,' says Robin
  Hood,
'Nor I'll none of it have.'

'But now I have slain the master,' he
  said,
'Let me go strike the knave;
This is all the reward I ask,
Nor no other will I have.'

'Thou art a madman,' said the sheriff,
'Thou shouldest have had a knight's
  fee;
Seeing thy asking hath been so bad,
Well granted it shall be.'

But Little John heard his master
  speak,
Well he knew that was his steven;
'Now shall I be loosed,' quoth Little
  John,
'With Christ's might in heaven.'

But Robin he hied him towards Little
  John,
He thought he would loose him belive;
The sheriff and all his company
Fast after him did drive.

'Stand aback! stand aback!' said
  Robin;
'Why draw you me so near?
It was never the use in our country
One's shrift another should hear.'

But Robin pulled forth an Irish knife,
And loosed John hand and foot,
And gave him Sir Guy's bow in his
  hand,
And bade it be his boot.

But John took Guy's bow in his hand
(His arrows were rawsty by the root);
The sheriff saw Little John draw a
  bow
And fettle him to shoot.

Towards his house in Nottingham
He fled full fast away,
And so did all his company,
Not one behind did stay.

But he could neither so fast go,
Nor away so fast run,
But Little John, with an arrow broad,
Did cleave his heart in twain.

Robin Hood's Death

'I will never eat nor drink,' Robin
   Hood said,
'Nor meat will do me no good,
Till I have been at merry Churchlees,
My veins for to let blood.'

'That I rede not,' said Will Scarlett,
'Master, by the assent of me,
Without half a hundred of your best
   bowmen
You take to go with ye.

'For there a good yeoman doth abide,
Will be sure to quarrel with thee,
And if thou have need of us, master,

'And thou be fear'd, thou William
   Scarlett,
At home I rede thee be.'
'And you be wroth, my dear master,
You shall never hear more of me.'

For there shall no man with me go,
Nor man with me ride,
And Little John shall be my man,
And bear my benbow by my side.'

'You'st bear your bow, master, yourself,
And shoot for a penny with me.'
'To that I do assent,' Robin Hood said,
'And so, John, let it be.'

They two bold children shotten together,
All day theirself in rank,
Until they came to black water,
And over it laid a plank.

Upon it there kneeled an old woman,
Was banning Robin Hood,
'Why dost thou ban Robin Hood?'
   said Robin,
Knowst thou of him no good?

...

To give to Robin Hood;
We weepen for his dear body,
That this day must be let blood.'

'The dame prior is my aunt's daughter,
And nigh unto my kin;
I know she would me no harm this day,
For all the world to win.'

Forth then shotten these children two,
And they did never lin,
Until they came to merry Churchlees,
To merry Churchlees within.

And when they came to merry Churchlees,
They knocked upon a pin;
Up then rose dame prioress,
And let good Robin in.

Then Robin gave to dame prioress
Twenty pound in gold,
And bade her spend while that would
   last,
And she should have more when she wold.

And down then came dame prioress,
Down she came in that ilk,
With a pair of blood-irons in her hands,
Were wrapped all in silk.

'Set a chafing-dish to the fire,' said
   dame prioress,
'And strip thou up thy sleeve!'
I hold him but an unwise man
That will no warning 'lieve.

She laid the blood-irons to Robin
   Hood's vein,
Alack, the more pity!
And pierced the vein, and let out the
   blood,
That full red was to see.

And first it bled the thick, thick blood,
And afterwards the thin,
And well then wist good Robin Hood
Treason there was within.

'What cheer, my master?' said Little
   John;
'In faith, Little John, little good;
...
...

'I have upon a gown of green,
Is cut short by my knee,
And in my hand a bright brown brand
That will well bite of thee.'

But forth then of a shot-window,
Good Robin Hood he could glide;
Red Roger, with a grounden glaive,
Thrust him through the milk-white side.

But Robin was light and nimble of foot,
And thought to abate his pride,

For between his head and his
   shoulders
He made a wound full wide.

Says, 'Lie there, lie there, Red Roger,
The dogs they must thee eat;
For I may have my housel,' he said,
'For I may both go and speak.

'Now give me mood,' Robin said to
   Little John,
'Give me mood with thy hand;
I trust to God in heaven so high
My housel will me bestand.'

'Now give me leave, give me leave,
   master,' he said,
'For Christ's love give leave to me
To set a fire within this hall,
And to burn up all Churchlee.'

'That I rede not,' said Robin Hood
   then,
'Little John, for it may not be;
If I should do any widow hurt, at my
   latter end,
God,' he said, 'would blame me;

'But take me upon thy back, Little John,
And bear me to yonder street,
And there make me a full fair grave
Of gravel and of greet.

And set my bright sword at my head,
Mine arrows at my feet,
And lay my yew-bow by my side,
My met-yard wi [...]'

Adam Bell, Clym of the Clough and William of Cloudesly

Merry it was in grene forest
Among the leves grene,
Wher that men walke both east and
    west
Wyth bowes and arrowes kene;

To ryse the dere out of theyr denne;
Suche sightes as hath ofte bene sene,
As by thre yemen of the north
    countrey,
By them it is as I meane.

The one of them hight Adam Bel,
The other Clym of the Clough,
The thyrd was William of Cloudesly,
An archer good ynough.

They were outlawed for venyson,
These thre yemen everychone;
They swore them brethren upon a
    day,
To Ingle-wood for to gone.

Now lith and lysten, gentylmen,
And that of myrthes loveth to here;
Two of them were single men,
The third had a wedded fere.

Wyllyam was the wedded man,
Muche more then was hys care:
He sayde to hys brethren upon a day,
To Carlile he would fare,

For to speke with fayre Alyce his wife,
And with hys chyldren thre:

'By my trouth,' sayde Adam Bel,
'Not by the counsell of me:

'For if ye go to Carlile, brother,
And from thys wylde wode wende,
If that the justice may you take,
Your lyfe were at an ende.'

'If that I come not to-morrowe,
    brother,
By pryme to you agayne,
Truste not els but that I am take,
Or else that I am slayne.'

He toke hys leave of hys brethren
    two,
And to Carlel he is gone;
There he knocked at his owne
    windowe

Shortlye and anone.
'Wher be you, fayre Alyce, my wyfe,
And my chyldren three?
Lyghtly let in thyne husbande,
Wyllyam of Cloudeslee.'

'Alas!' then sayde fayre Alyce,
And syghed wonderous sore,
'Thys place hath ben besette
    for you
Thys halfe yere and more.'

'Now am I here,' sayde Cloudeslee,
'I would that in I were.

Now feche us meate and drynke
  ynough,
And let us make good chere.'

She feched hym meate and drynke
  plenty,
Lyke a true wedded wyfe;
And pleased hym with that she had,
Whome she loved as her lyfe.

There lay an old wyfe in that place,
A lytle besyde the fyre,
Whych Wyllyam had found of
  cherytye
More then seven yere.

Up she rose, and walked full still,
Evel mote shee spede therfore!
For she had not set no fote
  on ground
In seven yere before.

She went unto the justice hall,
As fast as she could hye:
'Thys night is come unto this town
Wyllyam of Cloudesle.'

Thereof the justice was full fayne,
And so was the shirife also:
'Thou shalt not travaile hither, dame,
  for nought,
Thy meed thou shalt have er thou go.'

They gave to her a ryght good goune,
Of scarlat it was, as I heard sayne;
She toke the gyft, and home she wente,
And couched her doune agayne.

They rysed the towne of mery Carlel,
In all the hast that they can;
And came thronging to Wyllyames
  house,
As fast as they might gone.

There they besette that good yeman
Round about on every syde:
Wyllyam hearde great noyse of folkes,
That heyther-ward they hyed.

Alyce opened a shot-windowe,
And loked all aboute,
She was ware of the justice and the
  shirife bothe,
Wyth a full great route.

'Alas! treason,' cryed Alyce,
'Ever wo may thou be!
Goe into my chamber, my husband,'
  she sayd,
'Swete Wyllyam of Cloudesle.'

He toke his sweard and hys bucler,
Hys bow and hys chyldren thre,
And wente into hys strongest chamber,
Where he thought surest to be.

Fayre Alyce followed him as a lover true,
With a pollaxe in her hande:
'He shall be deade that here cometh in
Thys dore, while I may stand.'

Cloudeslee bente a wel good bowe,
That was of trusty tre,
He smot the justise on the brest,
That hys arowe brest in thre.

'God's curse on his hart,' saide William,
'Thys day thy cote dyd on!
If it had ben no better then myne,
It had gone nere thy bone.'

'Yelde thee, Cloudesle,' sayd the justise,
'And thy bowe and thy arrowes the fro.'
'God's curse on hys hart,' sayd fair
    Alyce,
'That my husband councelleth so.'

'Set fyre on the house,' saide the
    sherife,
'Syth it wyll no better be,
And brenne we therin William,' he
    saide,
'Hys wyfe and chyldren thre.'

They fyred the house in many a place,
The fyre flew up on hye:
'Alas!' than cryed fayr Alice.
'I se we shall here dye.'

William openyd hys backe wyndow,
That was in hys chamber on hie,
And with sheetes let hys wyfe downe
And hys children three.

'Have here my treasure,' sayde William,
'My wyfe and my chyldren thre:
For Christes love do them no harme,
But wreke you all on me.'

Wyllyam shot so wonderous well,
Tyll hys arrowes were all go,
And the fyre so fast upon hym fell,
That hys bowstryng brent in two.

The spercles brent and fell hym on,
Good Wyllyam of Cloudesle;
But than was he a wofull man, and
    sayde,
'Thys is a cowardes death to me.

'Lever I had,' sayde Wyllyam,
'With my sworde in the route to renne,
Then here among myne enemyes wode
Thus cruelly to bren.'

He toke hys sweard and hys buckler,
And among them all he ran,
Where the people were most in prece
He smote downe many a man.

There myght no man stand hys stroke,
So fersly on them he ran:
Then they threw wyndowes and dores
    on him
And so toke that good yeman.

There they hym bounde both hand
    and fote,
And in a deepe dongeon him cast:
'Now, Cloudesle,' sayd the hye justice,
'Thou shalt be hanged in hast.'

'One vow shal I make,' sayde the
    sherife,
'A payre of new gallowes shal I for
    thee make;
And all the gates of Carlile shal be
    shutte:
There shall no man come in therat.

'Then shall not helpe Clym of the
   Cloughe,
Nor yet Adam Bell,
Though they came with a thousand mo,
Nor all the devels in hell.'

Early in the mornyng the justice uprose,
To the gates fast gan he gon,
And commaunded to be shut full close
Lightile everychone.

Then went he to the markett place,
As fast as he coulde hye;
A payre of new gallowes there dyd he
   up set,
Besyde the pyllorye.

A lytle boy stood them among,
And asked what meaned that gallow-tre?
They sayde, 'To hange a good yeman,
Called Wyllyam of Cloudesle.'

That lytle boye was the towne
   swyne-heard,
And kept fayre Alyce swyne;
Full oft he had seene Cloudesle in the
   wodde,
And geven hym there to dyne.

He went out of a crevis in the wall,
And lightly to the woode dyd gone;
There met he with these wight yonge men
Shortly and anone.

'Alas!' then sayde that lytle boye,
'Ye tary here all too longe;

Cloudeslee is taken, and dampned to
   death,
All readye for to honge.'

'Alas!' then sayd good Adam Bell,
'That ever we see thys daye!
He might here with us have dwelled,
So ofte as we dyd him praye.

'He myght have taryed in grene foreste,
Under the shadowes sheene,
And have kepte both hym and us in
   reste,
Out of trouble and teene.'

Adam bent a ryght good bow,
A great hart sone had he slayne:
'Take that, chylde,' he sayde, 'to thy
   dynner,
And bryng me myne arrowe agayne.'

'Now go we hence,' sayed these wight
   yong men,
'Tarry we no longer here;
We shall hym borowe, by God's grace,
Though we buy itt full dere.'

To Caerlel wente these good yemen,
In a mery mornyng of Maye.
Here is a fyt of Cloudesly,
And another is for to saye.

And when they came to mery Caerlell,
In a fayre mornyng-tyde,
They founde the gates shut them
   untyll
Round about on every syde.

'Alas!' than sayd good Adam Bell,
'That ever we were made men!
These gates be shut so wonderly well,
That we may not come herein.'

Than spake Clym of the Clough,
'Wyth a wyle we wyl us in bryng;
Let us saye we be messengers,
Streyght comen from our king.'

Adam said, 'I have a letter written
    wele,
Now let us wysely werke,
We wyl saye we have the kynges seale;
I holde the porter no clerke.'

Than Adam Bell bete on the gate
With strokes great and stronge:
The porter herde suche a noyse therat,
And to the gate faste he thronge.

'Who is there now,' sayde the porter,
'That maketh all this knockinge?'
'We be two messengers,' sayd Clim of
    the Clough,
'Be comen streyght from our kyng.'

'We have a letter,' sayd Adam Bell,
'To the justice we must it bryng;
Let us in our message to do,
That we were agayne to our kyng.'

'Here commeth no man in,' sayd the
    porter,
'By hym that dyed on a tre,
Tyll a false thefe be hanged
Called Wyllyam of Cloudesle.'

Than spake that good yeman Clym of
    the Clough,
And swore by Mary fre,
'If that we stande long wythout,
Lyke a thefe hanged shalt thou be.

'Lo! here we have got the kynges
    seale:
What, lordane, art thou wode?'
The porter had wende it had ben so,
And lyghtly dyd off hys hode.

'Welcome be my lordes seale,' saide he;
'For that ye shall come in.'
He opened the gate right shortly:
An evyl openyng for him!

'Now we are in,' sayde Adam Bell,
'Therof we are full faine;
But Christ knoweth, that harowed
    hell,
How we shall com out agayne.'
'Had we the keys,' said Clim of the
    Clough,
'Ryght wel than shoulde we spede,
Than might we come out wel ynough
Whan we se tyme and nede.'

They called the porter to a councell,
And wrong his necke in two,
And caste hym in a depe dongeon,
And toke the keys hym fro.

'Now am I porter,' sayd Adam Bel,
'Se, brother, the keys have we here,
The worst porter to mery Carlile
That ye had thys hondreth yere.

'Now wyll we our bowes bend,
Into the towne wyll we go,
For to delyver our dere brother,
Where he lyeth in care and wo.'

Then they bent theyr good yew
  bowes,
And loked theyr stringes were round;
The markett place of mery Carlile
They beset in that stound.

And, as they loked them besyde,
A paire of new galowes there they
  see,
And the justice with a quest of
  squyers,
That judged William hanged to be.

And Cloudesle hymselfe lay ready in
  a cart
Fast bound both fote and hand;
And a stronge rope about hys necke,
All readye for to be hangde.

The justice called to him a ladde,
Cloudesles clothes shold he have,
To take the measure of that good
  yoman,
And thereafter to make hys grave.

'I have sene as great a mervaile,' said
  Cloudesle,
'As betweyne thys and pryme,
He that maketh thys grave for me,
Hymselfe may lye therin.'

'Thou speakest proudlye,' said the justice,
'I shall hange thee with my hande.'
Full wel that herd his brethren two
There styl as they dyd stande.

Then Cloudesle cast his eyen asyde,
And saw hys brethren stande
At a corner of the market place,
With theyr good bowes bent in theyr
  hand,
Redy the justyce for to chase.

'I se good comfort,' sayd Cloudesle,
'Yet hope I well to fare,
If I might have my handes at wyll
Ryght lytel wold I care.'

Than bespake good Adam Bell
To Clym of the Clough so free,
'Brother, se ye marke the justyce wel;
Lo! yonder ye may him se:

'And at the shyrife shote I wyll
Strongly wyth an arrowe kene;
A better shote in mery Carlile
Thys seven yere was not sene.'

They loosed their arrowes both at once,
Of no man had they drede;
The one hyt the justice, the other the
  sheryfe,
That both theyr sides gan blede.

All men voyded, that them stode nye,
Whan the justice fell to the grounde,
And the sherife fell nye hym by;
Eyther had his deathes wounde.

All the citezens fast gan fle,
They durst no longer abyde:
There lyghtly they loosed Cloudeslee,
Where he with ropes lay tyde.

Wyllyam stert to an officer of the
  towne,
Hys axe out hys hand he wronge,
On eche syde he smote them downe,
Hym thought he had taryed too long.

Wyllyam sayde to hys brethren two,
'Thys daye let us lyve and die,
If ever you have nede, as I have now,
The same shall you finde by me.'

They shot so well in that tyde,
For theyr stringes were of silke ful sure,
That they kept the stretes on every
  side;
That batayle did long endure.

They fought together as brethren true,
Lyke hardy men and bolde,
Many a man to the ground they
  threw,
And made many an herte colde.

But whan their arrowes were all gon,
Men presyd on them full fast,
They drew theyr swordes than anone,
And theyr bowes from them cast.

They went lyghtlye on theyr way,
Wyth swordes and buclers round;
By that it was the myddes of the day,
They had made many a wound.

There was many an out-horne in
  Carleil blowen,
And the belles backward dyd they
  ryng,
Many a woman sayde 'Alas!'
And many theyr handes dyd wryng.

The mayre of Carlile forth com was,
And wyth hym a full great route:
These three yemen dred hym full sore,
For theyr lyves stode in doute.

The mayre came armed, a full great
  pace,
With a polaxe in hys hande;
Many a strong man wyth him was,
There in that stoure to stande.

The mayre smote at Cloudesle with
  his bil,
Hys bucler he brast in two,
Full many a yoman with great yll,
'Alas! Treason,' they cryed for wo.
'Kepe we the gates fast,' they bad,
'That these traytours therout not go.'

But al for nought was that they
  wrought,
For so fast they downe were layde,
Tyll they all thre, that so manfully
  fought,
Were gotten without at a braide.

'Have here your keys,' sayd Adam Bel,
'Myne office I here forsake,
Yf you do by my councell
A newe porter ye make.'

He threw the keys there at theyr
    heads,
And bad them evil to thryve,
And all that letteth any good yoman
To come and comfort his wyfe.

Thus be these good yomen gon to the
    wode,
As lyghtly as lefe on lynde;
They laugh and be mery in theyr
    mode,
Theyr enemyes were farr behynde.

Whan they came to Inglyswode,
Under their trysty-tre,
There they found bowes full good,
And arrowes great plente.

'So help me God,' sayd Adam Bell,
And Clym of the Clough so fre,
'I would we were nowe in mery
    Carlile,
Before that fayre meyne.'

They set them downe, and made good
    chere,
And eate and dranke full well.
Here is a fytte of the wight yongemen:
And another I shall you tell.

As they sat in Inglyswood,
Under theyr trysty-tre,
They thought they herd a woman
    wepe,
But her they myght not se.

Sore syghed there fayre Alyce, and
    sayd,
'Alas, that ever I see thys day!
For nowe is my dere husband slayne:
Alas! and wel-a-way!

'Myght I have spoken wyth hys dere
    brethren,
With eyther of them twayne,
To show to them what him befell,
My hart were out of payne.'

Cloudesle walked a lytle beside,
And looked under the grene wood
    lynde,
He was ware of his wife and chyldren
    three,
Full wo in herte and mynde.

'Welcome, wyfe,' than sayde Wyllyam,
'Unto this trysty-tre:
I had wende yesterday, by swete saynt
    John,
Thou sholde me never have se.'

'Now well is me,' she sayd, 'that ye
    be here,
My harte is out of wo.'
'Dame,' he sayde, 'be mery and glad,
And thanke my brethren two.'

'Herof to speake,' said Adam Bell,
'I-wis it is no bote:
The meate, that we must supp withall,
It runneth yet fast on fote.'

Then went they downe into a launde,
These noble archares all thre;
Eche of them slew a hart of grece,
The best they cold there se.

'Have here the best, Alyce my wyfe,'
Sayde Wyllyam of Cloudeslye,
'By cause ye so boldly stode me by
Whan I was slayne full nye.'

Than went they to theyr suppere
Wyth suche meate as they had;
And thanked God of ther fortune:
They were both mery and glad.

And when they had supped well,
Certayne withouten lease,
Cloudesle sayd, 'We wyll to our kyng,
To get us a charter of peace.

'Alyce shal be at sojournyng
In a nunnery here besyde;
My two sonnes shall wyth her go,
And there they shall abyde.

'Myne eldest son shall go wyth me;
For hym have I no care:
And he shall bring you worde agayn,
How that we do fare.'

Thus be these wight men to London
    gone,
As fast as they maye hye,
Tyll they came to the kynges pallace;
There they woulde nedes be.

And whan they came to the kynges
    courte,
Unto the pallace gate,
Of no man wold they aske leave,
But boldly went in therat.

They presyd prestly into the hall,
Of no man had they dreade:
The porter came after, and dyd them
    calle,
And with them began to chyde.

The usher sayde, 'Yemen, what wold
    ye have?
I pray you tell to me:
You myght thus make offycers shent:
Good syrs, of whence be ye?'

'Syr, we be outlawes of the forest
Certayne withouten lease;
And hyther we be come to our kyng,
To get us a charter of peace.'

And whan they came before the kyng,
As it was the lawe of the lande,
They kneled downe without lettyng,
And eche held up his hand.

They sayed, 'Lord, we beseche you here,
That ye wyll graunt us grace;
For we have slayne your fat falow dere
In many a sondry place.'

'What is your names,' than said our king,
'Anone that you tell me?'

They sayd, 'Adam Bell, Clim of the
  Clough,
And Wyllyam of Cloudesle.'

'Be ye those theves,' than sayd our
  kyng,
'That men have tolde of to me?
Here to God I make a vowe,
Ye shal be hanged al thre.

'Ye shal be dead without mercy,
As I am kynge of this lande.'
He commanded his officers
  everichone,
Fast on them to lay hande.

There they toke these good yemen,
And arested them al thre:
'So may I thryve,' sayd Adam Bell,
'Thys game lyketh not me.

'But, good lorde, we beseche you now,
That ye wyll graunt us grace,
Insomuche as we be to you comen,
Or elles that we may fro you passe,

'With such weapons, as we have here,
Tyll we be out of your place;
And yf we lyve this hondred yere,
We wyll aske you no grace.'

'Ye speake proudly,' sayd the kynge;
'Ye shall be hanged all thre.'
'That were great pitye,' sayd the
  quene,
'If any grace myght be.

'My lorde, whan I came fyrst into this
  lande
To be your wedded wyfe,
The fyrst boone that I would aske,
Ye would graunt me belyfe:

'And I asked you never none tyll now;
Therefore, good lorde, graunt it me.'
'Now aske it, madam,' sayd the kynge,
'And graunted shal it be.'

'Than, good lord, I you beseche,
These yemen graunt you me.'
'Madame, ye myght have asked a boone,
That shuld have been worth them thre.

'Ye myght have asked towres, and
  townes,
Parkes and forestes plentie.'
'None soe pleasant to my pay,' shee
  sayd;
'Nor none so lefe to me.'

'Madame, sith it is your desyre,
Your askyng graunted shal be;
But I had lever have given you
Good market townes thre.'

The quene was a glad woman,
And sayde, 'Lord, gramarcy;
I dare undertake for them,
That true men shal they be.

'But, good lord, speke som mery word,
That comfort they may se.'
'I graunt you grace,' than sayd our kyng;
'Washe, felos, and to meate go ye.'

They had not setten but a whyle
Certayne without lesynge,
There came messengers out of the north
With letters to our kyng.

And whan they came before the
   kynge,
They kneled downe upon theyr kne;
And sayd, 'Lord, your officers grete
   you well,
Of Carlile in the north cuntre.'

'How fareth my justice,' sayd the kyng,
'And my sherife also?'
'Syr, they be slayne, without lesynge,
And many an officer mo.'

'Who hath them slayne?' sayd the kyng;
'Anone thou tell me.'
'Adam Bell, and Clim of the Clough,
And Wyllyam of Cloudesle.'

'Alas for rewth!' than said our kynge:
'My hart is wonderous sore;
I had lever than a thousande pounde,
I had knowne of thys before;

'For I have y-graunted them grace,
And that forthynketh me:
But had I knowne all thys before,
They had been hanged all thre.'

The kyng opened the letter anone,
Himselfe he red it tho,
And founde how these thre outlawes
   had slain
Thre hundred men and mo:

Fyrst the justice, and the sheryfe,
And the mayre of Carlile towne;
Of all the constables and catchipolles
Alyve were left not one:

The baylyes, and the bedyls both,
And the sergeauntes of the law,
And forty fosters of the fe,
These outlawes had y-slaw:

And broke his parks, and slayne his
   dere;
Over all they chose the best;
So perelous out-lawes as they were
Walked not by easte nor west.

When the kynge this letter had red,
In hys harte he syghed sore:
'Take up the table,' anone he bad,
'For I may eat no more.'

The kyng called his best archars
To the buttes wyth hym to go:
'I wyll se these felowes shote,' he sayd,
'That in the north have wrought this
   wo.'

The kynges bowmen buske them blyve.
And the quenes archers also;
So dyd these thre wyght yemen;
With them they thought to go.

There twyse or thryse they shote about
For to assay theyr hande;
There was no shote these thre yemen
   shot.
That any prycke myght them stand.

Then spake Wyllyam of Cloudesle;
'By God that for me dyed,
I hold hym never no good archar,
That shoteth at buttes so wyde.'

'Whereat?' than sayd our king,
'I pray thee tell me.'
'At suche a but, syr,' he sayd.
'As men use in my countree.'

Wyllyam wente into a fyeld,
And his two brethren with him:
There they set up two hasell roddes
Twenty score paces betwene.

'I hold him an archar,' said Cloudesle,
'That yonder wande cleveth in two.'
'Here is none suche,' sayd the kyng,
'Nor none that can so do.'

'I shall assaye, syr,' sayd Cloudesle,
'Or that I farther go.'
Cloudesly with a bearyng arowe
Clave the wand in two.

'Thou art the best archer,' then said
    the king,
'Forsothe that ever I se.'
'And yet for your love,' sayd
    Wyllyam,
'I wyll do more maystry.

'I have a sonne is seven yere olde,
He is to me full deare;
I wyll hym tye to a stake;
All shall se, that be here;

'And lay an apple upon hys head,
And go syxe score paces hym fro,
And I my selfe with a brode arow
Shall cleve the apple in two.'

'Now haste thee then sayd the kyng,
'By hym that dyed on a tre;
But yf thou do not as thou hest sayde,
Hanged shalt thou be.

'And [if] thou touche his head or
    gowne,
In syght that men may se,
By all the sayntes that be in heaven,
I shall hange you all thre.'

'That I have promised,' said William,
'I wyll it never forsake.'
And there even before the kynge
In the earth he drove a stake:

And bound therto his eldest sonne,
And bad hym stand styll thereat;
And turned the childes face fro him,
Because he should not stert.

An apple upon his head he set,
And then his bowe he bent:
Syxe score paces they were outmet,
And thether Cloudesle went.

There he drew out fayre brode
    arrowe,
Hys bowe was great and longe,
He set that arrowe in his bowe,
That was both styffe and stronge.

He prayed the people, that wer there,
That they wold still stand,
For he that shoteth for such a wager
Behoveth a stedfast hand.

Muche people prayed for Cloudesle,
That his lyfe saved myght be,
And whan he made hym redy to shote,
There was many a weeping eye.

Thus Cloudesle clefte the apple in two,
That many a man it se:
'Over Gods forbode,' sayde the kinge,
'That thou sholdest shote at me.

'I geve thee eightene pence a day,
And my bowe shalt thou bere,
And over all the north countre
I make the chyfe rydere.'

'And I give thee twelve pence a day,'
said the quene,
'By God and by my fay;
Come feche thy payment whan thou
wylt,
No man shall say thee nay.'

'Wyllyam, I make thee gentleman
Of clothyng and of fe:
And thy two brethren yemen of my
chambre,
For they are so semely to see.

'Your sonne, for he is tendre of age,
Of my wyne-seller shall he be;
And whan he commeth to mannes
state,
Better avaunced shall he be.'

Robin Hood and the Beggar

Lyth and listen, gentlemen,
That be of high born blood,
I'll tell you of a brave booting
That befell Robin Hood.

Robin Hood upon a day,
He went forth him alone.
And as he came from Barnsdale
Into fair evening,

He met a beggar on the way.
Who sturdily could gang;
He had a pike-staff in his hand
That was both stark and Strang;

A clouted clock about him was,
That held him frae the cold,
The thinnest bit of it, I guess.
Was more than twenty fold.

His meal poke hang about his neck,
Into a leathern whang.
Well fasten'd to a broad bucle,
That was both stark and Strang.

He had three hats upon his head,
Together sticked fast.
He car'd neither for wind nor wet,
In lands where'er he past.

Good Robin cast him in the way,
To see what he might be,
If any beggar had mony,
He thought some part had he.

Tarry, tarry, good Robin says,
Tarry, and speak with me.
He heard him as he heard him not,
And fast on his way can hy.

'Tis be not so, says [good] Robin,
Nay, thou must tarry stil
By my troth, said the bold beggir,
Of that I have no will.

It is far to my lodging house.
And it is growing late.
If they have supt e'er I come in
I will look wondrous blate.

Now, by my truth, says good Robin,
I see well by thy fare,
If thou shares well to thy supper,

Of mine thou dost not care.
Who wants my dinner all this day
And wots not where to ly,
And would I to the tavern go,
I want money to buy.

Sir, you must lend me some mony
Till we meet again.
The beggar answer'd cankardly,
I have no money to lend:

Thou art a young man as I,
And seems to be as sweer;

If thou fast till thou get from me,
Thou shalt eat none this year.

Now, by my truth, says [good] Robin,
Since we are assembled so,
If thou hast but a small farthing,
I'll have it e'er thou go.

Come, lay down thy clouted cloak,
And do no longer stand,
And loose the strings of all thy pokes,
I'll ripe them with my hand.

And now to thee I make a vow,
If thou make any din,
I shall see a broad arrow,
Can pierce a beggar's skin.

The beggar smil'd, and answer made.
Far better let me be;
Think not that I will be afraid.
For thy nip crooked tree;

Or that I fear thee any whit,
For thy cum nips of sticks,
I know no use for them so meet
As to be puding-pricks.

Here I defy thee to do me ill,
For all thy boisterous fair,
Thou's get nothing from me but ill,
Would'st thou seek evermair.

Good Robin bent his noble bow,
He was an angery man,
And in it set a broad arrow;
Lo e'er 'twas drawn a span.

The beggar, with his noble tree,
Reach'd him so round a rout,
That his bow and his broad arr6w
In flinders flew about.

Good Robin bound him to his brand,
But that prov'd likewise vain,
The beggar lighted on his hand
With his pike-staff again:

[I] wot he might not draw a sword
For forty days and main
Good Robin could not speak a word.
His heart was ne'er so sair.

He could not fight, he could not flee,
He wist not what to do;
The beggar with his noble tree
Laid lusty slaps him to.

He paid good Robin back and side,
And baist him up and down.
And with his pyke-staff laid on loud.
Till he fell in a swoon.

Stand up, man, the beggar said,
'Tis shame to go to rest;
Stay till thou get thy money told,
I think it were the best:

And syne go to the tavern house,
And buy both wine and ale;
Hereat thy friends will crack full crouse,
Thou hast been at the dale.

Good Robin answer'd ne'er a word.
But lay still as a stane;

His cheeks were pale as any clay.
And closed were his een.

The beggar thought him dead but
fail.
And boldly bound his way. —
I would ye had been at the dale.
And gotten part of the play.

THE SECOND PART

Now three of Robin's men, by chance,
Came walking by the way,
And found their master in a trance,
On ground where that he lay.

Up have they taken good Robin,
Making a piteous bear.
Yet saw they no man there at whom
They might the matter spear.

They looked him all round about,
But wound on him saw nane,
Yet at his mouth came bocking out
The blood of a good vain.

Cold water they have gotten syne,
And cast unto his face;
Then he began to hitch his ear.
And speak within short space.

Tell us, dear master, said his men,
How with you stands the case.
Good Robin sigh'd e'er he began
To tell of his disgrace.

I have been watchman in this wood
Near hand this twenty year,

Yet I was never so hard bestead
As ye have found me here;

A beggar with a clouted clock,
Of whom I fear'd no ill
Hath with his pyke-staff cla'd my
    back,
I fear 'twill never be well.

See, where he goes o'er yon hill,
With hat upon his head;
If e'er ye lov'd your master well,
Go now revenge this deed;

And bring him back again to me,
If it lie in your might.
That I may see, before I die,
Him punish'd in my sight:

And if you may not bring him back,
Let him not go loose on;
For to us all it were great shame
If he escape again,

One of us shall with you remain,
Because you're ill at ease.
The other two shall bring him back,
To use him as you please.

Now, by my truth, says good Robin,
I true there's enough said;
And he get scouth to wield his tree,
I fear you'll both be paid.

Be not fear'd, our master,
That we two can be dung

With any bluter base beggkr,
That has nought but a rung.

His staff shall stand him in no stead,
That you shall shortly see,
But back again he shall be led,

And fast bound shall he be,
To see if ye will have him slain,
Or hanged on a tree.
But cast you sliely in his way.

Before he be aware.
And on his pyke-staff first hands lay,
Ye'll speed the better far.
Now leave we Robin with this man.

Again to play the child,
And learn himself to stand and gang
By halds, for all his eild.
Now pass we to the bold beggkr.

That raked o'er the hill,
Then he had done no ill.
And they have taken another way,
Was nearer by miles three.

They stoutly ran with all their might,
Spared neither dub nor mire,
They started at neither how nor height,
No travel made them tire,

Till they before the beggar wan,
And cast them in his way;
A little wood lay in a glen,
And there they both did stay;

They stood up closely by a tree.
In each side of the gate,
Untill the beggar came them nigh.
That thought of no such late:

And as he was betwixt them past.
They leapt upon him baith;
The one his pyke staff gripped fast,
They feared for its skaith.

The other he held in his sight
A drawen durk to his breast,
And said. False carel, quit thy staff.
Or I shall be thy priest.

His pyke-staflf they have taken him
  frae,
And stuck it in the green,
He was full loath to let it gae,
An better might it been.

The beggar was the feardest man
Of any that e'er might be,
To win away no way he can,
Nor help him with his tree.

Nor wist he wherefore he was ta'en,
Nor how many was there;
He thought his life days had been
  gane,
He grew into dispair.

Grant me my life, the beggar said,
For him that dy'd on the tree.
And hold away that ugly knife,
Or else for fear I'll die.

I griev'd you never in all my life,
Neither by late or air,
You have great sin if you would slay
A silly poor beggkr.

Thou lies, false lown, they said again.
For all that may be sworn;
Thou hast near slain the gentlest man
Of one that e'er was born;

And back again thou shall be led,
And fast bound shalt thou be,
To see if he will have thee slain,
Or hanged on a tree.

The beggar then thought all was
  wrong,
They were set for his wrack,
He saw nothing appearing then
But ill upon warse back.

Were he out of their hands, he
  thought,
And had again his tree,
He should not be led back for nought,
With such as he did see.

Then he bethought him on a wile.
If it could take effect.
How he might the young men beguile,
And give them a begeck.

Thus to do them shame for ill
His beastly breast was bent.
He found the wind blew something
  shrill,
To further his intent.

He said. Brave gentlemen, be good.
And let a poor man be:
When ye have taken a beggar's blood.
It helps you not a flee.

It was but in my own defence,
If he has gotten skaith;
But I will make a recompence
Is better for you baith.

If ye will set me fair and free,
And do me no more dear,
An hundred pounds I will you give,
And much more odd silvr,

That I have gather'd this many years,
Under this clouted cloak,
And hid up wonder privately,
In bottom of my poke.

The young men to the council yeed,
And let the beggar gae;
They wist full well he had no speed
From them to run away.

They thought they would the money
　take,
Come after what so may;
And yet they would not take him
　back,
But in that place him slay.

By that good Robin would not know
That they had gotten coin,
It would content him [well] to sliow
That there they had him slain,

They said, False carel, soon have
　done,
And tell forth thy monfey.
For the ill turn that thou hast done
It's but a simple plee.

And yet we will not have thee back,
Come after what so may.
If thou will do that which thou spak,
And make us present pay.

Then he loosed his clouted clock,
And spread it on the ground.
And thereon lay he many a poke,
Betwixt them and the wind.

He took a great bag from his hals,
I was near full of meal.
Two pecks in it at least there was,
And more, I wot full well.

Upon this cloak he set it down,
The mouth he opened wide,
To turn the same he made him bown,
The young men ready spy'd;

In every hand he took a nook
Of that great leathren mail,
And with a fling the meal he shook
Into their face all hail:

Wherewith he blinded them so close,
A stime they could not see;
And then in heart he did rejoice,
And clap'd his lusty tree.

He thought if he had done them
    wrong,
In mealing of their cloaths,
For to strike off the meal again
With his pyke-staff he goes.

E'er any of them could red their een,
Or a glimmring might see,
like one of them a dozen had.
Well laid on with his tree.

The young men were right swift of
    foot,
And boldly bound away.
The beggar could them no more hit.
For all the haste he may.

What's all this haste ? the beggar said,
May not you tarry still,
Untill your money be received ?
I'll pay you with good will.

The shaking of my pokes, I fear,
Hath blown into your een;
But I have a good pyke-staff here
Can ripe them out full clean.

The young men answered never a word,
They were dum as a stane;
In the thick wood the beggar fled,
E'er they riped their een:

And syne the night became so late,
To seek him was in vain:
But judge ye if they looked blate
When they cam home again.

Good Robin speer'd how they had
    sped.
They answered him, full ill.
That can not be, good Robin says,
Ye have been at the mill.

The mill it is a meat-rife part,
They may lick what they please,
Most like ye have been at the art.
Who would look at your claiths.

They hang'd their heads, they drooped
    down,
A word they could not speak.
Robin said, Because I fell a-sound,
I think ye'd do the like.

Tell on the matter, less or more,
And tell me what and how
Ye have done with the bold beggkr
I sent you for right now.

And when they told him to an end,
As i have said before,
How that the beggar did them blind.
What mister presses more ?

...

...

And how in the thick woods he fled,
E'er they a stime could see;

And how they scarcely could win home,
Their bones were baste so sore;
Good Robin crd, Fy! Out ! For shame !
We're sham'd for evermore.

Altho good Robin would full fain
Of his wrath revenged be,
He smil'd to see his merry young men
Had gotten a taste of the tree.

A True Tale of Robin Hood by Martin Parker

Robert earl of Huntington
Lies under this little stone,
No archer was like him so good;
His wildness named him Robin Hood;

Full thirteen years, and something
   more,
These northern parts he vexed sore;
Such outlaws as he and his men
May England never know again.

Both gentlemen, and yeomen bold,
Or whatsoever you are.
To have a stately story told
Attention now prepare:

It is a tale of Robin Hood,
Which i to you will tell;
Which, being rightly understood,
I know will please you well.

This Robin (so much talked on)
Was once a man of fame.
Instiled earl of Huntington,
Lord Robin Hood by name.

In courtship and magnificence
His carriage won him praise.
And greater favour with his prince
Than any in those days.

In bounteous liberality
He too much did excell,
And loved men of quality
More than exceeding well.

His great revenues all he sold
For wine and costly chear;
He kept three hundred
   bow-men bold,
He shooting lov'd so dear.

No archer living in his time
With him might well compare;
He practis'd all his youthful prime
That exercise most rare.

At last, by his profuse expence,
He had consum'd his wealth;
And, being outlaw'd by his prince,
In woods he liv'd by stealth.

The abbot of Saint Maries rich,
To whom he money ought,
His hatred to the earl was such
That he his downfal wrought.

So being outlaw'd (as 'tis told)
He with a crew went forth
Of lusty cutters stout and bold.
And robbed in the North.

Among the rest one Little John,
A yeoman bold and free,
Who could (if it stood him upon)
With ease encounter three.

One hundred men in all he got,
With whom (the story says)
Three hundred common men durst
 not
Hold combat any waies.

They Yorkshire woods frequented
 much,
And Lancashire also.
Wherein their practises were such
That they wrought muckle woe.

None rich durst travel to and fro,
Though ne'r so strongly arm'd,
But by these thieves (so strong in show)
They still were rob'd and harm'd.

His chiefest spight to the clergy was,
That liv'd in monstrous pride:
No one of them he would let pass
Along the highway side,

But first they must to dinner go,
And afterwards to shrift:
Full many a one he served so,
Thus while he liv'd by theft.

No monks nor fryers he would let go
Without paying their fees:
If they thought much to be used so.
Their stones he made them lese.

For such as they the country fi'd
With bastards in those days:
Which to prevent, these sparks did
 geld
All that came in their ways.

But Robin Hood so gentle was,
And bore so brave a mind,
If any in distress did pass.
To them he was so kind,

That he would give and lend to them.
To help them in their need;
This made all poor men pray for
 him,
And wish he well might speed.

The widow and the fatherless
He would send means unto;
And those whom famine did oppress
Found him a friendly foe.

Nor would he do a woman wrong,
But see her safe convey'd:
He would protect with power strong
All those who crav'd his aid.

The abbot of Saint Maries then,
Who him undid before,
Was riding with two hundred men,
And gold and silver store:

But Robin Hood upon him set.
With his couragious sparks.
And all the coyn perforce did get.
Which was twelve thousand marks.

He bound the abbot to a tree,
And would not let him pass.
Before that to his men and he
His lordship had said mass:

Which being done, upon his horse
He set him fast astride.
And with his face towkrds his ass
He forced him to ride.

His men were forced to be his guide,
For he rode backward home:
The abbot, being thus villify'd.
Did sorely chafe and fume.

Thus Robin Hood did vindicate
His former wrongs receiv'd:
For 'twas this covetous prelate
That him of land bereav'd.

The abbot he rode to the king,
With all the haste he could;
And to his grace he every thing
Exactly did unfold:

And said that if no course
    were ta'n,
By force or stratagem,
To take this rebel and his train,
No man should pass for them.

The king protested by and by
Unto the abbot then,
That Robin Hood with speed should
    dye.
With all his merry men.

But e're the king did any send,
He did another feat,
Which did his grace much more
    offend,
The fact indeed was great:

For in a short time after that
The kings receivers went
Towards London with the coyn they
    got
For's highness northern rent:
Bold Robin Hood and Little John,
With the rest of their train,
Not dreading law, set them upon.
And did their gold obtain.

The king much moved at the same,
And the abbots talk also,
In this his anger did proclaim,
And sent word to and fro,

That whosoever alive or dead
Could bring bold Robin Hood,
Should have one thousand marks well
    paid
In gold and silver good.

This promise of the king did make
Full many yeomen bold
Attempt stout Robin Hood to take
With all the force they could.

But still when any came to him
Within the gay green wood.
He entertainment gave to them
With venison fat and good;

And shew'd to them such martial sport
With his long bow and arrow.
That they of him did give report,
How that it was great sorow

That such a worthy man as he
Should thus be put to shift,
Being a late lord of high degree,
Of living quite bereft.

The king to take him more and more
Sent men of mickle might;
But he and his still beat them sore,
And conquered them in fight:

Or else with love and courtesie,
To him he won their hearts.
Thus still he liv'd by robbery
Throughout the northern parts;

And all the country stood in dread
Of Robin Hood and's men:
For stouter lads ne'r liv'd by bread
In those days, nor since then.

The abbot, which before i nam'd,
Sought all the means he could
To have by force this rebel ta'n,
And his adherents bold.

Therefore he arm'd five hundred men,
With furniture compleat;
But the outlaws slew half of them.
And made the rest retreat,

The long bow and the arrow keen
They were so us'd unto

That still he kept the forest green
In spight o' th' proudest foe.

Twelve of the abbot's men he took,
Who came to have him ta'n,
When all the rest the field forsook,
These he did entertain

With banqueting and merriment,
And, having us'd them well,
He to their lord them safely sent,
And will'd them him to tell.

That if he would be pleas'd at last
To beg of our good king,
That he might pardon what was past,
And him to favour bring,

He would surrender back again
The mony which before
Was taken by him and his men
From him and many more.

Poor men might safely pass by him,
And some that way would chuse.
For well they knew that to help them
He evermore did use.

But where he knew a miser rich
That did the poor oppress,
To feel his coyn his hands did itch,
He'd have it, more or less:

And sometimes, when the high-way fail'd,
Then he his courage rouzes,
He and his men have oft assaild
Such rich men in their houses:

So that, through dread of Robin then,
And his adventurous crew,
The misers kept great store of men,
Which else maintain'd but few.

King Richard, of that name the first,
Simamed Ceur de Lyon,
Went to defeat the Pagans curst,
Who kept the coasts of Sion.

The bishop of Ely, chancellor.
Was left a vice-roy here.
Who, like a potent emperor.
Did proudly domineer.

Our chronicles of him report,
That commonly he rode
With a thousand horse from court to
    court,
Where he would make abode.

He, riding down towards the north,
With his aforesaid train,
Robin and his men did issue forth,
Them all to entertain;

And with the gallant gray-goose wing
They shew'd to them such play
That made their horses kick and
    fling,
And down their riders lay,

Full glad and fain the bishop was,
For all his thousand men,
So seek what means he could to pass
From out of Robin's ken.

Two hundred of his men were kill'd,
And fourscore horses good.
Thirty, who did as captives yield,
Were carried to the green wood;

Which afterwards were ransomed.
For twenty marks a man:
The rest set spurs to horse and fled
To the town of Warrington.

The bishop, sore inraged, then
Did, in king Richards name.
Muster up a power of northern men,
These outlaws bold to tame.

But Robin with his courtesie
So won the meaner sort,
That they were loath on him to try
What rigour did import.

So that bold Robin and his train
Did live unhurt of them,
Until king Richard came again
From fair Jerusalem:

And then the talk of Robin Hood
His royal ears did fill;
His grace admir'd that i' th' green
    wood
He was continued still.

So that the country far and near
Did give him great applause;
For none of them need stand in fear,
But such as broke the laws.

He wished well unto the king.
And prayed still for his health,
And never practis'd any thing
Against the common-wealth.

Only, because he was undone
By th' cruel clergy then,
All means that he could think upon
To vex such kind of men,

He enterpriz'd with hateful spleen;
For which he was to blame,
For fault of some to wreak his teen
On all that by him came.

With wealth that he by roguery got
Eight alms-houses he built,
Thinking thereby to purge the blot
Of blood which he had spilt.

Such was their blind devotion then,
Depending on their works;
Which if 'twere true, we Christian men
Inferiour were to Turks.

But, to speak true of Robin Hood,
And wrong him not a jot.
He never would shed any mans blood
That him invaded not.

Nor would he injure husbandmen,
That toil at cart and plough;
For well he knew wer't not for them
To live no man knew how.

The king in person, with some lords,
To Nottingham did ride.

To try what strength and skill affords
To crush this outlaws pride.

And, as he once before had done,
He did again proclaim,
That whosoever would take upon
To bring to Nottingham,

Or any place within the land,
Rebellious Robin Hood,
Should be preferr'd in place to stand
With those of noble blood.

When Robin Hood heard of the same,
Within a little space.
Into the town of Nottingham
A letter to his grace

He shot upon an arrow head,
One evening cunningly;
Which was brought to the king, and read
Before his majesty.

The tenour of this letter was
That Robin would submit.
And be true liegeman to his grace
In any thing that's fit,

So that his highness would forgive
Him and his merry men all;
If not, he must i' th' green wood live.
And take what chance did fall

The king would feign have pardoned him,
But that some lords did say,
This president will much condemn
Your grace another day.

While that the king and lords did stay
Debating on this thing,
Some of these outlaws fled away
Unto the Scottish king.

For they suppos'd, if he were ta'n
Or to the king did yield,
By th' commons all the rest of 's train
Full quickly would be quell'd.

Of more than full an hundred men,
But forty tarried still,
Who were resolv'd to stick to him,
Let Fortune work her will.

If none had fled, all for his sake
Had got their pardon free;
The king to favour meant to take
His merry men and he.

But e're the pardon to him came
This famous archer dy'd:
His death and manner of the same
Iie presently describe.

For, being vext to think upon
His followers revolt,
In melancholy passibn
He did recount his fault.

Perfidious traytors! said he then.
In all your dangers past
Have i you guarded as my men,
To leave me thus at last!

This sad perplexity did cause
A feaver, as some say.

Which him unto confusion draws,
Though by a stranger way.

This deadly danger to prevent.
He hie'd him with all speed
Unto a nunnery, with intent
For his healths-sake to bleed.

A faithless fryer did pretend
In love to let him blood.
But he by falshood wrought the end
Of famous Robin Hood.

The fryer, as some say, did this
To vindicate the wrong
Which to the clergy he and his
Had done by power strong.

Thus dyed he by treachery,
That could not die by force;
Had he liv'd longer, certainly
King Richard, in remorse.

Had unto favour him receiv'd,
His brave men elevated:
'Tis pitty he was of life bereav'd
By one which he so hated.

A treacherous leach this fryer was,
To let him bleed to death;
And Robin was, methinks, an ass
To trust him with his breath.

His corps the prioress of the place,
The next day that he did.
Caused to be buried, in mean case,
Close by the highway side.

And over him she caused a stone
To be fixt on the ground.
An epitaph was set thereon,
Wherein his name was found;

The date o' th' year and day also,
She made to be set there:
That all, who by the way did go,
 Might see it plain appear.

That such a man as Robin Hood
Was buried in that place;
And how he Hved in the
    green wood
And robbed for a space.

It seems that though the clergy he
Had put to mickle woe,
He should not quite forgotten be
Although he was their foe.

This woman, though she did him
    hate.
Yet loved his memory;
And thought it wondrous pitty that
His fame should with him dye.

This epitaph, as records tell,
Within this hundred years,
By many was discerned well.
But time all things out-wears.

His followers, when he was dead.
Were some repriev'd to grace;
The rest to foreign countries fled,
And left their native place.

Although his funeral was but mean,
This woman had in mind,
Least his fame should be buried clean
From those that came behind.

For certainly, before nor since,
No man e're understood,
Under the reign of any prince,
Of one like Robin Hood.

Full thirteen years, and something more,
These outlaws lived thus;
Feared of the rich, loved of the poor:
A thing most marvellous.

A thing impossible to us
This story seems to be;
None dares be now so venturous,
But times are chang'd we see.

We that live in these later days
Civil government.
If need be, have an hundred ways
Such outlaws to prevent.

In those days men more barbarous were,
And lived less in awe;
Now (god be thanked) people fear
More to offend the law.

No waring guns were then in use,
They dreamt of no such thing;
Our Englishmen in fight did use
The gallant gray-goose wing;

In which activity these men,
Through practise, were so good,

That in those days none equal'd them,
Especially Robin Hood.

So that, it seems, keeping in caves.
In woods and forests thick,
They'd beat a multitude with staves,
Their arrows did so prick:

And none durst neer unto them come.
Unless in courtesie;
All such he bravely would send home
With mirth and jollity:

Which courtesie won him such love,
As I before have told,
'Twas the chief cause that he did prove
More prosperous than he could.

Let us be thankful for these times
Of plenty, truth and peace;
And leave our great and horrid crimes,
Least they cause this to cease.

I know there's many feigned tales
Of Robin Hood and his crew;
But chronicles, which seldome fails.
Reports this to be true.

Let none then think this is a lye,
For, if 'twere put to th' worst.
They may the truth of all descry
In th' reign of Richard the first.

If any reader please to try,
As I direction show.
The truth of this brave history,
He'll find it true I know.

And I shall think my labour well
Bestow'd to purpose good,
When't shall be said that I did tell
True tales of Robin Hood.

Robin Hood's Birth, Breeding, Valour, and Marriage

Kind gentlemen, will you be patient
   awhile?
Ay, and then you shall hear anon
A very good ballad of bold Robin
   Hood,
And of his man brave Little John.

In Locksly town, in merry
   Nottinghamshire,
In merry sweet Locksly town,
There bold Robin Hood he was born
   and was bred,
Bold Robin of famous renown.

The father of Robin a forrester was,
And he shot in a lusty strong bow
Two north-country miles and an inch at
   a shot,
As the Pinder of Wakefield does know.

For he brought Adam Bell, and Clim of
   the Clugh,
And William of Clowdesle,
To shoot with our forrester for forty
   mark,
And the forrester beat them all three.

His mother was neece to the Coventry
    knight,
Which Warwickshire men call sir Guy;
For he slew the blue bore that hangs up at
    the gate.
Or mine host of the Bull tells a lie.

Her brother was Gamwel, of Great
    Gamwel hall,
A noble house-keeper was he,
Ay, as ever broke bread in sweet
    Nottinghamshire,
And a squire of famous degree.

The mother of Robin said to her husband,
My honey, my love, and my dear.
Let Robin and I ride this morning to
    Gamwel,
To taste of my brother's good cheer.

And he said, I grant thee thy boon, gentle
    Joan,
Take one of my horses, I pray:
The sun is arising, and therefore make
    haste.
For to-morrow is Christmas-day.

Then Robin Hood's father's grey gelding
    was brought.
And sadled and bridled was he;
God-wot a blue bonnet, his new suit of
    cloaths,
And a cloak that did reach to his knee.

She got on her holyday kirtle and gown.
They were of a light Lincoln green;

The cloath was homespun, but for colour
    and make
It might have beseemed our queen.

And then Robin got on his basket-hilt
    sword,
And his dagger on his tother side;
And said. My dear mother, let's haste to be
    gone.
We have forty long miles to ride.

When Robin had mounted his gelding so
    grey,
His father, without any trouble,
Set her up behind him, and bad her not
    fear,
For his gelding had oft carried double.

And when she was settled, they rode to
    their neighbours
And drank and shook hands with them all;
And then Robin gallopt, and never gave
    o're.
Till they lighted at Gamwel-hall.

And now you may think the right
    worshipful squire
Was joyful his sister to see;
For he kist her, and kist her, and swore a
    great oath.
Thou art welcome, kind sister, to me.

To-morrow, when mass had been said at
    the chappel,
Six tables were covered in the hall,
And in comes the squire, and makes a short
    speech,

It was. Neighbours, you're welcome all

But not a man here shall taste my March
  beer,
Till a Christmas carrol he does sing.
Then all clapt their hands, and theys houted
  and sung.
Till the hall and the parlour did ring.

Now mustard and brawn, roast beef and
  plumb pies
Were set upon every table;
And noble George Gamwel said, Eat and be
  merry.
Drink too as long as you're able.

When dinner was ended, his chaplain said
  grace,
And, Be merry, my friends, said the squire;
It rains and it blows, but call for more ale,
And lay some more wood on the fire.

And now call ye Little John hither to me,
For Little John is a fine lad.
At gambols and juggling, and twenty such
  tricks,
As shall make you both merry and glad.

When Little John came, to gambols they
  went.
Both gentlemen, yeomen, and clown;
And what do you think? Why, as true as I
  live.
Bold Robin Hood put them all down.

And now you may think the right
  worshipful squire

Was joyful this sight for to see;
For he said, Cousin Robin, thou'st go no
  more home.
But tarry and dwell here with me.

Thou shalt have my land when I die, and till
  then,
Thou shalt be the staff of my age.
Then grant me my boon, dear uncle, said
  Robin,
That Little John may be my page.

And he said. Kind cousin, I grant thee thy
  boon;
With all my heart, so let it be.
Then come hither, Little John, said Robin
  Hood,
Come hither my page unto me:

Go fetch me my bow, my longest long bow,
And broad arrows, one, two, or three.
For when 'tis fair weather we'll into
  Sherwood,
Some merry pastime to see.

When Robin Hood came into merry
  Sherwood,
He winded his bugle so clear;
And twice five and twenty good yeomen and
  bold,
Before Robin Hood did appear.

Where are your companions all? said Robin
  Hood,
For still I want forty and three.
Then said a bold yeoman, Lo, yonder they
  stand.

All under the green wood tree.

As that word was spoke, Clorinda came by,
The queen of the shepherds was she;
And her gown was of velvet as green as the
    grass.
And her buskin did reach to her knee.

Her gate it was graceful, her body was
    straight,
And her countenance free from pride;
A bow in her hand, and a quiver of arrows
Hung dangling by her sweet side.

Her eye-brows were black, ay, and so was
    her hair,
And her skin was as smooth as glass;
Her visage spoke wisdom, and modesty
    too:
Sets with Robin Hood such a lass!

Said Robin Hood, Lady fair, whither away?
Whither, fair lady, away?
And she made him answer. To kill a fat
    buck;
For to-morrow is Titbury day.

Said Robin Hood, Lady fair, wander with
    me
A little to yonder green bower;
There set down to rest you, and you shall
    be sure
Of a brace or a leash in an hour.

And as we were going towkrds the green
    bower.
Two hundred good bucks we espy'd;

She chose two out the fattest that was in
    the herd,
And she shot him through side and side.

By the faith of my body, said bold Robin
    Hood,
I never saw woman like thee;
And com'st thou from east, or com'st thou
    from west,
Thou needst not beg venison of me.

However, along to my bower you shall go.
And taste of a forrester's meat:
And when we came thither we found as
    good cheer
As any man needs for to eat.

For there was hot venison, and warden pies
    cold,
Cream clouted, and honey-combs plenty;
And the servitors they were, besides Little
    John,
Good yeomen, at least four and twenty.

Clorinda said. Tell me your name, gentle
    sir:
And he said, 'tis bold Robin Hood:
Squire Gamwel's my uncle, but all my
    delight
Is to dwell in the merry Sherwood;

For 'tis a fine life, and 'tis void of all strife.
So 'tis Sir, Clorinda replied,
But oh! said bold Robin, how sweet would
    it be,
If Clorinda would be my bride!

She blusht at the motion; yet, after a pause,
Said, Yes, sir, and with all my heart.
Then let us send for a priest, said Robin
    Hood,
And be married before we do part.

But she said, It may not be so, gentle sir,
For I must be at Titbury feast;
And if Robin Hood will go thither with me,
I'll make him the most welcome guest.

Said Robin Hood, Reach me that buck,
    Little John,
For I'll go along with my dear;
And bid my yeomen kill six brace of bucks,
And meet me to-morrow just here.
Before he had ridden five Staffordshire
    miles.
Eight yeomen, that were too bold,
Bid Robin Hood stand, and deliver his
    buck:
A truer tale never was told.

I will not, faith, said bold Robin; come,
    John,
Stand by me, and we'll beat 'em all
Then both drew their swords, and so cut
    'em, and slasht 'em
That five out of them did fall.

The three that remain'd call'd to Robin for
    quarter,
And pitiful John begg'd their lives:
When John's boon was granted, he gave
    them good councel
And sent them all home to their wives,

This battle was fought near to Titbury
    town,
When the bagpipes baited the bull;
I'm the king of the fidlers, and I swear 'tis
    truth,
And I call him that doubts it a gull:

For I saw them fighting, and fiddled the
    while
And Clorinda sung 'Hey derry down!
The bumkins are beaten, put up thy sword,
    Bob,
And now let's dance into the town.'

Before we came in we heard a great
    shouting,
And all that were in it look'd mad;
For some were on bull-back, some dancing
    a morris.
And some singing Arthur-a-Bradley.

And there we see Thomas, our justice's
    clerk,
And Mary, to whom he was kind;
For Tom rode before her, and call'd Mary
    madam,
And kiss'd her full sweetly behind:

And so may your worships. But we went
    to dinner,
With Thomas and Mary, and Nan;
They all drank a health to Clorinda, and
    told her,
Bold Robin Hood was a fine man.

When dinner was ended, sir Roger, the
    parson

Of Dubbridge, was sent for in haste:
He brought his mass-book, and he bad
    them take hands
And joyn'd them in marriage full fast.

And then, as bold Robin Hood and his
    sweet bride
Went hand in hand to the green bower.
The birds sung with pleasure in merry
    Sherwood,
And 'twas a most joyful hour.

And when Robin came in sight of the
    bower.
Where are my yeomen? said he:
And Little John answer'd, Lo, yonder they
    stand,
All under the green-wood-tree.

Then a garland they brought her by two
    and by two,
And plac'd them all on the bride's head:

The music struck up, and we all fell to dance,
Till the bride and bridegroom were a-bed.

And what they did there must be counsel
    to me,
Because they lay long the next day;
And I had haste home, but I got a good
    piece
Of bride-cake, and so came away.

Now, out, alas! I had forgotten to tell ye.
That marry'd they were with a ring;
And so will Nan Knight, or be buried a
    maiden:
And now let us pray for the king;

That he may get children, and they may get
    more,
To govern and do us some good:
And then I'll make ballads in Robin Hood's
    bower
And sing 'em in merry Sherwood.

Robin Hood's Progress to Nottingham

Robin Hood he was and a tall young man,
Derry derry down,
And fifteen Winters old;
And Robin Hood he was a proper young
    man,
Of courage stout and bold.
Hey down, derry derry down.

Robin hee would and to fair
    Nottingham,
With the general for to dine;

There was hee aware of fifteen forresters,
And a drinking bear, ale, and wine.

What news? What news? said bold Robin
        Hood.
'What news fain wouldest thou know?'
Our king hath provided a shooting match,
And I'm ready with my bow.

We hold it in scorn, said the forresters,
That ever a boy so young

236

Should bear a bow before our king,
That's not able to draw one string,

Iie hold you twenty marks, said bold
    Robin Hood,
By the leave of our lady.
That I'le hit a mark a hundred rod,
And I'le cause a hart to dye.

We'l hold you twenty mark, then said
    the forresters,
By the leave of our lady.
Thou hit'st not the marke a hundred rod,
Nor causest a hart to dye.

Robin he bent up a noble bow.
And a broad arrow he let flye.
He hit the mark a hundred rod.
And he caused a hart to dye.

Some say hee brake ribs one or two,
And some say hee brake three;
The arrow within the hart would not
    abide,
But it glanced in two or three.

The hart did skip, and the hart did leap,
And the hart lay on the ground;
The wager is mine, said bold Robin Hood,
Ift were for a thousand pound.

The wager's none of thine, then said the
    forresters.
Although thou beest in haste;
Take up thy bow, and get thee hence.
Lest wee thy sides do baste.

Robin Hood hee took up his noble
    bow,
And his broad arrows all amain;
And Robin he laught, and begun [for]
    to smile,
As hee went over the plain.

Then Robin he bent his noble bow.
And his broad arrows he let flye.
Till fourteen of these fifteen forresters
Upon the ground did lye.

He that did this quarrel first begin
Went tripping over the plain;
But Robin he bent his noble bow,
And hee fetcht him back again.

You said I was no archer, said Robin
    Hood,
But say so now again:
With that he sent another arrow,
That split his head in twain.

You have found mee an archer, saith
    Robin Hood,
Which will make your wives for to
    wring,
And wish that you had never spoke the
    word.
That I could not draw one string.

The people that lived in fair Nottinghkm
Came running out amain.
Supposing to have taken bold Robin
    Hood,
With the forresters that were slain.

Some lost legs, and some lost arms.
And some did lose their blood;
But Robin hee took up his noble bow,
And is gone to the merry green
   wood.

They carried these forresters into fair
   Nottinghkm,
As many there did know;
They dig'd them graves in their church-yard.
And they buried them all a-row.

The Jolly Pinder of Wakefield, with Robin Hood, Scarlet and John

In Wakefield there lives a jolly pinder,
In Wakefield all on a green,
In Wakefield all on a green:

There is neither knight nor squire, said the
   pinder,
Nor baron that is so bold,
Nor baron that is so bold,
Dare make a trespiss to the town of Wakefield,

All this beheard three witty young men,
'Twas Robin Hood, Scarlet, and John;
With that they espy'd the jolly pinder,
As he sat under a thorn.

Now turn again, turn again, said the pinder,
For a wrong way you have gone;
For you have forsaken the king's highway.
And made a path over the comon.

O that were a shame, said jolly Robin,
We being three, and thou but one.
The pinder leapt back then thirty good foot,
'Twas thirty good foot and one.

He leaned his back fast unto a thorn,
And his foot against a stone,
And there he fought a long Summers day,

A Summer's day so long,
Till that their swords on their broad
   bucklers
Were broke fast into their hands.

Hold thy hand, hold thy hand, said bold
   Robin Hood,
And my merry men every one;
For this is one of the best pinders,
That ever I tryed with sword.

And wilt thou forsake thy pinders craft,
And live in the green-wood with me?
'At Michaelmas next my cov'nant comes out,
When every man gathers his fee;

Then I'le take my blew blade all in my hand,
And plod to the green-wood with thee.'
Hast thou either meat or drink, said Robin
   Hood,
For my merry men and me?

'I have both bread and beef, said the pinder,
And good ale of the best.'
'And that is meat good enough,' said Robin
   Hood,
For such unbidden 'guests'.

'O wilt thou forsake the pinder his craft,
And go to the green-wood with me?
Thou shalt have a livery twice in the year,
The one green, the other brown.'

'If Michaelmas day was come and gone.
And my master had paid me my fee.
Then would I set as little by him,
As my master doth by me.'

Robin Hood and the Bishop

Come, gentlemen all, and listen awhile,
Hey down, down an a down.
And a story I'le to you unfold;
I'll tell you how Robin Hood served the
    bishop,
When he robbed him of his gold.

As it fell out on a sun-shining day,
When Phoebus was in his prime,
Then Robin Hood, that archer good,
In mirth would spend some time.

And as he walk'd the forrest along,
Some pastime for to spy.
There was he aware of a proud bishop,
And all his company.

O what shall I do, said Robin Hood the,
If the bishop he doth take me
No mercy he'l show unto me, I know,
But hanged I shall be.

Then Robin was stout, and turned him
    about.
And a little house there he did spy;
And to an old wife, for to save his life.
He loud began for to cry.

Why, who art thou? said the old womkn,
Come tell to me for good.

'I am an out-law, as many do know.
My name it is Robin Hood;

And yonder's the bishop and all his men.
And if that I taken be.
Then day and night he'l work my spight,
And hanged I shall be.'

If thou be Robin Hood, said the old wife,
As thou dost seem to be,
Iie for thee provide, and thee I will hide,
From the bishop and his company.
For I remember one Saturday night,
Thou brought me both shoos and hose;
Therefore I'le provide thy person to hide,
And keep thee from thy foes.

'Then give me soon thy coat of gray,
And take thou my mantle of green;
Thy spindle and twine unto me resign,
And take thou my arrows so keen.'

And when Robin Hood was so araid.
He went straight to his company.
With his spindle and twine, he oft lookt
    behind,
For the bishop and his company.

O who is yonder, quoth little John,
That now comes over the lee?

Robin Hood

An arrow I will at her let flie.
So like an old witch looks she.

Hold thy hand, hold thy hand, said Robin
    Hood then
And shoot not thy arrows so keen;
I am Robin Hood, thy master good,
And quickly it shall be seen.

The bishop he came to the old womans
    house,
And called, with furious mood.
Come let me soon see, and bring unto me
That traitor Robin Hood.

The old woman he set on a milk-white
    steed,
Himselfe on a dapple gray;
And for joy he had got Robin Hood,
He went laughing all the way.

But as they were riding the forrest along,
The bishop he chanc'd for to see
A hundred brave bowmen bold.
Stand under the green-wood tree.

O who is yonder, the bishop then said.
That's ranging within yonder wood?
Marry, says the old woman, I think it to
    be
A man call'd Robin Hood.

Why, who art thou, the bishop he said.
Which I have here with me?

'Why, I am an old woman, thou cuckoldly
    bishop.
Lift up my leg and see.'

'Then woe is me', the bishop he said.
'That ever I saw this day!'
He turn'd him about, but Robin stout
Call'd him, and bid him stay.

Then Robin took hold of the bishop's horse,
And ty'd him fast to a tree;
Then Little John smil'd his master upon,
For joy of that company.

Robin Hood took his mantle from his back,
And spread it upon the ground,
And out of the bishop's portmantle he
Soon told five hundred pound.

Now let him go, said Robin Hood.
Said little John, That may not be;
For I vow and protest he shall sing us a mass,
Before that he goe from me.

Then Robin Hood took the bishop by the
    hand,
And bound him fast to a tree,
And made him sing a mass, god wot,
To him and his yeomandree.

And then they brought him through the
    wood,
And set him on his dapple gray.
And gave him the tail within his hand.
And bade him for Robin Hood pray.

Robin Hood and the Butcher

Come, all you brave gallants, listen awhile,
   With hey down, down, an a down.
That are this bower within;
For of Robin Hood, that archer good,
A song I intend for to sing.

Upon a time it chanced so,
Bold Robin in [the] forrest did spy
A jolly butcher, with a bonny fine mare.
With his flesh to the market did hye.

Good morrow, good fellow, said jolly
   Robin,
What food hast [thou], tell unto me ?
Thy trade to me tell, and where thou dost
   dwell,
For I like well thy company.

The butcher he answer'd jolly Robin,
No matter where I dwell;
For a butcher I am, and to Nottingham
I am going, my flesh to sell.

What is [the] price of thy flesh? said jolly
   Robin,
Come tell it soon unto me;
And the price of thy mare, be she never so
   dear,
For a butcher fain would I be.

The price of my flesh, the butcher repli'd,
I soon will tell unto thee;
With my bonny mare, and they are not
   too dear.
Four mark thou must give unto me.

Four mark I will give me, saith jolly Robin,
Four mark it shall be thy fee;
The mony come count, and let me mount.
For a butcher I fain would be.

Now Robin he is to Nottingham gone,
His butchers trade to begin;
With good intent to the sheriff he went,
And there he took up his inn.
When other butchers they opened their
   meat,
Bold Robin he then begun;
But how for to sell he knew not well,
For a butcher he was but young.

When other butchers no meat could sell,
Robin got both gold and fee;
For he sold more meat for one peny
Then others could do for three.

But when he sold his meat so fast.
No butcher by him could thrive;
For he sold more meat for one peny
Than others could do for five.

Which made the butchers of Nottingham
To study as they did stand,
Saying, Surely he is some prodigal,
That hath sold his fathers land.

The butchers stepped to jolly Robin,
Acquainted with him for to be;
Come, brother, one said, we be all of one
   trade.
Come, will you go dine with me?

Accurst of his heart, said jolly Robin,
That a butcher doth deny;
I will go with you, my brethren true,
As fast as I can hie.

But when to the sheriffs house they came.
To dinner they hied apace,
And Robin Hood he the man must be
Before them all to say grace.

Pray god bless us all, said jolly Robin,
And our meat within this place;
A cup of sack so good will nourish our
    blood
And so I do end my grace.

Come fill us more wine, said jolly Robin,
Let us be merry while we do stay;
For wine and good cheer, be it never so
    dear,
I vow I the reckning will pay.

Come, brothers, be merry, said jolly Robin,
Let us drink, and never give ore;
For the shot I will pay, ere I go my way,
If it cost me five pounds and more.

This is a mad blade, the butchers then said.
Sales the sheriff, He is some prodigal,
That some land has sold for silver and gold,
And now he doth mean to spend all.

Hast thou any horn beasts, the sheriff
    repli'd,
Good fellow, to sell unto me?
'Yes, that I have, good master sheriff,
I have hundreds two or three.

And a hundred aker of good free land,
If you please it to see:
And he make you as good assurance of
    it,
As ever my father made me.'

The sheriff he saddled his good palfrey,
And, with three hundred pound in gold.
Away he went with bold Robin Hood,
His homed beasts to behold.

Away then the sheriff and Robin did ride,
To the forrest of merry Sherwood,
Then the sheriff did say, God bless us this
    day.
From a man they call Robin Hood!

But when a little farther they came,
Bold Robin he chanced to spy
A hundred head of good red deer,
Come tripping the sheriff full nigh.

'How like you my horn'd beasts, good
    master sheriff –
They be fat and fair for to see.'
'I tell thee, good fellow, I would I were
    gone,
For I like not thy company.'

Then Robin set his horn to his mouth.
And blew but blasts three;
Then quickly anon there came Little John,
And all his company.

What is your will, master? then said Little
    John,
Good master, come tell unto me.

'I have brought hither the sheriff of
   Nottingham
This day to dine with thee.'

He is welcome to me, then said Little
   John,
I hope he will honestly pay;
I know he has gold, if it be but well
   told,
Will serve us to drink a whole day.

Then Robin took his mantle from his back,
And laid it upon the ground;
And out of the sheriffs portmantle
He told three hundred pound.

Then Robin he brought him thorow the
   wood.
And set him on his dapple gray;
'O have me commended to your wife at
   home:'
So Robin went laughing away.

Robin Hood and the Tanner; Or, Robin Hood Met With His Match

In Nottingham there lives a jolly tanner,
a hey downy down, a down down,
His name is Arthur-a-Bland;
There is nere a squire in Nottinghamshire
Dare bid bold Arthur stand.

With a long pike-staff upon his shoulder,
So well he can clear his way;
By two and by three he makes them to flee,
For he hath no list to stay.

And as he went forth, in a Summer's
   morning.
Into the forest of merry Sherwood,
To view the red deer, that range here and
   there.
There met he with bold Robin Hood.

As soon as bold Robin he did I espy,
He thought some sport he would make.
Therefore out of hand he bid him to stand,
And thus to him he spake:

Why, what art thou, thou bold fellow.
That ranges so boldly here?
In sooth, to be brief, thou lookst like a
   thief.
That comes to steal our kings deer.

For I am a keeper in this forrest,
The king puts me in trust
To look to his deer, that range here and
   there;
Therefore stay thee I must.

'If thou beest a keeper in this forest.
And hast such a great command,
Yet thou must have more partakers in
   store,
Before thou make me to stand.'

'Nay, I have no more partakers in store,
Or any that I do not need;
But I have a staff of another oke graff,
I know it will do the deed.

For thy sword and thy bow I care not a
    straw,
Nor all thine arrows to boot;
If I get a knop upon the bare scop,
Thou can'st as well shit as shoote.'

Speak cleanly, good fellow, said jolly
    Robin,
And give better terms to me;
Else he thee correct for thy neglect,
And make thee more mannerly.

Marry gep with a wenion! quod
    Arthur-a-Bland,
Art thou such a goodly man?
I care not a fig for thy looking so big.
Mend thou thyself where thou can.

Then Robin Hood he unbuckled his belt,
And laid down his bow so long;
He took up a staff of another oke graff,
That was both stiff and strong.

He yield to thy weapon, said jolly Robin,
Since thou wilt not yield to mine;
For I have a staff of another
    oke graff,
Not half a foot longer then thine.

But let me measure, said jolly Robin,
Before we begin our fray;
For I'le not have mine to be longer then
    thine,
For that will be counted foul play.

I pass not for length, bold Arthur reply'd,
My staflf is of oke so free;

Eight foot and a half, it will knock down
    a calf,
And I hope it will knock down thee.

Then Robin could no longer forbear,
He gave him such a knock.
Quickly and soon the blood came down.
Before it was ten a clock.

Then Arthur he soon recovered himself.
And gave him such a knock on the crown,
That from every side of bold Robin
    Hood's head.
The blood came trickling down.

Then Robin raged like a wild boar,
As soon as he saw his own blood:
Then Bland was in haste he laid on so fast.
As though he had been cleaving of wood.

And about, and about, and about they
    went.
Like two wild bores in a chase.
Striving to aim each other to maim,
Leg, arm, or any other place.

And knock for knock they lustily dealt,
Which held for two hours and more;
That all the wood rang at every bang,
They ply'd their work so sore.

Hold thy hand, hold thy hand, said Robin
    Hood,
And let thy quarrel fall;
For here we may thrash our bones all to
    mesh,
And get no coyn at all:

And in the forest of merry Sherwood
Heareafter thou shalt be free.
'God a mercy for nought, my freedom I
    bought,
I may thank my staff, and not thee.'

What tradesman art thou? said jolly Robin,
Good fellow, I prithee me show;
And also me tell, in what place thou dost
    dwel:
For both of these fain would I know.

I am a tanner, bold Arthur reply'd,
In Nottingham long have I wrought;
And if thou'lt come there, I vow and swear,
I will tan thy hide for nought

God-a-mercy, good fellow, said jolly Robin,
Since thou art so kind and free;
And if thou wilt tan my hide for nought,
I will do as much for thee.

And if thou'lt forsake thy tanners trade,
And live in the green wood with me,
My name's Robin Hood, I swear by the rood,
I will give thee both gold and fee.

If thou be Robin Hood, bold Arthur reply'd.
As I think well thou art.
Then here's my hand, my name's
    Arthur-a-Bland,
We two will never depart.

But tell me, O tell me, where is Little John?
Of him fain would I hear;
For we are alide by the mother's side.
And he is my kinsman dear.

Then Robin Hood blew on the beugle horn.
He blew full lowd and shrill;
But quickly anon appear'd Little John,
Come tripping down a green hill;

O what is the matter then said Little John,
Master, I pray you tell:
Why do you stand with your staff in your
    hand?
I fear all is not well.

'O man I do stand, and he makes me to
    stand.
The tanner that stands thee beside;
He is a bonny blade, and master of his trade.
For soundly he hath tan'd my hide.'

He is to be commended, then said Little John,
If such a feat he can do;
If he be so stout, we will have a bout,
And he shall tan my hide too.

Hold thy hand, hold thy hand, said Robin
    Hood,
For as I do understand,
He's a yeoman good, of thine own blood,
For his name is Arthur-a-Bland.

Then Little John threw his staff away,
As far as he could it fling,
And ran out of hand to Arthur-a-Bland,
And about his neck did cling.

With loving respect, there was no neglect,
They were neither nice nor coy,
Each other did face with a lovely grace,
And both did weep for joy.

Then Robin Hood took them both by the
  hands,
And danc'd round about the oke tree:
'For three merry men, and three merry men,
And three merry men we be:

And ever hereafter as long as we live,
We three will be as one;
The wood it shall ring, and the old wife
  sing,
Of Robin Hood, Arthur, and John.'

Robin Hood and the Tinker

In Summer time, when leaves grow green,
  Down, a down, a down.
And birds sing on every tree,
  Hey down, a down, a down.

Robin Hood went to Nottingham,
  Down, a down, a down.
As fast as hee could dree.
  Hey down, a down, a down.

And as hee came to Nottingham,
A tinker he did meet.
And seeing him a lusty blade,
He did him kindly greet

Where dost thou live? quoth Robin Hood,
I pray thee now mee tell:
Sad news I hear there is abroad,
I fear all is not well.

What is that news? the tinker said.
Tell mee without delay:
I am a tinker by my trade.
And do live at Banbura.

As for the news, quoth Robin Hood,
It is but as I hear.
Two tinkers were set ith' stocks.
For drinking ale and beer.

If that be all, the tinker he said,
As I may say to you,
Your news is not worth a fart,
Since that they all bee true.

For drinking good ale and beer,
You will not lose your part.
No, by my faith, quoth Robin Hood,
I love it with all my heart.

What news abroad? quoth Robin Hood,
Tell me what thou dost hear:
Seeing thou goest from town to town,
Some news thou need not fear.

All the news I have, the tinker said,
I hear it is for good.
It is to seek a bold outlaw,
Which they call Robin Hood.

I have a warrand from the king.
To take him where I can;
If you can tell me where hee is,
I will make you a man.

The king would give a hundred pound
That he could but him see;
And if wee can but now him get,
It will serve thee and mee.

Let me see that warrant, said
   Robin Hood,
He see if it bee right;
And I will do the best I can
For to take him this night.

That will I not, the tinker said,
None with it I will trust;
And where hee is if you'll not tell,
Take him by force I must.

But Robin Hood perceiving well
How then the game would go,
'If you would go to Nottinghnm,
We shall find him I know.'

The tinker had a crab-tree staff,
Which was both good and strong,
Robin hee had a good strong blade;
So they went both along.

And when they came to
   Nottingham,
There they both tooke their inn;
And they called for ale and wine,
To drink it was no sin.

But ale and wine they drank so fast.
That the tinker hee forgot
What thing he was about to do;
It fell so to his lot.

That, while the tinker fell asleep,
Robin made haste away.
And left the tinker in the lurch,
For the great shot to pay.

But when the tinker wakened,
And saw that he was gone,
He call'd then even for his host,
And thus hee made his moan:

I had a warrant from the king,
Which might have done me good,
That is to take a bold outlaw.
Some call him Robin Hood

But now my warrant and mony's
   gone,
Nothing I have to pay;
And he that promis'd to be my friend,
He is gone and fled away.

That friend you tell on, said the host.
They call him Robin Hood;
And when that first hee met with you,
He ment you little good.

'Had I but known it had been hee,
When that I had him here,
Th' one of us should have tri'd our
   might
Which should have paid full dear.

In the mean time I will away.
No longer here He bide.
But I will go and seek him out.
Whatever do me betide.

But one thing I would gladly know,
What here I have to pay.'
Ten shillings just, then said the host.
'He pay without delay;

Or elce take here my working-bag,
And my good hammer too;
And if that I light but on the knave,
I will then soon pay you.'

The onely way, then said the host.
And not to stand in fear.
Is to seek him among the parks.
Killing of the kings deer.

The tinker hee then went with speed.
And made then no delay,
Till he had found bold Robin Hood,
That they might have a fray.

At last hee spy'd him in a park,
Hunting then of the deer.
What knave is that, quoth Robin Hood,
That doth come mee so nea ?

No knave, no knave, the tinker said.
And that you soon shall know;
Whether of us hath done any wrong,
My crab-tree staff shall show.

Then Robin drew his gallant blade,
Made then of trusty steel:
But the tinker he laid on so fast,
That he made Robin reel.

Then Robin's anger did arise,
He fought right manfully,
Until he had made the tinker
Almost then fit to fly.

With that they had a bout again,
They ply'd their weapons fast;

The tinker threshed his bones so sore,
He made him yeeld at last.

A boon, a boon, Robin hee cryes,
If thou wilt grant it mee.
Before I do it, the tinker said,
He hang thee on this tree.

But the tinker looking him about,
Robin his horn did blow;
Then came unto him Little John,
And William Scadlock too.

What is the matter, quoth Little John,
You sit on th' highway side?
'Here is a tinker that stands by,
That hath paid well my hide.'

That tinker then, said Little John,
Fain that blade I would see,
And I would try what I could do,
If hee'l do as much for me.

But Robin hee then wish'd them both
They should the quarrel cease,
'That henceforth wee may bee as one,
And ever live in peace.'

And for the jovial tinkers part,
A hundred pounds He give
In th' year [for] to maintain him on,
As long as he doth live.

In manhood he is a mettled man,
And a mettle man by trade;
Never thought I that any man
Should have made mee so afraid.

And if hee will bee one of us.
Wee will take all one fare;
And whatsoever wee do get
He shall have his full share.'

So the tinker was content
With them to go along,
And with them a part to take:
And so I end my song.

Robin Hood and Allin 'A' Dale

Come listen to me, you gallants so free,
All you that love mirth for to hear.
And I will tell you of a bold outlaw.
That lived in Nottinghamshire.

Stand off, stand off, the young man said.
What is your will with me?
'You must come before our master straight,
Under yon green wood tree.'

As Robin Hood in the forest stood,
All under the green wood tree,
There he was aware of a brave young man,
As fine as fine might be.

And when he came bold Robin before,
Robin askt him courteously,
O, hast thou any money to spare
For my merry men and me?

The youngster was cloathed in scarlet red,
In scarlet fine and gay;
And he did frisk it over the plain,
And chanted a round-de-lay.

I have no money, the young man said,
But five shillings and a ring;
And that I have kept this seven long years,
To have it at my wedding.

As Robin Hood next morning stood
Amongst the leaves so gay,
There did [he] espy the same young man
Come drooping along the way.

Yesterday I should have married a maid,
But she from me was tane,
And chosen to be an old knights delight.
Whereby my poor heart is slain.

The scarlet he wore the day before
It was clean cast away;
And at every step he fetcht a sigh,
'Alack and a well a day'

What is thy name? then said Robin Hood,
Come tell me, without any fail.
By the faith of my body, then said the
     young man.
My name it is Allin a Dale.

Then stepped forth brave Little John,
And Midge the miller's son,
Which made the young man bend his
     bow,
When as he see them come.

What will thou give me, said Robin Hood,
In ready gold or fee,
To help thee to thy true love again.
And deliver her unto thee?

I have no money, then quoth the
    young man,
No ready gold nor fee.
But I will swear upon a book
Thy true servant for to be.

'How many miles is it to thy true love?
Come tell me without guile.'
By the faith of my body, then said the
    young man,
It is but five little mile.

Then Robin he hasted over the plain.
He did neither stint nor lin,
Until he came unto the church,
Where Allin should keep his
    wedding.

What hast thou here ? the bishop then
    said,
I prithee now tell unto me.
I am a bold harper, quoth Robin Hood,
And the best in the north country.

O welcome, O welcome, the bishop
    he said,
That musick best pleaseth me.
You shall have no musick, quoth
    Robin Hood,
Till the bride and the bridegroom
    I see.

With that came in a wealthy knight,
Which was both grave and old.
And after him a finikin lass.
Did shine like the glistering gold.

This is not a fit match, quod bold
    Robin Hood,
That you do seem to make here,
For since we are come into the church.
The bride shall chuse her own dear.

Then Robin Hood put his horn to his
    mouth,
And blew blasts two or three;
When four and twenty bowmen bold
Came leaping over the lee.

And when they came into the
    church-yard,
Marching all on a row,
The first man was Allin a Dale,
To give bold Robin his bow.

This is thy true love, Robin he said,
Young Allin, as I hear say.
And you shall be married at this same
    time,
Before we depart away.

That shall not be, the bishop he said,
For thy word shall not stand;
They shall be three times askt in the
    church,
As the law is of our land.

Robin Hood pull'd off the bishop's
    coat.
And put it upon Little John;
By the faith of my body, then Robin
    said.
'This cloth does make thee a man.'

When Little John went into the quire.
The people began to laugh;
He askt them seven times in the church.
Lest three times should not be enough.

Who gives me this maid? said Little John.
Quoth Robin Hood, That do I;
And he that takes her from Alin-a-Dale,
Full dearly he shall her buy.

Robin Hood and the Shepherd

All gentlemen, and yeomen good,
    Down, a down, a down, a down,
I wish you to draw near;
For a story of gallant bold Robin Hood
Unto you I will declare.
    Down, a down, a down, a down,

As Robin Hood walkt the forrest along,
Some pastime for to spie,
There he was aware of a jolly shephard,
That on the ground did lie.

Arise, arise, cried jolly Robin,
And now come let me see
What's in thy bag and bottle; I say,
Come tell it unto me.

'What's that to thee? thou proud fellow,
Tell me as I do stand:
What hast thou to do with by bag and
    bottle?
Let me see thy command.'

And thus having ended this merry
    wedding.
The bride lookt like a queen;
And so they return'd to the merry
    green-wood,
Amongst the leaves so green.

'My sword, which hangeth by my side,
Is my command I know;
Come, and let me taste of thy bottle,
Or it may breed thy woe.'

'The devil a drop, thou proud fellow.
Of my bottle thou shalt see,
Until thy valour here be tried.
Whether thou wilt fight or flee.'

What shall we fight for? cries Robin
    Hood,
Come tell it soon to me;
Here is twenty pound in good red gold.
Win it and take it thee.

The shepherd stood all in a maze,
And knew not what to say:
'I have no money, thou proud fellbw,
But bag and bottle ile lay.'

'I am content, thou shepherd swain,
Fling them down on the ground;

But it will breed thee mickle pain.
To win my twenty pound.'

'Come draw thy sword, thou proud
    fellow,
Thou standest too long to prate;
This hook of mine shall let thee know,
A coward I do hate.'

So they fell to it, full hardy and sore,
It was on a Summers day,
From ten till four in the afternoon
The shepherd held him play.

Robins buckler prov'd his chief
    defence.
And saved him many a bang.
For every blow the shepherd gave
Made Robin's sword cry twang.

Many a sturdie blow the shepherd
    gave,
And that bold Robin found,
Till the blood ran trickling from his
    head,
Then he fell to the ground.

'Arise, arise, thou proud fellow,
And thou shalt have fair play.
If thou wilt yield before thou go,
That I have won the day.'

A boon, a boon, cry'd bold Robin,
If that a man thou be.
Then let me have my beugle horn,
And blow but blasts three.

Then said the shepherd to bold Robin,
'To that I will agree;'
'For if thou shouldst blow till
    to-morrow morn,
I scorn one foot to flee.'

Then Robin he set his horn to his
    mouth,
And he blew with mickle main,
Until he espied Little John
Come tripping over the plain.

'O who is yonder, thou proud fellow.
That comes down yonder hill?'
'Yonder is John, bold Robin Hoods
    man,
Shall fight with thee thy fill.'

What is the matter? sayes Little John,
Master, come tell to me.
My case is bad, cries Robin Hood,
For the shepherd hath conquered me.

I am glad of that, cries Little John:
Shepherd, turn thou to me;
For a bout with thee I mean to have,
Either come fight or flee.

'With all my lieart, thou proud fell6w,
For it never shall be said
That a shepherd's hook of thy sturdy look
Will one jot be dismaied.'

So they fell to it, full hardy and sore.
Striving for victorie.
He know, says John, ere we give o'er,
Whether thou wilt fight or flee.

The shepherd gave John a sturdie blow,
With his hook under the chin.
Beshrew thy heart, said little John,
Thou basely dost begin.

Nay, that is nothing, said the
 shepherd,
Either yield to me the daie,
Or I will bang thy back and sides,
Before thou goest thy way.

What! dost thou think, thou proud
 fellow,
That thou canst conquer me?
Nay, thou shall know, bfore you go,
Iie fight before ile flee.

Again the shepherd laid on him,
Just as he first begun.
Hold thy hand, cry'd bold Robin,
I will yield the wager won.

With all my heart, said Little John,
To that I will agree;
For he is the flower of shepherd
 swains,
The like I did never see.

Thus have you heard of Robin Hood,
Also of Little John
How a shepherd swain did conquer
 them
The like was never known.

Robin Hood and the Curtall Fryer

In Summer time, when leaves grow green,
And flowers are fresh and gay,
Robin Hood and his merry men
[They] were disposed to play.

Then some would leape, and some
 would runne,
And some would use artillery:
'Which of you can a good bow draw,
A good archer for to be?

Which of you can kill a bucke,
Or who can kill a doe;
Or who can kill a hart of Greece
Five hundreth foot him fro?'

Will Scadlocke he kild a bucke
And Midge he kild a doe;

And Little John kild a hart of Greece,
Five hundreth foot him fro.

Gods blessing on thy heart, said
 Robin Hood,
That hath such a shot for me;
I would ride my horse a hundred
 miles,
find one could match thee.

That caused Will Scadlocke to laugh,
He laught full heartily:
'There lives a curtail fryer in
 Fountaines-Abbey
Will beate both him and thee.

The curtail fryer in Fountaines-Abbey
Well can a strong bow draw,

He will beat you and your yeomen,
Set them all on a row.'

Robin Hood he tooke a solemne oath,
It was by Mary free,
That he would neither eate nor
    drinke,
Till the fryer he did see.

Robin Hood put on his harnesse
    good,
On his head a cap of steel,
Broad sword and buckler by his side.
And they became him weele.

He tooke his bow into his hand,
It was made of a trusty tree.
With a sheafe of arrowes at his belt,
And to Fountaine-Dale went he.

And comming unto Fountaine-Dale,
No farther he would ride;
There he was aware of the curtail
    fryer.
Walking by the water side.

The fryer had on a harnesse good,
On his head a cap of steel.
Broad sword and buckler by
    his side,
And they became him weele.

Robin Hood lighted off his horse,
And tyed him to a thorne:
'Carry me over the water, thou curtail
    fryer,
Or else thy life's forlorne.'

The fryer tooke Robin Hood on his
    backe,
Deepe water he did bestride,
And spake neither good word nor bad.
Till he came at the other side.

Lightly leapt Robin offe the fryers backe;
The fryer said to him againe.
Carry me over this water, [thou] fine
    fellow,
Or it shall breed thy paine.

Robin Hood took the fryer on his
    backe,
Deepe water he did bestride.
And spake neither good word nor
    bad,
Till he came at the other side.

Lightly leapt the fryer off Robin
    Hoods backe,
Robin Hood said to him againe.
Carry me over this water, thou curtail
    fryer,
Or it shall breede thy pain.

The fryer tooke Robin on's backe
    againe.
And stept in to the knee.
Till he came at the middle streame,
Neither good nor bad spake he,

And comming to the middle streame,
There he threw Robin in:
'And chuse thee, chuse thee, fine
    fellow,
Whether thou wilt sink or swim.'

Robin Hood swam to a bush of broome,
The fryer to a wigger-wand;
Bold Robin Hood is gone to shore,
And took his bow in his hand.

One of his best arrowes under his belt
To the fryer he let fly;
The curtail fryer, with his Steele buckler.
Did put that arrow by.

'Shoot on, shoot on, thou fine fellow,
Shoot as thou hast begun.
If thou shoot here a Summers day,
Thy marke I will not shun.'

Robin Hood shot passing well,
Till his arrows all were game;
They tooke their swords and Steele
    bucklers,
They fought with might and maine,

From ten o'th' clock that [very] day,
Till four I' th' afternoon;
Then Robin Hood came to his knees,
Of the fryer to beg a boon.

'A boone, a boone, thou curtail fryer,
I beg it on my knee;
Give me leave to set my borne to my
    mouth,
And to blow blasts three.'

That I will do, said the curtail fryer,
Of my blasts I have no doubt;
I hope thoult blow so passing well,
Till both thy eyes fall out.

Robin Hood set his home to his mouth,
He blew out blasts three;
Halfe a hundreth yeomen, with bowes bent,
Came raking over the lee.

Whose men are these, said the fryer.
That come so hastily?
These men are mine, said Robin Hood;
Fryer, what is that to thee.

A boone, a boone, said the curtail fryer.
The like I gave to thee;
Give me leave to set my fist to my
    mouth.
And to whute whues three.

That will I doe, said Robin Hood,
Or else I were to blame;
Three whues in a fryers fist
Would make me glad and faine.

The fryer set his fist to his mouth,
And whuted whues three:
Haifa hundred good band-dogs
Came running over the lee.

'Here's for every man a dog,
And I myselfe for thee.'
Nay, by my faith, said Robin Hood,
Fryer, that may not be.

Two dogs at once to Robin Hood did
    goe,
The one behind, the other before,
Robin Hoods mantle of Lincolne greene
Off from his backe they tore.

And whether his men shot east or
    west,
Or they shot north or south.
The curtail dogs, so taught they were,
They kept the arrows in their mouth.

Take up thy dogs, said Little John,
Fryer, at my bidding be.
Whose man art thou, said the curtail
    fryer,
Comes here to prate with me?

'I am Little John, Robin Hoods man,
Fryer, I will not lie;
If thou take not up thy dogs soone,
Iie take up them and thee.'

Little John had a bow in his hand,
He shot with might and main;
Soon halfe a score of the fryers dogs
Lay dead upon the plain.

Hold thy hand, good fellow, said the
    curtail fryer,
Thy master and I will agree;
And we will have new orders taken,
With all the hast may be.

'If thou wilt forsake fair
    Fountaines-dale,
And Fountaines-Abbey free,
Every sunday throwout the yeere,
A noble shall be thy fee:

And every holiday through the yeere,
Changed shall thy garment be.
If thou wilt goe to faire Nottingham,
And there remaine with me.'

This curtail fryer had kept Fountaines-dale
Seven long yeeres and more,
There was neither knight, lord, nor earle,
Could make him yeeld before.

Robin Hood and the Stranger

Come listen awhile, you gentlemen all,
With a hey down, down, a down, down,
That are this bower within,
For a story of gallant bold Robin Hood,
I purpose now to begin.

What time of day? quod Robin Hood
    then.
Quoth Little John, 'tis in the prime.
'Why then we will to the green wood
    gang,
For we have no vittles to dine.'

As Robin Hood walkt the forrest along,
It was in the mid of the day,
There he was met of a deft young man.
As ever walkt on the way.

His doublet was of silk 'tis said.
His stockings like scarlet shone;
And he walked on along the way.
To Robin Hood then unknown.

A herd of deer was in the bend,
All feeding before his face:

'Now the best of you ile have to my
  dinner.
And that in a little space.'

Now the stranger he made no mickle
  adoe.
But he bends and a right good bow,
And the best of all the herd he slew,
Forty good yards him froe.

Well shot, well shot, quod Robin
  Hood then,
That shot it was shot in time;
And if thou wilt accept of the place,
Thou shalt be a bold yeoman of mine.

Go play the chiven, the stranger said,
Make haste and quickly go,
Or with my fist, be sure of this,
He give thee bufifets sto'.

Thou had'st not best buffet me, quod
  Robin Hood,
For though I seem forlorn,
Yet I have those will take my part.
If I but blow my horn.

Thou wast not best wind thy horn,
  the stranger said,
Beest thou never so much in haste.
For I can draw out a good broad sword,
And quickly cut the blast.

Then Robin Hood bent a very good bow,
To shoot, and that he would fain;
The stranger he bent a very good bow,
To shoot at bold Robin again.

Hold thy hand, hold thy hand, quod
  Robin Hood,
To shoot it would be in vain;
For if we should shoot the one at, the
  other,
The one of us may be slain.

But let's take our swords and our
  broad bucklers.
And gang under yonder tree,
As I hope to be sav'd, the stranger he
  said,
One foot I will not fice.

Then Robin Hood lent the stranger a
  blow,
Most scar'd him out of his wit:
Thou never felt blow, the stranger he
  said,
That shall be better quit.

The stranger he drew out a good
  broad sword.
And hit Robin on the crown,
That from every haire of bold Robin's
  head
The blood ran trickling down.

God a mercy, good fellow! quod
  Robin Hood then.
And for this that thou hast done,
Tell me, good fellow, what thou art.
Tell me where thou doest won.

The stranger then answered bold
  Robin Hood,
He tell thee where I do dwell;

In Maxwell town I was bred and born,
My name is young Gamwell.

For killing of my own fathers steward,
I am forc'd to this English wood,
And for to seek an uncle of mine,
Some call him Robin Hood.

'But art thou a cousin of Robin Hood
then?
The sooner we should have done.'
As I hope to be sav'd, the stranger
then said,
I am his own sister's son.

But, lord ! what kissing and courting
was there,
When these two cousins did greet !
And they went all that Summers day,
And Little John did [not] meet.

But when they met with Little John,
He unto them did say,
master, pray where have you been,
You have tarried so long away?

I met with a stranger, quod Robin
Hood,
Full sore he hath beaten me.
Then I'le have a bout with him, quod
Little John,
And try if he can beat me.

Oh [no], oh no, quoth Robin Hood then
Little John, it may [not] be so;
For he is my own dear sisters son,
And cousins I have no mo.

But he shall be a bold yeoman of
mine,
My chief man next to thee;
And I Robin Hood, and thou Little
John,
And Scadlock he shall be.

And we'el be three of the bravest
outlaws
That live in the north country,
If you will hear more of bold Robin
Hood,
In the second part it will be.

PART THE SECOND
Now Robin Hood, Will Scadlock, and
Little John
Are walking over the plain,
With a good fat buck, which Will
Scadlock
With his strong bow had slain.

Then bold Robin Hood to the north
he would go,
With valour and mickle might.
With sword by his side, which oft had
been tri'd,
To fight and recover his right.

The first that he met was a bonny
bold Scot,
His servant he said he would be.
No, quoth Robin Hood, it cannot be
good,
For thou wilt prove false unto me;

Thou hast not been true to sire nor cuz.
Nay, marry, the Scot he said.
As true as your heart, He never part,
Gude master, be not afraid.

Jog on, jog on, cries Robin Hood,
The day it runs full fast;
For tho' my nephew me a breakfast gave,
I have not yet broke my fast

Then to yonder lodge let us take our way,
I think it wondrous good,
Where my nephew by my bold yeoman
Shall be welcom'd unto the green-wood.

Then Robin turned his face to the east,
Fight on, my merry men stout:
Our cause is good, quod brave Robin
    Hood,
And we shall not be beaten out.

The battel grows hot on every side,
The Scotchman made great moan;
Quoth Jockey, Gude faith, they fight on
    each side.
Would I were with my wife Joan!

The enemy compast brave Robin about,
'Tis long ere the battel ends;
Ther's neither will yield, nor give up the
    field.
For both are supplied with friends.

This song it was made in Robin Hoods
    dayes:
Let's pray unto Jove above,

To give us true peace, that mischief may
    cease,
And war may give place unto love.

With that he took his bugle-horn,
Full well he could it blow;
Slreight from the woods came marching
    down
One hundred tall fellows and mo.

Stand, stand to your arms, says Will Scadlbck,
Lo ! the enemies are within ken.
With that Robin Hood he laugh'd aloud,
Crying, They are my bold yeomfen.

Who, when they arriv'd, and Robin
    espy'd,
Cry'd, Master, what is your will?
We thought you had in danger been.
Your horn did sound so shrill.

Nay nay, now nay, quoth Robin Hood,
The danger is past and gone;
I would have you welcome my nephew
    here,
That has paid me two for one.

In feasting and sporting they passed the
    day,
Till Phoebus sunk into the deep;
Then each one to his quarters hy'd.
His guard there for to keep.

Long had they not walked within the
    green-wood,
But Robin he soon espy'd,

A beautiful damsel all alone.
That on a black palfrey did ride.

Her riding-suit was of a sable hew black,
Cypress over her face,
Through which her rose-like cheeks did
    blush,
All with a comely grace.

Come tell me the cause, thou pretty
    one.
Quoth Robin, and tell me aright,
From whence thou comest, and whither
    thou goest
All in this mournful plight?

From London I came, the damsel reply'd,
From London upon the Thames,
Which circled is, O grief to tell!
Besieg'd with foreign arms,

By the proud prince of Arragon,
Who swears by his martial hand
To have the princess to his spouse,
Or else to waste this land;

Except such champions can be found,
That dare fight three to three.
Against the prince, and giants twain.
Most horrid for to see;

Whose grisly looks, and eyes like
    brands.
Strike terrour where they come,
With serpents hissing on their helms,
Instead of feathered plume.

The princess shall be the victor's prize,
The king hath vow'd and said,
And he that shall the conquest win,
Shall have her to his bride.

Now we are four damsels sent abroad,
To the east, west, north, and south.
To try whose fortune is so good
To find these champions out.

But all in vain we have sought about,
For none so bold there are
That dare adventure life and blood,
To free a lady fair.

When is the day? quoth Robin Hood,
Tell me this and no more.
On Midsummer next, the dam'sel said.
Which is June the twenty-four.

With that the tears trickled down her
    cheeks,
And silent was her tongue;
With sighs and sobs she took her leave,
Away her palfrey sprung.

The news struck Robin to the heart,
He fell down on the grass,
His actions and his troubled mind
Shew'd he perplexed was.

Where lies your grief? quoth Will Scadloc
O, master, tell to me:
If the damsels eyes have pierc'd your
    heart,
I'll fetch her back to thee.

Now nay, now nay, quoth Robin Hood,
She doth not cause my smart;
But 'tis the poor distressed princess,
That wounds me to the heart;

I'll go fight the [prince and] giants all,
To set the lady free.
The devil take my soul, quoth Little
   John,
If I part with thy company.

Must I stay behind? quoth Will
   Scadlbeck,
No, no, that must not be;
Iie make the third man in the fight,
So we shall be three to three.

These words cheer'd Robin to the heart,
Joy shone within his face,
Within his arms he hugg'd them both,
And kindly did imbrace.

Quoth he, We'll put on mothley grey.
And long staves in our hands,
A scrip and bottle by our sides,
As come from the holy land.

So may we pass along the high-way,
None will ask us from whence we came,
But take us pilgrims for to be,
Or else some holy men.

Now they are on their journey gone,
As fast as they may speed,
Yet for all their haste, ere they arriv'd,
The princess forth was led,

To be deliver'd to the prince,
Who in the list did stand,
Prepar'd to fight, or else receive
His lady by the hand.

With that he walk'd about the lists.
With giants by his side:
Bring forth, said he, your
   champions.
Or bring me forth my bride.

This is the four and twentieth day,
The day prefixt upon:
Bring forth my bride, or London
   burns,
I swear by Alcaron.

Then cries the king, and queen likewise,
Both weeping as they spake,
'Whan Laban herde of this myschief,
A sorry man was he,

He trumped his men to relefe,
For to cease that tyme mente he.
Mersadage kinge of Barbarye
He did carye to his tente,

And beryed him by right of Sarsenye,
With brennynge fire riche oynemenfe;
And songe the dirige of Alkaron,
That bibill is of here laye;

And wayled his deth everychon,
Seven nyghtis and seven dayes.'
'Now shall ye here of Laban:
Whan tidynges to him were comen,

Tho was he a fulle sory man.
Whan he herde howe his vitaile were
   nomen,
And howe his men were slayne,
And Gye was go safe hem froo;

He defyed Mahounde, and Apolyne,
Jubiter, Astarol, and Alcaron also,'
Lo! we have brought our daughter dear,
Whom we are forc'd to forsake.

With that stept out bold Robin Hood,
Crys, My liege, it must not be so:
Such beauty as the fair princess
Is not for a tyrants mow.

The prince he then began to storm,
Cries, Fool, fanatick, baboon!
How dare thou stop my valours prize?
I'll kill thee with a frown.

Thou tyrant Turk, thou infidel,
Thus Robin began to reply.
Thy frowns I scorn and lo ! here's my
   gage,
And thus I thee defie.

And for those two Goliahs there.
That stand on either side,
Here are two little Davids by,
That soon can tame their pride.

Then the king did for armour send,
For lances, swords, and shields;
And thus all three in armour bright,
Came marching to the field.

The trumpets began to sound a charge,
Each singled out his man;
Their arms in pieces soon were hew'd,
Blood sprang from every vain.

The prince he reacht Robin Hood a
   blow,
He struck with might and main,
Which forc'd him to reel about the field,
As though he had been slain.

God-a-mercy, quoth Robin, for that blow!
The quarrel shall soon be try'd;
This stroke shall shew a full divorce
Betwixt thee and thy bride.

So from his shoulders he's cut his head,
Which on the ground did fall.
And grumbling sore at Robin Hood,
To be so dealt withaL

The giants then began to rage
To see their prince lie dead:
Thou's be the next, quoth Little
   John,
Unless thou well guard thy head.

With that his faulchion he wherl'd about,
It was both keen and sharp;
He clave the giant to the belt,
And cut in twain his heart.

Will Scadlock well had play'd his part,
The giant he had brought to his knee;
Quoth Will, The devil cannot break his fast,
Unless he have you all three.

So with his faulchion he run him through,
A deep and ghastly wound;
Who dam'd and foam'd, curst and
    blasphem'd,
And then fell to the ground.

Now all the lists with shouts were fill'd,
The skies they did resound,
Which brought the princess to herself,
Who had fal'n in a swound.

The king and queen, and princess fair,
Came walking to the place.
And gave the champions many thanks,
And did them further grace.

Tell me, quoth the king, whence you are.
That thus disguised came,
Whose valour speaks that noble blood
Doth run through every vain.

A boon, a boon, quoth Robin Hood,
On my knees I beg and crave.
By my crown, quoth the king, I grant.
Ask what, and thou shalt have.

Then pardon I beg for my merry men,
Which are in the green-wood,
For Little John and Will Scadlock,
And for me, bold Robin Hood.

Art thou Robin Hood? quoth the king;
For the valour thou hast shewn,
Your pardons I do freely grant,
And welcome every one,

The princess I promise the victor's prize,
She cannot have you all three.
She shall chuse, quoth Robin. Said
    Little John,
Then little share falls to me.

Then did the princess view all three.
With a comely lovely grace.
And took Will Scadlock by the hand,
Saying, Here I make my choice.

With that a noble lord stept forth.
Of Maxfield earl was he.
Who look'd Will Scadlock in the face,
And wept most bitterly.

Quoth he, I had a son like thee,
Whom I lov'd wondrous well,
But he is gone, or rather dead,
His name it is young Gamwell.

Then did Will Scadlock fall on his
    knees,
Cries, Father! father! here,
Here kneels your son, your young
    Gamwell,
You said you lov'd so dear.

But, lord! what imbracing and kissing
    was there,
When all these friends were met!
They are gone to the wedding, and so
    to [the] bedding
And so I bid you good night.

Robin Hood and Queen Katherine

Gold tane from the king's harbengers,
Downe, a downe, a downe.
As seldome hath beene scene,
Downe, a downe, a downe,
And carried by bold Robin Hood
For a present to the queene,
Downe, a downe, a downe.

If that I live a yeare to an end,
Thus gan queene Katharine say,
Bold Robin Hood, I will be thy friend,
And all thy yeomen gay.

The queene is to her chamber gone,
As fast as she can wen;
She calls unto her lovely page,
His name was Richard Patrington.

'Come thou hither to mee, thou lovely
    page,
Come thou hither to mee;
For thou must post to Nottingham.
As fast as thou can dree;

And as thou goest to Nottingham,
Search all the English wood.
Enquire of one good yeoman or
    another,
That can tell thee of Robin Hood.'

Sometimes hee went, sometimes hee ran,
As fast as hee could win;
And when hee came to Nottingham,
There hee tooke up his inne.

And when he came to Nottingham,
And had tooke up his inne,
He cals for a pottle of Rhenish wine,
And dranke a health to his queene.

There sate a yeoman by his side,
Tell mee, sweet page, said hee,
What is thy businesse and the cause,
So far in the north countrey?

This is my businesse and the cause.
Sir, I tell it you for good.
To enquire of one good yeoman or
    another,
To tell mee of Robin Hood.

'Get my horse betimes in the morne,
By it be break of day,
And I will shew thee bold Robin
    Hood,
And all his yeomen gay.'

When that he came at Robin Hoods
    place,
Hee fell down on his knee:
'Queen Katherine she doth greet you
    well,
She greets you well by mee;

She bids you post to fair London
    court,
Not fearing any thing;
For there shall be a little sport,
And she hath sent you her ring.'

Robin Hood tooke his mantle from his
  back.
It was of the Lincolne greene,
And sent it by this lovely page.
For a present unto the queene.

In Summer time, when leaves grow green,
It's a seemely sight to see.
How Robin Hood himselfe had drest,
And all his yeomandry.

He clothed his men in Lincolne greene,
And himselfe in scarlet red;
Blacke hats, white feathers, all alike.
Now bold Robin Hood is rid:

And when hee came at London's court,
Hee fell downe on his knee.
Thou art welcome, Locksly, said the
  queen,
And all thy good yeomandree.

The king is into Finsbury field
Marching in battle-ray.
And after follows bold Robin Hood,
And all his yeomen gay.

Come hither, Tepus, said the king,
Bow-bearer after mee;
Come measure me out with this line,
How long our mark must be.

What is the wager? said the queene,
That must I now know here.
'Three hundred tun of Rhenish wine.
Three hundred tun of beere;

Three hundred of the fattest harts
That run on Dallom-lee.'
That's a princely wager, said the king.
That needs must I tell thee.

With that bespake one Clifton then,
Full quickly and full soone,
Measure no markes for us, most
  soveraigne liege,
Wee'l shoot at sun and moone.

'Full fifteene score your marke shall be,
Full fifteene score shall stand.'
I lay my bow, said Clifton then,
He cleave the willow wand.

With that the king's archers led about,
While it was three, and none;
With that the ladies began to shout,
'Madam, your game is gone.'

A boone, a boone, queene Katherine
  cries,
I crave it on my bare knee;
Is there any knight of your privy counsel
Of queen Katherines part will be?

Come hither to mee, Sir Richard Lee,
Thou art a knight full good;
For I do knowe by thy pedigree
Thou sprung'st from Gowers blood.

Come hither to me, thou bishop of
  Herefordshire;
For a noble priest was hee.
By my silver miter, said the bishop then,
I'le not bet one peny.

The king hath archers of his own,
Full ready and full light,
And these be strangers every one,
No man knowes what they hight.

What wilt thou bet? said Robin Hood,
Thou seest our game the worse.
By my silver miter, then said the bishop,
All the money within my purse.

What is in thy purse? said Robin Hood,
Throw it downe on the ground.
Fifteen score nobles, said the bishop;
It's neere an hundred pound,

Robin Hood took his bagge from his
    side,
And threw it downe on the greene:
William Scadlocke then went smiling
    away,
'I know who this money must win.'

With that the king's archers led about,
While it was three and three;
With that the ladies gave a shout,
'Woodcock, beware thy knee!'

It is three pounds he has in hand
The next three pays for all.
Robin Hood went and whisper'd the
    queen,
The king's part shall be but small,

Robin Hood hee led about,
Hee shot it under hand;
And Clifton with a bearing arrow,
Hee clave the willow wand.

And little Midge, the millers son,
Hee shot not much the worse;
He shot within a finger of the prick:
'Now, bishop, beware thy purse!'

A boone, a boone, queene Katherine cries,
I crave it on my bare knee,
That you will angry be with none
That are of my partie,

'They shall have forty daies to come.
And forty daies to goe.
And three times forty to sport and play;
Then welcome friend or foe,'

Thou art welcome, Robin Hood, said
    the queene,
And so is Little John,
And so is Midge, the millers son;
Thrice welcome every one.

Is this Robin Hood ? now said the
    king,
For it was told to me
That he was slain in the palace gates,
So far in the north country.

Is this Robin Hood? quoth the bishop then,
As it seems well to be:
Had I knowne it had been that bold
    outlaw,
I would not [have] bet one peny.

Hee tooke me late one Saturday at night,
And bound mee fast to a tree.
And made mee sing a masse, God wot,
To him and his yeomandree.

What, an if I did, sales Robin Hood,
Of that masse I was faine;
For recompence of that, he sales,
Here's halfe thy gold againe.

Robin Hood's Chase

Come, you gallants all, to you I do call,
With hey down, down, an a down,
That now are in this place;
For a song I will sing of Henry the
    king,
How he did Robin Hood chase.

Queen Katherin she a match did
    make,
As plainly doth appear,
For three hundred tun of good red
    wine.
And three [hundred] tun of beere.

But yet her archers she had to seek,
With their bows and arrows so good;
But her mind it was bent with a good
    intent,
To send for bold Robin Hood.

But when bold Robin he came there,
Queen Katherin she did say,
Thou art welcome, Locksley, said the
    queen,
And all thy yeomen gay.

For a match of shooting I have made,
And thou on my part must be.
'If I miss the mark, be it light or
    dark,

Now nay, now nay, sayes Little John,
Master, that shall not be;
We must give gifts to the kings officers;
That gold will serve thee and mee.

Then hanged I will be.'

But when the game came to be
    played.
Bold Robin he then drew nigh.
With his mantle of green, most brave
    to be seen,
He let his arrows fly.

And when the game it ended was,
Bold Robin wan it with a grace;
But after the king was angry with
    him,
And vowed he would him chace.

What though his pardon granted was,
While he with him did stay;
But yet the king was vexed at him,
When as he was gone his way.

Soon after the king from the court
    did hye,
In a furious angry mood,
And often enquired both far and near
After bold Robin Hood.

But when the king to Nottingham came,
Bold Robin was in the wood:
O, come now, said he, and let me see
Who can find me bold Robin Hood.

But when that bold Robin he did hear
The king had him in chase,
Then said Little John, 'tis time to be gone.
And go to some other place.

And away they went from merry Sherwood,
And into Yorkshire he did hye;
And the king did follow, with a hoop
     and a hallow,
But could not come him nigh.

Yet jolly Robin he passed along,
And went strait to Newcastle town;
And there he stayed hours two or three,
And then to Barwick is gone.

When the king did see how Robin did
     flee,
He was vexed wondrous sore;
With a hoop and a hallow he vowed to
     follow,
And take him, or never give ore.

Come now let's away, then crys Little
     John,
Let any man follow that dare;
To Carlisle we'l hye, with our company,
And so then to Lancaster.

From Lancaster then to Chester they went,
And so did king Henry;
But Robin [went] away, for he durst not
     stay,
For fear of some treachery.

Says Robin, Come let us for London goe,
To see our noble queens face,
It may be she wants our company,
Which makes the king so us chase.

When Robin he came queene Katherin
     before,
He fell low upon his knee:
'If it please your grace, I am come to this
     place
For to speak with king Henry.'

Queen Katherine answered bold Robin
     again,
The king is gone to merry Sherwood;
And when he went away to me he did say.
He would go and seek Robin Hood.

'Then fare you well, my gracious queen,
For to Sherwood I will hye apace;
For fain would I see what he would with
     me,
If I could but meet with his grace.'

But when king Henry he came home,
Full weary, and vexed in mind,
And that he did hear Robin had been there,
He blamed dame Fortune unkind.

You're welcome home, queen Katherin
     cryed,
Henry, my soveraign liege;
Bold Robin Hood, that archer good.
Your person hath been to seek.

But when king Henry he did hear,
That Robin had been there him to seeke.
This answer he gave, He's a cunning knave.
For I have sought him this whole three weeks.

A boon! a boon! queen Katherin cry'd,
I beg it here of your grace,
To pardon his life, and seek not strife:
And so endeth Robin Hoods chase.

Robin Hood's Golden Prize

I have heard talk of Robin Hood,
Derry, derry down,
And of brave Little John,
Of fryer Tuck, and Will Scarlet,
Loxley, and maid Marian.

But such a tale as this before
I think was never known:
For Robin Hood disguised himself,
And from the wood is gone.

Like to a fryer bold Robin Hood
Was accoutered in his array;
With hood, gown, beeds, and crucifix.
He past upon the way.

He had not gone miles two or three,
But it was his chance to spy
Two lusty priests, clad all in black,
Come riding gallantly.

Benedicite, then said Robin Hood,
Some pitty on me take;
Cross you my hand with a silver groat,
For our dear ladies sake.

For I have been wandring all this day.
And nothing could I get;
Not so much as one poor cup of drink,
Nor bit of bread to eat.

Now, by our holy dame, the priest's
repli'd,
We never a peny have;
For we this morning have been rob'd.
And could no money save.

I am much afraid, said bold Robin Hood,
That you both do tell a lie;
And now before you do go hence,
I am resolv'd to try.

When as the priests heard him say so,
Then they rode away amain;
But Robin Hood betook to his heels,
And soon overtook them again.

Then Robin Hood laid hold of them both.
And pull'd them down from their horse:
O spare us, fryer! the priests cry'd out,
On us have some remorse!

You said you had no mony, quoth he,
Wherefore, without delay,
We three will fall down on our knees,
And for mony we will pray.

The priests they could not him gainsay.
But down they kneeled with speed:
Send us, O send us, then quoth they,
Some mony to serve our need.

The priests did pray with a mournful chear.
Sometimes their hands did wring;
Sometimes they wept, and cried aloud.
Whilst Robin did merrily sing.

When they had been praying an hour's
    space,
The priests did still lament;
Then quoth bold Robin, Now let's see
What mony heaven hath us sent.

We will be sharers all alike
Of [the] mony that we have;
And there is never a one of us
That his fellow shall deceive.

The priests their hands in their pockets
    put,
But mony would find none:
We'l search ourselves, said Robin Hood,
Each other, one by one.

Then Robin took pains to search them
    both,
And he found good store of gold.
Five hundred peeces presently
Upon the grass was told.

Here is a brave show, said Robin Hood,
Such store of gold to see,
And you shall each one have a part.
Cause you prayed so heartily.

He gave them fifty pounds a-peece,
And the rest for himself did keep:
The priests [they] durst not speak one word,
But they sighed wondrous deep.
With that the priests rose up from their
    knees,
Thinking to have parted so:
Nay, nay, says Robin Hood, one thing
    more
I have to say ere you go.

You shall be sworn, said bold Robin
    Hood,
Upon this holy grass,
That you will never tell lies again,
Which way soever you pass.

The second oath that you here must take,
That all the days of your lives,
You shall never tempt maids to sin,
Nor lie with other mens wives.

The last oath you shall take, it is this,
Be charitable to the poor;
Say, you have met with a holy fryar.
And I desire no more.

He set them on their horses again,
And away then they did ride;
And he return'd to the merry
    green-wood.
With great joy, mirth, and pride.

Robin Hood's Rescuing Will Stutly

When Robin Hood in the green wood
   liv'd,
Derry derry down.
Under the green wood tree,
Tidings there came to him with speed,
Tidings for certainty;
Hey down, derry, derry down;

That Will Stutly surprized was,
And eke in prison lay;
Three varlets that the sheriff had hired,
Did likely him betray:

'I, and to-morrow hanged must be,
To-morrow as soon as it is day;
Before they could this victory get,
Two of them did Stutly slay.'

When Robin Hood he heard this news,
Lord! he was grieved sore;
And to his merry men he did say,
(Who altogether swore),

That Will Stutly should rescued be,
And be brought back again;
Or else should many a gallant wight
For his sake there be slain.

He cloathed himself in scarlet red,
His men were all in green;
A finer shew, throughout the world.
In no place could be seen.

Good lord! it was a gallant sight
To see them all on a row;
With every man a good broad sword,
And eke a good yew bow.

Forth of the green wood are they gone,
Yea all couragiously,
Resolving to bring Stutly home,
Or every man to die.

And when they came the castle neer.
Whereas Will Stutly lay,
I hold it good, saith Robin Hood,
Wee here in ambush stay,

And send one forth some news to hear,
To yonder palmer fair,
That stands under the castle wall,
Some news he may declare.

With that steps forth a brave young man.
Which was of courage bold,
Thus did hee speak to the old man:
I pray thee, palmer old.

Tell me, if that thou rightly ken.
When must Will Stutly die,
Who is one of bold Robin's men,
And here doth prisoner lie?

Alack! alas! the palmer said,
And for ever woe is me!
Will Stutly hanged must be this day,
On yonder gallows-tree.

O had his noble master known,
He would some succour send;
A few of his bold yeomandree
Full soon would fetch him hence.

I, that is true, the young man said;
I, that is true, said he;
Or, if they were neer to this place,
They soon would set him free.

But fare thee well, thou good old man,
Farewell, and thanks to thee;
If Stutly hanged be this day,
Reveng'd his death will be.

Hee was no sooner from the palmer
    gone,
But the gates were open'd wide,
And out of the castle Will Stutly came.
Guarded on every side.

When hee was forth of the castle come,
And saw no help was nigh,
Thus he did say to the sheriff,
Thus he said gallantly:

Now seeing that I needs must die,
Grant me one boon, said he,
For my noble master nere had a man,
That yet was hang'd on the tree.

Give me a sword all in my hand,
And let mee be unbound,
And with thee and thy men He fight,
Till I lie dead on the ground.

But his desire he would not grant,
His wishes were in vain;
For the sheriff had sworn he hanged
    should be,
And not by the sword be slain.

Do but unbind my hands, he sales,
I will no weapons crave.
And if I hanged be this day,
Damnation let me have.

O no, O no, the sheriff said.
Thou shalt on the gallows die,
I, and so shall thy master too.
If ever in me it lie.

O, dastard coward ! Stutly cries,
Thou faint-heart pesant slave!
If ever my master do thee meet,
Thou shalt thy paiment have,

My noble master doth thee scorn,
And all thy coward crew;
Such silly imps unable are,
Bold Robin to subdue.

But when he was to the gallows come,
And ready to bid adiew,
Out of a bush leaps Little John,
And comes Will Stutly to:

'I pray thee, Will, before thou die,
Of thy dear friends take leave: —
I needs must borrow him for a while,
How say you, master shrieve?'

Now, as I live, the sheriff he said,
That varlet will I know;
Some sturdy rebell is that same,
Therefore let him not go.

Then Little John most hastily,
Away cut Stutly's bands,
And from one of the sheriff's men,
A sword twicht from his hands.

'Here, Will, here, take thou this same.
Thou canst it better sway;
And here defend thyself awhile,
For aid will come straightway.'

And there they turn'd them back to back.
In the middle of them that day.
Till Robin Hood approached near.
With many an archer gay.

With that an arrow by them flew,
I wist from Robin Hood;
Make haste, make haste, the sheriff
   he said,
Make haste, for it is good.

The sheriff is gone, his doughty men
Thought it no boot to stay,

But, as their master had them taught,
They run full fast away.

O stay, O stay, Will Stutly said,
Take leave ere you depart;
You neere will catch bold Robin Hood,
Unless you dare him meet.

Ill betide you, quoth Robin Hood,
That you so soon are gone;
My sword may in the scabbord rest,
For here our work is done.

I little thought, Will Stutly said
When I came to this place,
For to have met with Little John,
Or seen my masters face.

Thus Stutly was at liberty set.
And safe brought from his foe:
'O thanks, O thanks to my master,
Since here it was not so:

And once again, my fellows [all],
We shall in the green woods meet,
Where we [will] make our bow-strings
   twang,
Musick for us most sweet.'

The Noble Fisher-Man or, Robin Hood's Preferment

In Summer-time, when leaves grow green,
When they doe grow both green and
   long,
Of a bold outlaw, call'd Robin Hood,
It is of him I sing this song.

When the lilly leafe, and the eglantine
Doth bud and spring with a merry
   cheere,
This outlaw was weary of the wood-side,
And chasing of the fallow-deere.

'The fisher-men brave more mony have
Than any merchants two or three;
Therefore I will to Scarborough go,
That I a fisherman brave may be.'

This outlaw called his merry men all,
As they sate under the green-wood tree:
'If any of you have gold to spend,
I pray you heartily spend it with me.'

Now, quoth Robin Hood, I'll to
    Scarborough go,
It seems to be a very faire day,
He tooke up his inne at a
    widdow-womans
Hard by upon the water gray:

Who asked of him, 'Where wert thou
    borne?
Or tell to me where dost thou fare?'
'I am a poor fisherman,' said he then.
'This day intrapped all in care.'

'What is thy name, thou fine fellow,
I pray thee heartily tell it to mee?'
'In my own country, where I was borne,
Men call me Simon over the Lee.'

'Simon, Simon,' said the good-wife,
'I wish thou mayest well brook thy name.'
The out-law was ware of her courtesie,
And rejoyced he had got such a dame.

'Simon, wilt thou be my man?
And good round wages I'll give thee;
I have as good a ship of my own,
As any sails upon the sea:

Anchors and planks thou shalt not want,
Masts and ropes that are so long.
And if you thus do furnish me.'
Said Simon, 'Nothing shall goe wrong.'

They pluckt up anchor, and away did
    sayle,
More of a day then two or three;
When others cast in their baited hooks.
The bare lines into the sea cast he.

It will be long, said the master then,
Ere this great lubber do thrive on the sea;
I'le assure you he shall have no part
    of our fish,
For in truth he is no part worthy.

Woe is me! said Simon then,
This day that ever I came here!
I wish I were in Plompton parke.
In chasing of the fallow deere.

For every clowne laughs me to scorne,
And they by me set nought at all;
If I had them in Plompton park,
I would set as little by them all.

They pluckt up anchor, and away did
    sayle,
More of a day then two or three:
But Simon espyed a ship of warre,
That sayled towards them most valorously.

O woe is me! said the master then,
This day that ever I was borne!
For all our fish we have got to day,
Is every bit lost and forlorne.

For your French robbers on the sea.
They will not spare of us one man,
But carry us to the coast of France,
And ligge us in the prison strong.

But Simon said. Doe not feare them,
Neither, master, take you no care;
Give me my bent bow in my hand.
And never a Frenchman will I spare.

'Hold thy peace, thou long lubber,
For thou art nought but brags and
   boast;
If I should cast thee over-board.
There's but a simple lubber lost'

Simon grew angry at these words,
And so angry then was he,
That he took his bent bow in his hand,
And in the ship-hatch goe doth he.

Master, tye me to the mast, saith he.
That at my mark I may stand fair,
And give me my bent bow in my
   hand,
And never a Frenchman will I spare.

He drew his arrow to the very head,
And drew it with all might and maine,
And straightway in the twinkling of
   an eye,
To the Frenchmans heart the arrow's
   gane.

The Frenchman fell down on the
   ship-hatch,
And under the hatches there below;
Another Frenchman, that him espy'd,
The dead corpse into the sea doth throw.
O master, loose me from the mast, he said,
And for them all take you no care;
For give me my bent bow in my hand,
And never a Frenchman will I spare.

Then streight [they] boarded the
   French ship.
They lyeing all dead in their sight;
They found within that ship of warre.
Twelve thousand pound of mony bright.

The one halfe of the ship, said Simon
   then,
He give to my dame and [her]
   children small;
The other halfe of the ship I'll bestow
On you that are my fellowes all.

But now bespake the master then,
For so, Simon, it shall not be.
For you have won it with your own
   hand,
And the owner of it you shall bee.

'It shall be so, as I have said;
And, with this gold, for the opprest
An habitation I will build,
Where they shall live in peace and rest.'

Robin Hood's Delight

There's some will talk of lords and
   knights,
Doun, a doun, a doun,
And some of yeomen good;
But I will tell you of Will Scarlock,
Little John, and Robin Hood.
Doun, a doun, a doun, a doun.

They were outlaws, 'tis well known,
And men of a noble blood;
And many a time was their valour
   shown
In the forrest of merry Sheerwood.

Upon a time it chanced so.
As Robin would have it be.
They all three would a walking go,
The pastime for to see.

And as they walked the forest along,
Upon a Midsummer day,
There was they aware of three keepers,
Clad all in green aray.

With brave long faucheons by their
   sides
And forrest-bills in hand.
They call'd aloud to those bold outlkws,
And charged them to stand.

Why, who are you, cry'd bold Robin,
That speak so boldly here?
'We three belong to King Henry,
And are keepers of his deer.'
'

The devil you are!' sayes Robin Hood,
I am sure that it is not so;
We be the keepers of this forrest,
And that you soon shall know.

Come, your coats of green lay on the
   ground.
And so will we all three,
And take your swords and bucklers
   round.
And try the victory.

We be content, the keepers said,
We be three, and you no less,
Then why should we be of you
   afraid,
As we never did transgress?

'Why, if you be three keepers in this
   forrest.
Then we be three rangers good,
And will make you know before you do go,
You meet with bold Robin Hood.'

'We be content, thou bold outlkw,
Our valour here to try.
And will make you know, before we
   do go,
We will fight before we will fly.

Then, come draw your swords, you
   bold outlaws,
No longer stand to prate,
But let us try it out with blows,
For cowards we do hate.

Here is one of us for Will Scarlock,
And another for Little John,
And I myself for Robin Hood,
Because he is stout and strong,'

So they fell to it hard and sore,
It was on a Midsummers day;
From eight of the clock till two and
    past.
They all shewed gallant play.

There Robin, and Will, and Little
    John,
They fought most manfully,
Till all their winde was spent and
    gone,
Then Robin aloud did cry:

O hold, O hold, cries bold Robin,
I see you be stout men;
Let me blow one blast on my
    bugle-horn,
Then I'll fight with you again.

'That bargain's to make, bold Robin
    Hood,
Therefore we it deny;
Thy blast upon the bugle-horn
Cannot make us fight or fly.

Therefore fall on, or else be gone,
And yield to us the day:
It never shall be said that we are afraid
Of thee, nor thy yeomen gay.'

If that be so, cries bold Robin,
Let me but know your names,
And in the forrest of merry
    Sheerwood,

I shall extol your fames.
And with our names, one of them
    said.
What hast thou here to do?
Except that you wilt fight it out.
Our names thou shalt not know.

We will fight no more, sayes bold
    Robin,
You be men of valour stout;
Come and go with me to Nottingham,
And there we will fight it out.

With a but of sack we will bang it
    about,
To see who wins the day;
And for the cost make you no doubt,
I have gold enough to pay.

And ever hereafter so long as we live.
We all will brethren be;
For I love these men with heart and
    hand,
That will fight and never flee.

So, away they went to Nottinghkm,
With sack to make amends;
For three days they the wine did chase,
And drank themselves good friends.

Robin Hood and the Beggar (2)

Come and listen, you gentlemen all,
Hey down, down, an a down,
That mirth do love for to hear,
And a story true He tell unto you,
If that you will but draw near.

In elder times, when merriment was,
And archery was holden good.
There was an outlaw, as many know,
Which men called Robin Hood.

Upon a time it chanced so,
Bold Robin was merry disposed,
His time for to spend he did intend
Either with friends or foes.

Then he got upon a gallant brave steed,
The which was worth angels ten.
With a mantle of green, most brave to
  be seen.
He left all his merry men.

And riding towards Nottingham,
Some pastime for to spy.
There was he aware of a jolly beggar,
As ere he beheld with his eye.

An old pacht coat the beggar had on,
Which he daily did use to wear;
And many a bag about him did wag.
Which made Robin to him repair.

God speed, God speed, said Robin
  Hood,
What countryman? tell to me,
'I am Yorkshire, sir; but, ere you go far,
Some charity give unto me.'

Why, what wouldst thou have? said
  Robin Hood,
I pray thee tell unto me.
No lands nor livings, the beggar he said,
But a penny for charitie.

I have no money, said Robin Hood
  then,
But a ranger within the wood;
I am an outlaw, as many do know,
My name it is Robin Hood.

But yet I must tell the, bonny beggkr,
That a bout with [thee] I must try;
Thy coat of grey, lay down I say,
And my mantle of green shall lye by.

Content, content, the beggar he cry'd,
Thy part it will be the worse;
For I hope this bout to give thee the rout,
And then have at thy purse.

So the beggar he had a mickle long staffe,
And Robin a nut-brown sword;
So the beggar drew nigh, and at Robin
  let fly.
But gave him never a word.

Fight on, fight on, said Robin Hood then.
This game well pleaseth me.
For every blow that Robin gave,
The beggar gave buffets three.

And fighting there full hard and sore,
Not far from Nottingham town,
They never fled, till from Robin Hoods
  head
The blood came trickling down.

O, hold thy hand, said Robin Hood
  then,
And thou and I will agree.
If that be true, the beggar he said,
Thy mantle come give unto me.

Now a change, a change, cri'd Robin
  Hood,
Thy bags and coat give me;
And this mantle of mine He to thee resign,
My horse and my braverie.

When Robin had got the beggars clothes.
He looked round about;
Methinks, said he, I seem to be
A beggar brave and stout

For now I have a bag for my bread,
So I have another for corn;
I have one for salt, and another for malt.
And one for my little horn.

And now I will a begging goe,
Some charitie for to find.
And if any more of Robin you'll know,
In the second part 'tis behind.

Now Robin he is to Nottingham bound,
With his bag hanging down to his knee,
His staff, and his coat, scarce worth a
  groat,
Yet merrilie passed he.

As Robin he passed the streets along,
He heard a pittiful cry;
Three brethren dear, as he did hear,
Condemned were to dye.

Then Robin he highed to the sherififs
  [house],
Some reliefe for to seek;
He skipt, and leapt, and capered full high,
As he went along the street.

But when to the sheriff's doore he came,
There a gentleman fine and brave,
Thou beggar, said he, come tell unto me
What it is thou wouldest have.

No meat, nor drink, said Robin Hood
  then,
That I come here to crave;
But to get the lives of yeomen three,
And that I fain would have.

That cannot be, thou bold beggkr.
Their fact it is so clear;
I tell to thee, they hanged must be,
For stealing of our king's deer.

But when to the gallows they did come,
There was many a weeping eye:
O, hold your peace, said Robin Hood then,
For certain they shall not dye.

Then Robin he set his horn to his mouth,
And he blew out Wastes three,
Till a hundred bold archers brave
Came kneeling down to his knee.

What is your will, master? they said,
We are at your command.
Shoot east, shoot west, said Robin
   Hood then,
And see you spare no man.

Then they shot east, and they shot west,
Their arrows were so keen;
The sheriffe he, and his companie.
No longer could be seen.

Then he stept to those brethren three,
And away he has them tane;
The sheriffe was crost, and many a
   man lost,
That dead lay on the plain.

And away they went into the merry
   green wood,
And sung with a merry glee;
And Robin Hood took these brethren
   good
To be of his yeomandrie.

Little John and the Four Beggars

All you that delight to spend some
   time,
With a hey down, down, a down,
   down,
A merry song for to sing,
Unto me draw neer, and you shall
   hear
How Little John went a begging.

As Robin Hood walked the forest along,
And all his yeomandree.
Sayes Robin, Some of you must a
   begging go.
And, Little John, it must be thee.

Sayes John, If I must a begging go,
I will have a palmer's weed,
With a staff and a coat, and bags of
   all sort.

The better then I may speed.

Come, give me now a bag for my
   bread,
And another for my cheese.
And one for a peny, when as I get
   any,
So nothing I may leese.

Now Little John he is a begging gone,
Seeking for some relief;
But of all the beggers he met on the way,
Little John he was the chief.

But as he was walking himself alone,
Four beggers he chanced to spy,
Some deaf, and some blind, and some
   came behind;
Sayes John, Heres a brave company.

Good-morrow, said John, my brethren
  dear.
Good fortune I had you to see;
Which way do you go? pray let me know,
For I want some company.

O! what is here to do? then said Little
  John:
Why ring all these bells? said he;
What dog is a hanging? Come, let us be
  ganging,
That we the truth may see.

Here is no dog a hanging, then one of
  them said,
Good fellow, we tell unto thee;
But here is one dead, that will give us
  cheese and bread,
And it may be one single penny,

We have brethren in London, another he
  said.
So have we in Coventry,
In Barwick and Dover, and all the world
  over,
But ne'er a crookt carril like thee.

Therefore stand thee back, thou crooked
  carhl,
And take that knock on the crown.
Nay, said Little John, He not yet be gone,
For a bout will I have of you round.

Now have at you all, then said Little
  John,
If you be so full of your blows;

Fight on all four, and nere give ore.
Whether you be friends or foes.

John nipped the dumb, and made him to
  rore,
And the blind he made to see;
And he that a cripple had been seven
  years.
He made run then faster than he.

And flinging them all against the wall,
With many a sturdie bang,
It made John sing, to hear the gold ring,
Which again the walls cryed twang.

Then he got out of the beggers cloak,
Three hundred pound in gold,
Good fortune had I, then said Little
  John,
Such a good sight to behold.

But what found he in the beggar's bag
But three hundred pound and three?
If I drink water while this doth last.
Then an ill death may I dye:

And my begging trade I will now give ore,
My fortune hath bin so good;
Therefore He not stay, but I will away,
To the forrest of merry Sherwood.'

And when to the forrest of Sherwood he
  came.
He quickly there did see
His master good, bold Robin Hood,
And all his company.

What news? What news? then said
  Robin Hood
Come, Little John, tell unto me,
How hast thou sped with thy beggers trade?
For that I fain would see.

No news but good, said Little John,
With begging ful wel I have sped;
Six hundred and three I have here for thee,
In silver and gold so red.

Then Robin Hood took Little John by
  the hand
And danced about the oak tree:
'If we drink water while this doth last,
Then an ill death may we die.'

So to conclude my merry new song,
All you that delight it to sing;
'Tis of Robin Hood, that archer good,
And how Little John went a begging.

Robin Hood and the Ranger – True Friendship after a Fierce Fight

When Phebus had melted the sickles of ice,
With a hey down, &c.
And likewise the mountains of snow,
Bold Robin Hood he would ramble away,
To frollick abroad with his bow.

He left all his merry men waiting behind,
Whilst through the green vallies he pass'd,
Where he did behold a forester bold,
Who cry'd out. Friend, whither so fast?

I am going, quoth Robin, to kill a fat buck.
For me and my merry men all;
Besides, ere I go, I'll have a fat doe,
Or else it shall cost me a fall.

You'd best have a care, said the forester
  then,
For these are his majesty's deer;
Before you shall shoot, the thing I'll dispute,
For I am head forester here.

These thirteen long Summers, quoth
  Robin, I'm sure.
My arrows I here have let fly,
Where freely I range; methinks it is strange
You should have more power than I.

This forest, quoth Robin, I think is my own.
And so are the nimble deer too;
Therefore I declare, and solemnly swear,
I'll not be affronted by you.

The forester he had a long quarter-staff.
Likewise a broad sword by his side;
Without more ado, he presently drew
Declaring the truth should be try'd.

Bold Robin Hood had a sword of the best,
Thus, ere he would take any wrong.
His courage was flush, he'd venture a
  brush,
And thus they fell to it ding dong.

The very first blow that the forester gave,
He made his broad weapon cry twang;
'Twas over the head, he fell down for dead,
O that was a damnable bang!

But Robin he soon recovered himself,
And bravely fell to it again;
The very next stroke their weapons they
   broke,
Yet never a man there was slain.

At quarter-staff then they resolved to play,
Because they would have the other bout;
And brave Robin Hood right valiantly
   stood,
Unwilling he was to give out.

Bold Robin he gave him very hard blows,
The other return'd them as fast;
At every stroke their jackets did smoke;
Three hours the combat did last.

At length in a rage the forester grew,
And cudgel'd bold Robin so sore.
That he could not stand, so shaking his hand,
He cry'd, Let us freely give o'er.

Thou art a brave fellow, I needs must confess
I never knew any so good;
Thou art fitting to be a yeoman for me,
And range in the merry green wood.

I'll give thee this ring as a token of love.
For bravely thou hast acted thy part;
That man that can fight, in him I delight,
And love him with all my whole heart.

Robin Hood set his bugle-horn to his
   mouth,
A blast then he merrily blows;
His yeomen did hear, and strait did appear
A hundred with trusty long bows.

Now Little John came at the head of them all,
Cloath'd in a rich mantle of green;
And likewise the rest were gloriously drest,
A delicate sight to be seen!

Lo! these are my yeomen, said bold
   Robin Hood,
And thou shalt be one of the train:
A mantle and bow, and quiver also,
I give them whom I entertain.

The forester willingly enter'd the list.
They were such a beautiful sight;
Then with a long bow they shot a fat doe.
And made a rich supper that night.

What singing and dancing was in the
   green wood,
For joy of another new mate!
With might and delight they spent all the
   night,
And liv'd at a plentiful rate.

The forester ne'er was so merry before,
As then he was with these brave souls,
Who never would fail, in wine, beer, or
   ale,
To take off their cherishing bowls.

Then Robin Hood gave him a mantle of
    green,
Broad arrows, and curious long bow:
This done, the next day, so gallant and
    gay,
He marched them all on a row.

Quoth he. My brave yeomen, be true to
    your trust,
And then we may range the woods wide.
They all did declare, and solemnly
    swear,
They would conquer, or die by his side.

Robin Hood and Little John

When Robin Hood was about twenty
    years old,
With a hey down, down, and a down;
He happen'd to meet Little John,
A jolly brisk blade, right fit for the trade,
For he was a lusty young man.

Tho' he was call'd Little, his limbs they
    were large
And his stature was seven foot high;
Whereever he came, they quak'd at his
    name,
For soon he would make them to fly.

How they came acquainted, I'll tell you
    in brief,
If you would but listen awhile;
For this very jest, among all the rest,
I think it may cause you to smile.

For Robin Hood said to his jolly bowman.
Pray tarry you here in this grove;
And see that you all observe well my call.
While thorough the forest I rove.

We have had no sport for these fourteen
    long days,
Therefore now abroad will I go;

Now should I be beat, and cannot retreat,
My horn I will presently blow.

Then did he shake hands with his merry
    men all,
And bid them at present good bye;
Then, as near the brook his journey he took,
A stranger he chanc'd to espy.

They happen'd to meet on a long
    narrow bridge,
And neither of them would give way;
Quoth bold Robin Hood, and sturdily
    stood,
I'll shew you right Nottingham-play.

With that from his quiver an arrow he
    drew,
A broad arrow with a goose-wing.
The stranger reply'd, I'll liquor thy hide,
If thou offer to touch the string.

Quoth bold Robin Hood, Thou dost
    prate like an ass.
For were I to bend but my bow,
I could send a dart, quite thro' thy
    proud heart.
Before thou could'st strike me one blow.

Thou talk'st like a coward, the stranger
   reply'd;
Well arm'd with a long bow you stand,
To shoot at my breast, while I, I protest
Have nought but a staff in my hand.

The name of a coward, quoth Robin, I
   scorn,
Therefore my long bow I'll lay by thee
And now, for thy sake, a staff will I take,
The truth of thy manhood to try.

Then Robin Hood stept to a thicket of trees.
And chose him a staff of ground oak;
Now this being done, away he did run
To the stranger, and merrily spoke:

Lo ! see my staff is lusty and tough,
Now here on the bridge we will play;
Whoever falls in, the other shall win
The battle, and so we'll away.

With all my whole heart, the stranger
   reply'd,
I scorn in the least to give out;
This said, they fell to't without more
   dispute,
And their staffs they did flourish about.

At first Robin he gave the stranger a bang,
So hard that he made his bones ring:
The stranger he said, This must be
   repaid,
I'll give you as good as you bring.

So long as I am able to handle a staff,
To die in your debt, friend, I scorn.
Then to it each goes, and follow'd their
   blows,
As if they'd been threshing of corn.

The stranger gave Robin a crack on the
   crown,
Which caused the blood to appear;
Then Robin enrag'd, more fiercely engag'd.
And follow'd his blows more severe.

So thick and so fast did he lay it on him.
With a passionate fury and ire;
At every stroke he made him to smoke,
As if he had been all on fire.

O then into fury the stranger he grew.
And gave him a damnable look.
And with it a blow that laid him full low,
And tumbl'd him into the brook.

I prithee, good fellow, O where art thou
   now?
The stranger, in laughter, he cry'd.
Quoth bold Robin Hood, Good faith, in
   the flood,
And floating along with the tide.

I needs must acknowledge thou art a
   brave soul,
With thee I'll no longer contend;
For needs must I say, thou hast got the day,
Our battel shall be at an end.

Then unto the bank he did presently wade.
And pull'd himself out by a thorn;
Which done, at the last he blow'd a loud
blast
Straitway on his fine bugle-horn:

The eccho of which through the vallies
did fly,
At which his stout bowmen appear'd,
All cloathed in green, most gay to be seen,
So up to their master they steer'd.

O, what's the matter? quoth William Stutly,
Good master, you are wet to the skin.
No matter, quoth he, the lad which you see
In fighting hath tumbl'd me in.

He shall not go scot-free, the others reply'd;
So strait they were seizing him there.
To duck him likewise: but Robin Hood
cries.
He is a stout fellow forbear.

There's no one shall wrong thee, friend,
be not afraid;
These bowmen upon me do wait;
There's threescore and nine; if thou wilt
be mine.
Thou shalt have my livery strait,

And other accoutrements fit for a man;
Speak up, jolly blade, never fear:
I'll teach you also the use of the bow,
To shoot at the fat fallow deer.

O, here is my hand, the stranger reply'd,
I'll serve you with all my whole heart;

My name is John Little, a man of good
mettle;
Ne're doubt me, for I'll play my part.

His name shall be alter'd, quoth William
Stutly,
And I will his godfather be;
Prepare then a feast, and none of the least,
For we will be merry, quoth he.

They presently fetch'd him a brace of fat
does,
With humming strong liquor likewise;
They lov'd what was good; so, in the
green wood,
This pretty sweet babe they baptize.

He was, I must tell you, but seven foot
high,
And, may be, an ell in the waste;
A sweet pretty lad: much feasting they had;
Bold Robin the christ'ning grac'd,

With all his bowmen, which stood in a
ring,
And were of the Nottingham breed
Brave Stutly came then, with seven yeomen.
And did in this manner proceed:

This infant was called John Little, quoth he;
Which name shall be changed anon:
The words we'll transpose; so where ever
he goes.
His name shall be call'd Little John.

They all with a shout made the elements ring;
So soon as the office was ore,

To feasting they went, with true
  merriment,
And tippl'd strong liquor gillore.

Then Robin he took the pretty sweet
  babe,
And cloath'd him from top to the toe,
In garments of green, most gay to be seen,
And gave him a curious long bow.

'Thou shalt be an archer, as well as the best,
And range in the green wood with us;
Where we'll not want gold nor silver,
  behold.
While bishops have ought in their purse.

We live here like squires, or lords of renown.
Without ere a foot of free land;
We feast on good cheer, with wine, ale,
  and beer,
And everything at our command.'

Then musick and dancing did finish the day;
At length, when the sun waxed low,
Then all the whole train the grove did refrain.
And unto their caves they did go.

And so, ever after, as long as he liv'd,
Altho' he was proper and tall,
Yet, nevertheless, the truth to express.
Still Little John they did him call.

Robin Hood and the Bishop of Hereford

Some they will talk of bold Robin Hood,
And some of barons bold;
But I'll tell you how he serv'd the bishop
  of Here-
When he robb'd him of his gold.

As it befel, in merry Barnsdale,
All under the green-wood-tree,
The bishop of Hereford was to come by,
With all his company.

Come, kill [me] a ven'son, said bold
  Robin Hood,
Come, kill me a good fat deer,
The bishop of Hereford is to dine with
  me to-day,
And he shall pay well for his cheer.

We'll kill a fat ven'son, said bold Robin
  Hood,
And dress it by the highway side;
And we will watch the bishop narrowly.
Lest some other way he should ride.

Robin Hood dress'd himself in shepherd's
  attire.
With six of his men also
And, when the bishop of Hereford came by,
They about the fire did go.

O what is the matter? then said the
  bishbp,
Or for whom do you make this a-do?
Or why do you kill the king's ven'son,
When your company is so few?

We are shepherds, said bold Robin Hood,
And we keep sheep all the year,
And we are disposed to be merry this
    day.
And to kill of the king's fat deer.

You are brave fellows! said the bishop,
And the king of your doings shall know:
Therefore make haste, and come along
    with me,
For before the king you shall go,

O pardon, O pardon, said bold Robin Hood,
O pardon, I thee pray;
For it becomes not your lordships coat
To take so many lives away.

No pardon, no pardon, said the bishbp,
No pardon I thee owe;
Therefore make haste, and come along
    with me.
For before the king you shall go.

Then Robin set his back against a tree,
And his foot against a thorn,
And from underneath his shepherds coat
He pull'd out a bugle-horn.

He put the little end to his mouth.
And a loud blast did he blow.
Till threescore and ten of bold Robin's men
Came running all on a row;

All making obeysance to bold Robin
    Hood;
'Twas a comely sight for to see.
What is the matter, master, said Little John,

That you blow so hastily?

'O here is the bishop of Hereford,
And no pardon we shall have.'
Cut off his head, master, said
    Little John,
And throw him into his grave.

O pardon, O pardon, said the bishop,
O pardon I thee pray;
For if I had known it had been you,
I'd have gone some other way.

No pardon, no pardon, said bold Robin
    Hood,
No pardon I thee owe;
Therefore make haste, and come along
    with me,
For to merry Barnsdale you shall go.

Then Robin he took the bishop by the hand,
And led him to merry Barnsdale;
He made him to stay and sup with him
    that night,
And to drink wine, beer, and ale.

Call in a reckoning, said the bish6p.
For methinks it grows wond'rous high.
Lend me your purse, master, said Little
    John,
And I'll tell you bye and bye.

Then Little John took the bishop's cloak.
And spread it upon the ground.
And out of the bishop's portmantua
He told three hundred pound.

Here's money enough, master, said Little
    John,
And a comely sight 'tis to see;
It makes me in charity with the bishop,
Tho' he heartily loveth not me.

Robin Hood took the bishop by the
    hand,
And he caused the music to play;
And he made the [old] bishop to dance
    in his boots.
And glad he could so get away.

Robin Hood Rescuing the Widow's Three Sons from the Sheriff

There are twelve months in all the year,
As I hear many say,
But the merriest month in all the year
Is the merry month of May.

Now Robin Hood is to Nottingham
    gone
With a link a down, and a day,
And there he met a silly old woman
Was weeping on the way.

'What news? what news? thou silly old
    woman,
What news hast thou for me?'
Said she. There's three squires in
    Nottingham town,
To-day are they condemned to die.

Oh, have they parishes burnt? he said,
Or have they ministers slain?
Or have they robbed any virgin?
Or with other men's wives have lain?

'They have no parishes burnt, good sir.
Nor yet have ministers slain,
Nor have they robbed any virgin,
Nor with other men's wives have lain.'

Oh, what have they done? said Robin Hood,
I pray thee tell to me.
'It's for slaying of the kings fallow deer.
Bearing their long bows with thee.'

Dost thou not mind, old woman, he said.
Since thou made me sup and dine?
By the truth of my body, quoth bold
    Robin Hood,
You could not tell it in better time.

Now Robin Hood is to Nottingham
    gone,
With a link, a down, and a day
And there he met with a silly old
    palmer,
Was walking along the highway.

'What news, what news? thou silly old man,
What news, I do thee pray?'
Said he. Three squires in Nottingham town,
Are condemn'd to die this day.

'Come change thy apparel with me, old man,
Come change thy apparel for mine;
Here is forty shillings in good silver,
Go drink it in beer or wine.'

Oh, thine apparel is good, he said,
And mine is ragged and torn;
Wherever you go, wherever you ride.
Laugh ne'er an old man to scorn.

'Come change thy apparel with me, old
    churl,
Come change thy apparel with mine;
Here are twenty pieces of good broad gold,
Go feast thy brethren with wine.'

Then he put on the old man's hat,
It stood full high on the crown;
'The first bold bargain that I come at.
It shall make thee come down.'

Then he put on the old man's cloak,
Was patch'd black, blew, and red;
He thought it no shame, all the day long,
To wear the bags of bread.

Then he put on the old man's breeches,
Was patch'd from ballup to side:
By the truth of my body, bold Robin can
    say.
This man lov'd little pride.

Then he put on the old man's hose.
Were patch'd from knee to wrist:
By the truth of my body, said bold
    Robin Hood,
I'd laugh if I had any list.

Then he put on the old man's shoes,
Were patch'd both beneath and aboon;
Then Robin Hood swore a solemn oath,
It's good habit that makes a man.

Now Robin Hood is to Nottingham gone,
With a link a down and a down,
And there he met with the proud sheriff,
Was walking along the town.

Oh Christ you save, oh, sheriff, he said,
Oh Christ you save and see;
And what will you give to a silly old
    man
To-day will your hangman be.

Some suits, some suits, the sheriff he said.
Some suits, I'll give to thee;
Some suits, some suits, and pence thirteen.
To-day's a hangman's fee.

Then Robin he turns him round about,
And jumps from stock to stone:
By the truth of my body, the sheriff he said,
That's well jumpt, thou nimble old man.

I was ne'er a hangman in all my life.
Nor yet intends to trade;
But curst be he, said bold Robin,
That first a hangman was made.

I've a bag for meal, and a bag for
    malt.
And a bag for barley and corn;
A bag for bread, and a bag for beef.
And a bag for my little small horn.

I have a horn in my pocket,
I got it from Robin Hood,
And still when I set it to my mouth,
For thee it blows little good,

'Oh, wind thy horn, thou proud fellow,
Of thee I have no doubt;
I wish that thou give such a blast,
Till both thy eyes fall out.'

The first loud blast that he did blow,
He blew both loud and shrill;
A hundred and fifty of Robin Hood's
    men
Came riding over the hill.

The next loud blast that he did give,
He blew both loud and amain.

And quickly sixty of Robin Hoods men,
Came shining over the plain.

Oh, who are those, the sheriff he said,
Come tripping over the lee?
They're my attendants, brave Robin did
    say.
They'll pay a visit to thee.

They took the gallows from the slack,
They set it in the glen,
They hang'd the proud sheriff on that,
Releas'd their own three men.

Robin Hood and Maid Marian

A bonny fine maid of a noble degree,
With a hey down, down, a down, down
Maid Marian call'd by name,
Did live in the North, of excellent worth,
For shee was a gallant dame.

For favour and face, and beauty most rare,
Queen Hellen shee did excell:
For Marian then was prais'd of all men,
That did in the country dwell.

'Twas neither Rosamond nor Jane
    Shore,
Whose beauty was clear and bright,
That could surpass this country lass,
Beloved of lord and knight.

The earl of Huntington, nobly born.
That came of noble blood.
To Marian went, with a good intent.
By the name of Robin Hood.

With kisses sweet their red lips did meet.
For she and the earl did agree;
In every place, they kindly embrace,
With love and sweet unity.

But fortune bearing these lovers a spight.
That soon they were forced to part:
To the merry green wood then went
    Robin Hood,
With a sad and sorrowful heart.

And Marian, poor soul, was troubled in
    mind,
For the absence of her friend;
With finger in eye, shee often did cry,
And his person did much comend.

Perplexed and vexed, and troubled in mind,
Shoe drest herself like a page,
And ranged the wood, to find Robin Hood,
The bravest of men in that age.

With quiver and bow, sword, buckler, and all,
Thus armed was Marian most bold,
Still wandering about to find Robin out.
Whose person was better then gold.

But Robin Hood, hee himself had disguis'd,
And Marian was strangly attir'd.
That they prov'd foes, and so fell to blowes.
Whose vallour bold Robin admir'd.

They drew out their swords, and to
    cutting they went,
At least an hour or more,
That the blood ran apace from bold
    Robins face.
And Marian was wounded sore.

O hold thy hand, hold thy hand, said
    Robin Hood,
And thou shalt be one of my string.
To range in the wood with bold Robin
    Hood,
And hear the sweet nightingall sing.

When Marian did hear the voice of her
    love,
Herself shee did quickly discover.
And with kisses sweet she did him greet,
Like to a most loyall lover.

When bold Robin Hood his Marian did
    see,
Good lord, what clipping was there!
With kind embraces, and jobbing of faces,
Providing of gallant cheer.

For Little John took his bow in his hand,
And wandred in the wood,
To kill the deer, and make good chear.
For Marian and Robin Hood.

A stately banquet they had full soon,
All in a shaded bower,
Where venison sweet they had to eat.
And were merry that present hour.

Great flaggons of wine were set on the
    board,
And merrily they drunk round
Their boules of sack, to strengthen the
    back.
Whilst their knees did touch the
    ground.

First Robin Hood began a health
To Marian his onely dear;
And his yeomen all, both comly and
    tall.
Did quickly bring up the rear:

For in a brave venie they tost off the
    bouls.
Whilst thus they did remain;
And every cup, as they drunk up.
They filled with speed again.

At last they ended their merryment,
And went to walk in the wood,
Where Little John, and Maid Marikn,
Attended on bold Robin Hood.

In sollid content together they liv'd,
With all their yeomen gay;
They liv'd by their hands, without any
    lands,
And so they did many a day.

But now to conclude an end I will make,
In time as I think it good;
For the people that dwell in the North
    can tell
Of Marian and bold Robin Hood.

The King's Disguise and Friendship with Robin Hood

King Richard hearing of the pranks
Of Robin Hood and his men,
He much admir'd, and more desired
To see both him and them.

Then, with a dozen of his lords,
To Nottingham he rode;
When he came there, he made good cheer,
And took up his abode.

He having staid there some time.
But had no hopes to speed.
He and his lords, with one accord,
All put on monks weeds.

From Fountain-abbey they did ride,
Down to Barnsdale;
Where Robin Hood prepared stood
All company to assail.

The king was higher than the rest,
And Robin thought he had
An abbot been whom he had seen.
To rob him he was glad.

He took the king's horse by the head.
Abbot, says he, abide;
I am bound to rue such knaves as you.
That live in pomp and pride.

But we are messengers from the king,
The king himself did say;
Near to this place his royal grace
To speak with thee does stay.

God save the king, said Robin Hood,
And all that wish him well;
He that does deny his sovereignty,
I wish he was in hell.

Thyself thou cursedst, says the king,
For thou a traitor art.
'Nay, but that you are his messenger,
I swear you lie in heart.

For I never yet hurt any man
That honest is and true;
But those who give their minds to live
Upon other mens due.

I never hurt the husbandmen,
That use to till the ground:
Nor spill their blood who range the wood,
To follow hawk or hound.

My chiefest spite to clergy is,
Who in these days bear great sway;
With fryars and monks, with their fine sprunks,
I make my chiefest prey.'

But I am very glad, says Robin Hood,
That I have met you here;
Come, before we end, you shall, my friend,
Taste of our green-wood cheer.

The king he then did marvel much,
And so did all his men;
They thought with fear, what kind of cheer,
Robin would provide for them.

Robin took the kings horse by the head,
And led him to his tent:
Thou wouldst not be so us'd, quoth he.
But that my king thee sent.

Nay, more than that, quoth Robin Hood,
For good king Richards sake,
If you had as much gold as ever I told,
I would not one penny take.

Then Robin set his horn to his mouth,
And a loud blast he did blow,
Till a hundred and ten of Robin Hoods
     men,
Came marching all of a row.

And when they came bold Robin before,
Each man did bend his knee:
O, thought the king, 'tis a gallant thing.
And a seemly sight to see.

Within himself the king did say,
These men of Robin Hoods
More humble be than mine to me;
So the court may learn of the woods.

So then they all to dinner went,
Upon a carpet green;
Black, yellow, red, finely mingled.
Most curious to be seen.

Venison and fowls were plenty there,
With fish out of the river:
King Richard swore, on sea or shore.
He never was feasted better.

Then Robin takes a cann of ale:
'Come, let us now begin;
And every man shall have his cann:
Here's a health unto the king.'

The king himself drank to the king,
So round about it went;
Two barrels of ale, both stout and stale,
To pledge that health was spent.

And, after that, a bowl of wine
In his hand took Robin Hood;
Until I die, I'll drink wine, said he,
While I live in the green wood.

Bend all your bows, said Robin Hood,
And with the grey-goose-wing.
Such sport now show, as you would
     do
In the presence of the king.

They shewed such brave archery,
By cleaving sticks and wands,
That the king did say, such men as they
Live not in many lands.

Well, Robin Hood, then says the king,
If I could thy pardon get.
To serve the king in every thing
Would'st thou thy mind firm set?

Yes, with all my heart, bold Robin said.
So they flung off their hoods;
To serve the king in every thing,
They swore they would spend their bloods.

For a clergyman was first my bane,
Which makes me hate them all.
But if you will be so kind to me.
Love them again I shall.

The king no longer could forbear.
For he was mov'd with ruth
...
...

'I am the king, your sovereign king,
That appears before you all.'
When Robin saw that it was he.
Strait then he down did fall.

Stand up again, then said the king,
I'll thee thy pardon give;
Stand up, my friend, who can contend,
When I give leave to live?

So they are all gone to Nottingham,
All shouting as they came:
But when the people them did see.
They thought the king was slain;

And for that cause the outlaws were come,
To rule all as they list;
And for to shun, which way to run.
The people did not wist.

The plowman left the plow in the fields.
The smith ran from his shop;
Old folks also, that scarce could go,
Over their sticks did hop.

The king soon did let them understand
He had been in the green-wood.
And from that day, for evermore.
He'd forgiven Robin Hood.

Then [when] the people they did hear,
And [that] the truth was known,
They all did sing, God save the king!
Hang care, the town's our own!

What's that Robin Hood ? then said the
    sheriff,
That varlet I do hate;
Both me and mine he caused to dine,
And serv'd us all with one plate.

Ho, ho, said Robin Hood, I know what
    you mean,
Come, take your gold again;
Be friends with me, and I with thee.
And so with every man.

Now, master sheriff, you are paid,
And since you are beginner,
As well as you give me my due.
For you ne'er paid for that dinner.

But if that it should please the king,
So much your house to grace,
To sup with you, for, to speak true,
[I] know you ne'er was base.

The sheriff [this] could not gainsay.
For a trick was put upon him;
A supper was drest, the king was a guest,
But he thought 'twould have outdone him.

They are all gone to London court,
Robin Hood with all his train;
He once was there a noble peer.
And now he's there again.

Many such pranks brave Robin play'd,
While he liv'd in the green wood:
Now, my friend, attend, and hear an end
Of honest Robin Hood.

Robin Hood and the Golden Arrow

When as the sheriff of Nottingham
Was come with mickle grief,
He talk'd no good of Robin Hood,
That strong and sturdy thief.
Fal la dal de.

So unto London road he past,
His losses to unfold
To king Richard, who did regard
The tale that he had told.

Why, quoth the king, what shall I do?
Art thou not sheriff for me?
The law is in force, to take thy course
Of them that injure thee.

Go get thee gone, and by thyself
Devise some tricking game,
For to enthral yon rebels all,
Go take thy course with them.

So away the sheriff he return'd,
And by the way he thought
Of th' words of the king, and how the thing
To pass might well be brought.

For within his mind he imagin,
That when such matches were,
Those outlaws stout, without all doubt,
Would be the bowmen there.

So an arrow with a golden head,
And shaft of silver-white,
Who on the day should bear away
For his own proper right.

Tidings came to bold Robin Hood,
Under the green-wood tree:
'Come prepare you then, my merry men.
We'll go yon sport to see.'

With that stept forth a brave young
    man,
David of Doncaster,
Master, said he, be rul'd by me,
From the green wood we'll not stir.

To tell the truth, I'm well inform'd,
Yon match it is a wile;
The sheriff, I wiss, devises this
Us archers to beguile.

Thou smells of a coward, said Robin Hood,
Thy words do not please me;
Come on't what will, I'll try my skill.
At yon brave archery.

O then bespoke brave Little John,
Come let us thither gang;
Come listen to me, how it shall be,
That we need not be ken'd.

Our mantles all of Lincoln-green
Behind us we will leave;
We'll dress us all so several,
They shall not us perceive.

One shall wear white, another red,
One yellow, another blue;
Thus in disguise, to the exercise
We'll gang, whate'er insue.

Forth from the green wood they are gone,
With hearts all firm and stout,
Resolving [then] with the sheriflfs men
To have a hearty bout.

So themselves they mixed with the rest,
To prevent all suspicion;
For if they should together hold.
They thought it no discretion.

So the sheriff looked round about.
Amongst eight hundred men,
But could not see the sight that he
Had long suspected then.

Some said, If Robin Hood was here,
And all his men to boot,
Sure none of them could pass these men,
So bravely they do shoot.

Ay, quoth the sheriff, and scratch'd his head,
I thought he would have been here;
I thought he would, but tho' he's bold,
He durst not now appear.

O that word griev'd Robin Hood to the heart,
He vexed in his blood;
Ere long, thought he, thou shalt well see
That here was Robin Hood.

Some cried, Blue Jacket! another cried, Brown!
And a third cried, Brave yellow!
But the fourth man said, Yon man in red
In this place has no fellow.

For that was Robin Hood himself,
For he was cloath'd in red;
At every shot the prize he got,
For he was both sure and dead.

So the arrow with the golden head,
And shaft of silver-white,
Brave Robin Hood won, and bore with him,
For his own proper right.

These outlaws there, that very day.
To shun all kinds of doubt.
By three or four, no less nor more,
As they went in came out.

Until they all assembled were
Under the green-wood shade,
Where they report, in pleasant sport,
What brave pastime they made.

Says Robin Hood, all my care is,
How that yon sheriff may
Know certainly that it was I
That bore his arrow away.

Says Little John, My counsel good
Did take effect before,
So therefore now, if you'll allow,
I will advise once more.

Speak on, speak on, said Robin Hood,
Thy wit's both quick and sound
This I advise, said Little John,
That a letter shall be penn'd,

And when it is done, to Nottingham
You to the sheriff shall send.
That is well advised, said Robin Hood,
But how must it be sent

'Pugh! when you please, 'tis done with ease:
Master, be you content.
I'll stick it on my arrow's head,
And shoot it into the town;

The mark must show where it must go,
Whenever it lights down.'
The project it was well perform'd,
The sheriff that letter had.

Which when he read, he scratch'd his head.
And rav'd like one that's mad.
So we'll leave him chafing in his grease,
Which will do him no good.

Now, my friends, attend, and hear the end
Of honest Robin Hood

Robin Hood and the Valiant Knight

When Robin Hood, and his merry men all,
Derry down, down.
Had reigned many years,
The king was then told that they had
   been bold
To his bishops and noble peers.
Hey down, derry, derry down.

Therefore they called a council of state,
To know what was best to be done

For to quell their pride, or else they reply'd
The land would be over-run.

Having consulted a whole Summer's day,
At length it was agreed.
That one should be sent to try the event,
And fetch him away with speed.

Therefore a trusty and most worthy knight
The king was pleased to call,

Sir William by name; when to him he came,
He told him his pleasure all

'Go you from hence to bold Robin Hood,
And bid him, without more ado,
Surrender himself, or else the proud elf
Shall suffer with all his crew.

Take here a hundred bowmen brave.
All chosen men of great might.
Of excellent art to take thy part,
In glittering armour most bright.'

Then said the knight, My sovereign liege,
By me they shall be led;
I'll venture my blood against bold Robin Hood,
And bring him alive or dead.

One hundred men were chosen straight,
As proper as e'er men saw:
On Midsummer-day they marched away,
To conquer that brave outlaw.

With long yew bows, and shining spears,
They march'd with mickle pride.
And never delay'd, nor halted, nor stay'd
Till they came to the green-wood side.

Said he to his archers, Tarry here.
Your bows make ready all.
That if need should be, you may follow me,
And see you observe my call.

I'll go first in person, he cry'd,
With the letters of my good king.
Well sign'd and seal'd, and if he will yield,
We need not to draw one string.

He wander'd about till at length he came
To the tent of Robin Hood;
The letter he shows; bold Robin arose,
And there on his guard he stood.

They'd have me surrender, quoth bold Robin
    Hood
And lie at their mercy then
But tell them from me, that never shall be,
While I have full seven score men.

Sir William the knight, both hardy and bold,
He offer'd to seize him there.
Which William Locksley by fortune did
    see,
And bid him that trick to forbear.

Then Robin Hood set his horn to his mouth,
And blew a blast or twain.
And so did the knight, at which there in
    sight
The archers came all amain.

Sir William with care he drew up his men,
And plac'd them in battle-array;
Bold Robin, we find, he was not behind:
Now this was a bloody fray.

The archers on both sides bent their bows,
And the clouds of arrows flew;
The very first flight that honour'd knight
Did there bid the world adieu.

Yet nevertheless their fight did last
From morning till almost noon;
Both parties were stout, and loth to give out,
This was on the last day of June.

At length they left offf: one party they went
To London with right good will;
And Robin Hood he to the green-wood tree,
And there he was taken ill.

He sent for a monk, to let him blood,
Who took his life away;
Now this being done, his archers they run.
It was not a time to stay.

Some got on board, and cross'd the seas.
To Flanders, France, and Spain,
And others to Rome, for fear of their doom,
But soon return'd again.

The Death of Robin Hood (Variant Version)

When Robin Hood and Little John,
Down a down, a down, a down.
Went o'er yon bank of broom,
Said Robin Hood to Little John,
We have shot for many a pound:
Hey down, a down, a down.

But I am not able to shoot one shot more,
My arrows will not flee;
But I have a cousin lives down below,
Please god, she will bleed me.

Now Robin is to fair Kirkley gone.
As fast as he can win;
But before he came there, as we do hear,
He was taken very ill.

And when that he came to fair Kirkley-hall,
He knock'd all at the ring.
But none was so ready as his cousin herself
For to let bold Robin in.

Will you please to sit down, cousin
    Robin, she said,
And drink some beer with me?
'No, I will neither eat nor drink,
Till I am blooded by thee.'

Well, I have a room, cousin Robin, she said,
Which you did never see.
And if you please to walk therein,
You blooded by me shall be.'

She took him by the lilly-white hand,
And led him to a private room,
And there she blooded bold Robin Hood,
Whilst one drop of blood would run.

She blooded him in the vein of the arm,
And lock'd him up in the room;
There did he bleed all the live-long day,
Untill the next day at noon.

He then bethought him of a casement door,
Thinking for to be gone;
He was so weak he could not leap,
Nor he could not get down.

He then bethought him of his bugle-horn,
Which hung low down to his knee;
He set his horn unto his mouth,
And blew out weak blasts three.

Then Little John, when hearing him
As he sat under the tree,
'I fear my master is near dead,
He blows so wearily.'

Then Little John to fair Kirkley is gone,
As fast as he can dree;
But when he came to Kirkley-hall,
He broke locks two or three;

Untill he came bold Robin to,
Then he fell on his knee;
A boon, a boon, cries Little John,
Master, I beg of thee.

What is that boon, quoth Robin Hood,
Little John, thou begs of me?
'It is to burn fair Kirkley-hall,
And all their nunnery.'

Now nay, now nay, quoth Robin Hood,
That boon I'll not grant thee;
I never hurt woman in all my life,
Nor man in woman's company.

I never hurt fair maid in all my time,
Nor at my end shall it be;
But give me my bent bow in my hand.
And a broad arrow I'll let flee:
And where this arrow is taken up,
There shall my grave digg'd be.

Lay me a green sod under my head,
Another at my feet;
And lay my bent bow by my side,
Which was my music sweet;
And make my grave of gravel and green,
Which is most right and meet.

Let me have length and breadth enough.
With a green sod under my head;
With verdant sods most neatly put,
Sweet as the green wood tree.
That they may say, when I am dead,
Here lies bold Robin Hood.

These words they readily promis'd him,
Which did bold Robin please:
And there they buried bold Robin Hood,
Near to the fair Kirkleys.

GLOSSARY OF ANTIQUE WORDS

By no means all of the antique words found in the ballads are represented here, but in most cases, saying the lines out loud will persuade them to give up their meaning.

Angels, pieces of gold coin, value 10s

A-sound, in a swoon

Baist, belaboured

Baith, both

Bale, mischief, woe, sorrow, misery

Bear, moan, lamentation, outcry

Bearing, arrow

Begeck, trick. Give them a begeck, make fools of them

Benbow, a bent bow?

Bestead, beset

Blate, sheepish or foolish

Blyve, fast

Bocking, pouring

Bode, invited

Bolt, an arrow of a particular kind, used chiefly for shooting at birds

Borowe, pledge, surety, bail

Boskyd, prepared

Bottle, a small vessel, of wood or leather, in the shape of a cask

Breyde, quick or hasty step

Broke, enjoy, keep

Cankardly, peevishly, with ill-temper

Carril, carle, old fellow

Chaffare, merchandise, commodity

Chepe, cheapen, buy

Cla'd, scratched

Clouted, patched

Crack, boast

Crouse, brisk

Dame, mother
Dead, certain
Dub, shallow miry pool
Dung, beaten, overcome
Durk, dagger

Een, eyes
Eild, age

Fayne, glad
Feardest, most frightened
    or afraid
Finikin, finical, fine, spruce
Flinders, splinters
Force, care
Frae, from

Gae, go
Gan, gone
Gang, go
Gillore, plenty
God, good, goods, property
Graff, branch or sapling
Gramercy, thanks, or many
    thanks

Halds, holds, holding-places,
    supports
Hals, neck
Highed, hastened
Hight, called
Hew, hill

Kirtle, upper petticoat
Knave, servant, man
Late, lake, play, game
Lefe, willing.

Lever, rather
Lynde, Lyne, the lime or linden
    tree; or collectively lime trees

Meal, oat-meal
Meyne, attendants, retinue
Mot, Mote, might, may
Mote, meeting, assembly, court,
    audit
Morw, mouth
Myrthes, mirth, merriment

Nane, none

Paid, beat, beaten
Palmer, a pilgrim who had visited
    the Holy Land
Pinder, petty officer of a manor
Poke, bag
Prest, ready, ready to go
Puding-pricks, skewers that fasten
    the pudding-bag

Raked, walked apace
Ripe, cleanse
Rod, poles, perches. A rod, pole,
    or perch is usually 16½ feet,
    but in Sherwood Forest it is
    21 feet, the foot there being 18
    inches
Rung, staff

Sack, a kind of Spanish wine,
    perhaps sherry
Sair, sore
Scop, scalp, pate
Shawe, little wood

Shrift, confession

Shroggs, shrubs, thorns,
   briars

Skaith, harm

Slack, low ground

Slade, a slip of greensward
   between plow-lands, or woods

Stane, stone

Stark, stiff

Steven, some odd accident, by
   mere chance

Stime, spark, particle or ray of
   light

Stint, stop

Sweaven, dream

Syne, after, afterward, then

Syth, afterward

Tene, grief, sorrow, distress,
   vexation

Tene, grieve

Trow, true

Venie, jovial humour

Wan, got

Wed, pawn, pledge, or deposit.

Whang, leather thong or string

Whute, whistle

Wigger, wicker

Wight, strong

Wilfulle, doubtful

Wist, knew

Woodweele, the golden ouzle, a
   thrush

Wrack, ruin

Wroken, revenged

Wyght, strong, stout

Wynne, go

Wys, trow; there is no modern
   word precisely synonymous

Yede, went

Yeomandree, followers

Yode, went

BIBLIOGRAPHY AND RESOURCES

This is only a selection of the many hundreds of books on the subject of Robin Hood. It constitutes those that I have personally found most useful in writing this addition to the cannon. Many more titles will be found in the respective bibliographies of the works by Keen, Holt and Dobson & Taylor.

1. Alexander, M. *British Folklore, Myths and Legends* Weidenfeld & Nicholson, 1982
2. Anderson, W. *Green Man, the Archetype of our Oneness with the Earth* Harper Collins, 1990
3. Bailey, H. *Archaic England* Chapman and Hall, 1919
4. Barber, R. *Living Legends* British Broadcasting Corporation, 1980
5. Basford, K. *The Green Man* Boydell & Brewer, 1978
6. Basford, K. 'The Quest for the Green Man' *Symbols of Power* ed. by H. R. E. Davidson. Brewer/Roman & Littlefield, 1977
7. Bernheimer, R. *Wild Men in the Middle Ages* Cambridge, Mass., 1952
8. Bord, J. & C. *Earth Rites: Fertility Practices in Pre-Industrial Britain.* Granada, 1982
9. Bord, J. & C. *Mysterious Britain* Granada, 1974
10. Brand, J. *Observations on the Popular Antiquities of Great Britain* (3 vols.) George Bell & Sons, 1908
11. Briggs, K. *A Dictionary of Fairies* Alan Lane, 1976

12. Brodie, A. *The English Mummers and their Plays* Routledge & Kegan Paul, 1970

13. Burland, C. Echoes of Magic Rowman & Littlefield, 1972

14. Cawte, E. C. *Ritual Animal Disguise* Brewer/Roman and Littlefield, 1978

15. Chambers, E. *English Literature at the Close of the Middle Ages* Oxford University Press, 1947

16. Chambers, E. *The English Folk Play* OUP, 1933

17. Child, F. J. *English and Scottish Popular Ballads* New York: Houghton Mifflin, 1882–1898

18. Clawson, W. H. *The Gest of Robin Hood* Toronto, University of Toronto Library, 1909

19. Cooper, H. *Pastoral: Medieval into Renaissance* D. S. Brewer/ Rowman & Littlefield, 1977

20. Cooper, J. C. The *Aquarian Dictionary of Festivals* Aquarian Press, 1990

21. Cross, T. P. & C. H. Slover *Ancient Irish Tales* Dublin, C. W. Dunn, 1969

22. Crosby, R. *Robin Hood's Nottingham* Heritage Classics 1989

23. Dobson, R. B. & J. Taylor *Rymes of Robyn Hood: An Introduction to the English Outlaw,* Alan Sutton, 1989

24. Douce, F. *Illustrations of Shakespeare* London, 1807

25. Duffy, M. *The Erotic World of Faery* Hodder & Stoughton, 1972

26. Fowler, D. C. *A Literary History of the Popular Ballad* (Durham, North Carolina, 1968

27. Fraser, J. G. *The Golden Bough* (Abridged Edition) Macmillan, 1974

28. Geoffrey of Monmouth. *The History of the Kings of Britain* (trans. Sebastian Evans) J. M. Dent, 1963

29. Goulstone, J. *The Summer Solstice Games* Privately Printed, 1985

30. Green, B. *The Outlaw Robin Hood: His Yorkshire Legend.* Kirklees Cultural Services, 1991

31. Green, M. *A Harvest of Festivals* Longmans, 1980

32. Guest, Lady C. *The Mabinogion* J. M. Dent, 1937

33. Hampson, R. T. *Kalendars of the Middle Ages* Causton & Sons n.d.

34. Harris, P. V. *The Truth About Robin Hood,* Privately Printed, London, 1954

35. Harrison, J. *Ancient Art and Ritual* Thornton Butterworth, 1918

36. Harrowven, J. *Origins or Rhymes, Songs and Sayings*. Kaye & Ward, 1977
37. Henderson, H. 'The Green Man of Knowledge' *Scottish Studies* 2 (1958) pp. 47–85
38. Hilton, R. H. 'The Origins of Robin Hood' *Past & Present* 14 (1958) 30–44
39. Hodgart, M. J. C. *The Ballads* W. W. Norton, New York, n.d.
40. Hole, C. *A Dictionary of British Folk Customs* Hutchinson, 1976
41. Hole, C. *English Folk Heroes* Batsford, 1948
42. Holt, J. C. 'The Origins and Audience of the Ballads of Robin Hood' *Past & Present* 18 (1960) 89–110
43. Holt, J. C. *Robin Hood*, Thames & Hudson, 1983
44. Hull, E. Folklore of the British Isles Methuen, 1928
45. Husband, T. *The Wild Man: Medieval Myth & Symbolism* New York: Museum of Art, 1980
46. James, E. O. *Seasonal Feasts & Festivals* Thames & Hudson, 1961
47. Judge, R. *The Jack in the Green* Brewer/Roman & Littlefield, 1979
48. Keen, M. *The Outlaws of Medieval Legend* Routledge & Kegan Paul, 1977
49. Keen, M. 'Robin Hood: Peasant or Gentleman' *Past & Present* 19 (1961) pp. 7–15
50. Keightley, T. *The Fairy Mythology* Wildwood House, 1981
51. Kennedy, D. *England's Dances* G. Bell, 1950
52. Kightly, C. *The Customs & Ceremonies of Britain* Thames & Hudson, 1986
53. Kinsley, J. Ed. *The Oxford Book of Ballads* Oxford University Press, 1969
54. Kirtlan, E. J. B. *Sir Gawain & the Green Knight* Kelly, 1912
55. Lawman (Layamon) *The Brut* Trans by R. Allen Dent, 1992
56. Lees. J. *The Quest for Robin Hood* Temple Nostalgia Press, 1987
57. Lloyd, A. L. *Folk Song in England* Paladin, 1975
58. Malory, T. *Le Morte Darthur* Ed J. Matthews Carlton 2000
59. Matthews, C. *Arthur and the Sovereignty of Britain* Inner Traditions 2003
60. Matthews, C. *The Celtic Book of the Dead*, Thorsons, 1992
61. Matthews, C. *Mabon and the Mysteries of Britain*. Inner Traditions, 2004

62. Matthews, J. *The Celtic Shaman* Element Books, 1991
63. Matthews, J. *Gawain, Knight of the Goddess.* Inner Traditions, 2004
64. Matthews, J. *Taliesin: The Last Celtic Shaman,* Inner Traditions, 2005 HarperCollins, 1990
65. Matthews, J. (with R. J. Stewart) *Legendary Britain* Cassell, 1989
66. McNeill, F. M. *The Silver Bough* (4 Vols) William Maclellan, 1959
67. McPherson, J. M. *Primitive Beliefs is the North-East of Scotland* Longmans Green & Co, 1929
68. Mottram, E. *The Book of Herne* Arrowspire Press, 1981
69. Murray, M. *The Divine King in England* Faber & Faber, 1954
70. Murray, M. *The God of the Witches* OUP, 1952
71. Nutt, A. *The Fairy Mythology of Shakespeare.* David Nutt, 1900
72. Petry, M. J. *Herne the Hunter* Privately Printed, Reading, 1972
73. Raglan, Lord *The Hero* Watts & Co.1949
74. Rhys, E. *Fairy Gold: A Book of Old English Fairy Tales* J. M. Dent, n.d.
75. Ritson, J. *Robin Hood: A Collection of all the Ancient Poems, Songs and Ballads now extant ...* C. Stocking, 1823
76. Santillana, G. & H. Von Dechend *Hamlet's Mill* Macmillan, 1969
77. Simeone, W. E. 'The May-Games and the Robin Hood Legend' *Journal of American Folk-Lore* 64 (1951) 265–74
78. Sitwell, S. *Primitive Scenes & Festivals* Faber, 1942
79. Skelton, R & M. Blackwood. *Earth, Air, Fire, Water.* Arkana, 1991
80. Speak, H. & Forrester, J. *Robin Hood of Wakefield* (Pamphlet, no date or publisher)
81. Spence, L. *British Fairy Origins* Aquarian Press, 1981
82. Spence, L. *The Fairy Tradition in Britain* Rider, 1948
83. Spence, L. *The Minor Traditions in British Mythology* Rider, 1948
84. Spence, L. *Myth and Ritual in Dance, Game and Rhyme.* Watts, 1947
85. Spence, L. 'The Supernatural Character of Robin Hood' *Hibbert Journal* XL (1947) pp. 280–285
86. Sutcliff, R. *Heroes & History* Batsford, 1965
87. Thomas, K. *Religion & the Decline of Magic* Penguin Books, 1978
88. Thomas, W. J. *Early English Prose Romances* Routledge, 1898
89. Trevelyan, M. *Folk-Lore and Folk-Stories of Wales.* Eliot Stock, 1909
90. Vansittart, P. *Green Knights, Black Angels,* Macmillan, 1961
91. Vansittart, P. *Worlds & Underworlds* Peter Owen, 1974

92. Von dem Türlin, H. *The Crown (Diu Crone)*, Trans by J. W. Thomas. University of Nebraska, 1989

93. Wace & Layamon. *Arthurian Chronicles* (trans by E. Mason) J. M. Dent, 1962

94. Walker, J. W. *The True History of Robin Hood* E. P. Publishing, 1973

95. Webster, G. *The British Celts and their Gods Under Rome* Batsford, 1986

96. Welsford, E. *The Fool: His Social & Literary History* Faber, 1935

97. Wentz, W. Y. Evans *Fairy Faith in Celtic Countries* H. Frowde, 1911

98. Whitlock, R. *In Search of Lost Gods* Phaidon, 1979

99. Wiles, D. *The Early Plays of Robin Hood* D. S. Brewer/Roman & Littlefield, 1981

100. Williams, H. *Two Lives of Gildas* Llanerch Enterprises, 1990

101. Williamson, J. *The Oak King, the Holly King, and the Unicorn*. Harper & Row, 1986

Modern Retellings

Ever since Walter Scott's *Ivanhoe* in 1819 modern writers have been turning to the figure of Robin Hood for inspiration. Some very varied books have resulted, some good, some bad, some indifferent. A few of the best are listed here, though I have probably missed one or two.

102. Annand, V. *The King of the Wood* Headline, 1988

103. Carpenter, R. (with Robin May & Anthony Horowitz) *The Complete Adventures of Robin of Sherwood*. Penguin Books, 1991

104. Chase, N. *Locksley* Heinemann, 1983

105. Clifford, D. *The Affair of the Forest* Springwood Books, 1983

106. Emery, C. *Tales of Robin Hood* New York, Baen Books, 1988

107. Gilbert, H. *Robin Hood and the Men of the Greenwood* Jackson, Edinburgh, 1912

108. Godwin, P. *Sherwood* New York, William Morrow, 1992

109. Green, R. L. *The Adventures of Robin Hood* Penguin Books, 1956

110. Green, S. *Robin Hood, Prince of Thieves* New York, Berkley Books, 1992

111. Greenberg, M. H. Ed. *The Fantastic Adventures of Robin Hood* New York, Penguin Books USA, 1991

112. Hayes, S. Robin Hood Walker Books, 1989

113. James, G. P. R. *Forest Days: A Romance of Old Times*, 1843
114. Kipling, R. *Puck of Pook's Hill* Macmillan, 1987
115. McKinley, R. The Outlaws of Sherwood New York, Ace Books, 1989
116. Newbolt, H. *The Greenwood*, 1925
117. Noyes, A. 'Robin Hood: A Play in Five Acts' in *Collected Poems* vol. 1, William Blackwood, 1928
118. Oman, C. *Robin Hood, the Prince of Outlaws* J. M Dent (1939)1976
119. Peacock. T. L, 'Maid Marian' in *The Novels of Thomas Love Peacock* Thomas Hart Davis, 1958
120. Pyle, H. *The Merry Adventures of Robin Hood*, New York, Charles Scribners 1946
121. Rhead, L *Robin Hood and His Outlaw Band* 1923
122. Roberson, J. *Lady of the Forest* Zebra Books, 1992
123. Ryan, D. S. *The Lost Journal of Robyn Hood – Outlaw*. Kozmik Press, 1989
124. Serrallier, I. *Robin In the Greenwood* Oxford University Press, 1967
125. Stone, E. *Robin Hood's Arrow* Chicago, 1949
126. Sutcliff, R. *The Chronicles of Robin Hood* Oxford University Press, 1950
127. Tennyson, A. 'The Foresters' *Collected Poems* Oxford University Press, 1988
128. Vansittart, P. *The Death of Robin Hood* Peter Owen, 1981
129. White, T. H. *The Sword in the Stone* Collins, 1946

Music

Several musical treatments drawing their inspiration from the Robin Hood stories have appeared over the years. There follows a very brief selection of these.

A Tapestry of Music for Robin Hood and his King by St Georges Canzona (Enigma, VAR 1020, 1998)
The Ballad of Robin Hood by Anthony Quale (Caedmon, TC11177)
Merrie England by Sir Edward German. The Williams Singers with the Collins Orchestra conducted by Michael Collins (Silver Doubles, B000025VJ6, 1995)

Le Jeu De Robin et Marian by Adam de la Halle. Musicians of the Schola Cantorum Basiliensis (Arion B00002240BA, 1979, 2002)

Robin Hood Country (including music by Korngold, Coates, Nabarro, Goodwin and Curzon) by the East of England Orchestra conducted by Malcolm Nabarro (ASV WHL2069, 1992)

Robin Hood by Reginald De Koven with lyrics by Harry B. Smith. Ohio Light Opera (Albany Records, B0006A9FUA, 1891)

Robin Hood by George Alexander Macfarren, Victorian Opera Chorus and Orchestra conducted by Nicky Spence Naxos (B005KNODNM, 2012)

Robin Hood Ballads by Wallace House (Smithsonian Folkways, B00242W1S6, 2012)

Robin Hood – Elizabethan Ballad Settings by Paul O'Dette (Harmonia Mundi, B00005B5BP, 2001)

Websites and Organisations

Just a few of the best sites which offer many hundreds of pages of information and speculation on the great outlaw.

The Robin Hood Legend: http://hesternic.tripod.com/robinhood.htm

Robin Hood – Bold Outlaw of Sherwood and Barnsdale: http://www.boldoutlaw.com

Robin Hood – the Facts and the Fiction: http://www.robinhoodlegend.com/

Worldwide Robin Hood Society: http://www.robinhood.ltd.uk

The Outlaw Robin Hood – his Yorkshire Legend (Barbara Green): http://www.robinhoodyorkshire.co.uk

INDEX